TEACHER'S EDITION

Spelling
Workout

Phillip K. Trocki

Modern Curriculum Press
is an imprint of

Boston, Massachusetts

Chandler, Arizona

Glenview, Illinois

Upper Saddle River, New Jersey

COVER DESIGN: Pronk & Associates

ILLUSTRATIONS: Chris Knowles. 190: Jim Steck.

PHOTOGRAPHS: All photos © Pearson Learning unless otherwise noted.

Cover: Artbase Inc.
5: © Randy Harris/Fotolia.com. 8: Library of Congress. 9: © cyrano/Fotolia.com. 12: © Rudolf Tittelbach/Fotolia.com. 13: Library of Congress. 16: © Photos.com/Thinkstock. 17: © Photos.com/Thinkstock. 20: © SOMATUSCANI/Fotolia.com. 21: © Radu Razvan/Fotolia.com. 24: © Michael Matisse/PhotoDisc, Inc. 26: © Philipp Wininger/Fotolia.com. 29: © Brand X Pictures/Thinkstock. 32: © Maximilian Effgen/Fotolia.com. 33: © Gina Smith/Fotolia.com. 36: © Jean-Marie MAILLET/Fotolia.com. 37: © 2ndpic/Fotolia.com. 40: © godfer/Fotolia.com. 44: © Natalia Bratslavsky/Fotolia.com. 45: © chasingmoments/Fotolia.com. 48: © Dima/Fotolia.com. 53: © Comstock. 56: © BlueOrange Studio/Fotolia.com. 57: © Keith Brofsky/PhotoDisc, Inc. 60: © Piotr Marcinski/Fotolia.com. 61: NASA Jet Propulsion Laboratory Collection. 64: NASA Planetary Photo Journal Collection/JPL. 65: Library of Congress. 69: © Steve Mason/PhotoDisc, Inc. 72: Library of Congress Digital. 77: © nsphotography/Fotolia.com. 80: © oscar williams/Fotolia.com. 81: © Getty Images. 84: © Inna Sidorova/Fotolia.com. 85: © Medioimages/PhotoDisc/Thinkstock. 88: Library of Congress. 89: © Gary/Fotolia.com. 92: © Goodshoot/Thinkstock. 93: © Jupiterimages/Thinkstock. 96: © PhotoDisc, Inc. 99: © Jupiterimages/Thinkstock. 101: © Jupiterimages/Thinkstock. 104: © Michael Matisse/Thinkstock. 105: © Jupiterimages/Thinkstock. 109: © Juraj/Fotolia.com. 110: *pos. 1:* © Keith Wheatley/Fotolia.com. *pos. 2:* © Paul837/Fotolia.com. *pos. 3:* © Keith Wheatley/Fotolia.com. *pos. 4:* © c/Fotolia.com. 112: © PaulPaladin/Fotolia.com. 113: © NickR/Fotolia.com. 116: © bat104/Fotolia.com. 117: © outdoorsman/Fotolia.com. 120: © grabj/Fotolia.com. 123: © Stephen Oliver/Dorling Kindersley. 125: expsay/Fotolia.com. 128: © Artur Gabrysiak/Fotolia.com. 129: © Ryan McVay/Thinkstock. 132: © Comstock/Thinkstock. 133: © m hericher/Fotolia.com. 136: © Thinkstock. 137: © Jupiterimages/Thinkstock. 140: © PhotoDisc, Inc. 141: © Zoe/Fotolia.com. 144: Photos.com/Thinkstock. 145: NASA/Spacesuit and Spacewalk History Image Gallery.

Acknowledgments

ZB font Method Copyright © 1996 Zaner-Bloser.

Some content in this product is based upon WEBSTER'S NEW WORLD DICTIONARY, 4/E. Copyright ©2013 by Houghton Mifflin Harcourt Publishing Company. Reprinted by permission of Houghton Mifflin Harcourt Publishing Company. All rights reserved.

NOTE: Every effort has been made to locate the copyright owner of material reprinted in this book. Omissions brought to our attention will be corrected in subsequent editions.

Modern Curriculum Press
is an imprint of

ISBN–13: 978-0-7652-249
ISBN–10: 0-7652-249

13 V036 18 17 16 1

Table of Contents

Spelling Workout–Our Philosophy

Integration of Spelling with Writing

Spelling Workout provides for the integration of writing and spelling. In each lesson, students are asked to write about a topic related to the list words using various forms, such as poems, reports, advertisements, editorials, and letters.

The study of spelling should not be limited to a specific time in the school day. Use opportunities throughout the day to reinforce and maintain spelling skills by integrating spelling with other curriculum areas. Point out spelling words in books, texts, and the students' own writing. Encourage students to write, as they practice spelling through writing. Provide opportunities for writing with a purpose.

Across the Curriculum with Spelling Words

Each lesson of Spelling Workout contains a list of bonus words. These words were drawn from many subject areas including science, social studies, health, language arts, music, and art. Other bonus words feature terms related to more recent changes in technology.

Instructional Design

Spelling Workout takes a solid phonetic and structural approach to encoding. In each list of twenty words, all relate to the organizing principle or relationship that is the focus of the lesson. Of those list words, at least half are words that the student should be familiar with at that particular grade level. The remaining words introduce new vocabulary with emphasis on meaning, usage, and etymology.

Lessons have been organized as efficiently as possible with the degree of spelling difficulty in mind, and with as much diversity as possible. In addition to lessons based on phonetic and structural analysis, lessons containing challenging words, content words, and words adopted from other languages have been included in order to vary the focus from lesson to lesson.

Research-Based Teaching Strategies

Spelling Workout utilizes a test-study-test method of teaching spelling. The student first takes a pretest of words that have not yet been introduced. Under the direction of the teacher, the student then corrects the test, rewriting correctly any word that has been missed. This approach not only provides an opportunity to determine how many words a student can already spell, but also allows students to analyze spelling mistakes. In the process, students also discover patterns that make it easier to spell list words.

High-Utility List Words

Word lists for each lesson have been chosen with the following criteria in mind:

• Frequently misspelled words

• Application to the students' academic experiences

• Introduction to new or unfamiliar vocabulary

• Visible structural similarity (consonant and vowel patterns)

• Relationship groupings (prefixes, roots, subject areas, and so on)

Word lists have been compiled from the following:

Columbia University, N.Y. Bureau of Publications. Spelling Difficulties in 3,876 Words

Dolch. 2,000 Commonest Words for Spelling

Florida Department of Education. Lists for Assessment of Spelling

Fry, Fountokidis, and Polk. The New Reading Teacher's Book of Lists

Green. The New Iowa Spelling Scale

Hanna. Phoneme-Grapheme Correspondence as Cues to Spelling Improvement

Smith and Ingersoll. Written Vocabulary of Elementary School Pupils, Ages 6–14

S.C. Dept. of Education. South Carolina Word List, Grades 1–12

Thomas. Canadian Word Lists and Instructional Techniques

University of Iowa. The List of 1,000 Words Most Commonly Misspelled

A Format That Results in Success

Spelling Workout furnishes an intensive review of spelling skills previously taught and introduces the students to more sophisticated words and concepts. Lesson emphasis is on spelling strategies, developing vocabulary, practicing correct word usage, and understanding word derivations.

Sample Core Lesson

* The **Tip** explains the spelling rules or patterns, providing a focus for the lesson.

* The **List Words** box contains the spelling words for each lesson. Words were selected on the basis of meaning, usage, and origin.

* Each lesson begins with activities centering on vocabulary development, dictionary skills, and word analysis.

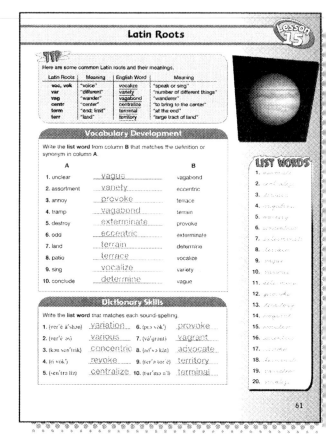

* **Did You Know?** exposes students to word origins and word histories while increasing vocabulary. An etymology is found in each lesson.

* **Spelling Practice** exercises give students an opportunity to practice the list words, focusing on their structure and meaning.

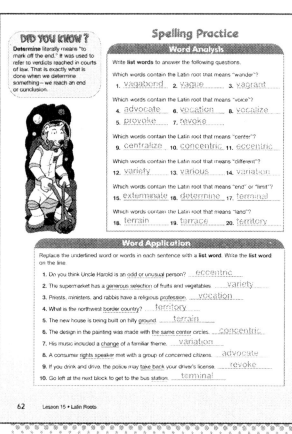

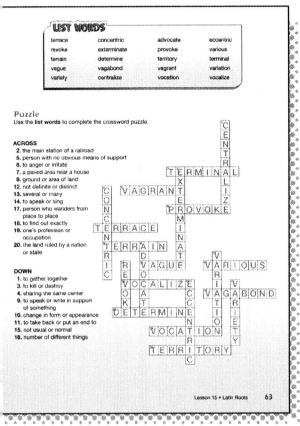

* Activities such as crossword puzzles, riddles, and games help motivate students by making learning fun.

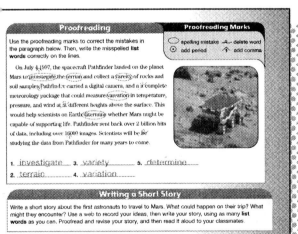

* **Spelling and Writing** reinforces the connection between spelling and everyday writing and encourages students to apply the list words in different contexts.

* **Proofreading** practice builds proofreading proficiency and encourages students to check their own writing.

* **Writing** activities provide opportunities for students to write their spelling words in a variety of writing forms and genres.

* **Bonus Words** offer more challenging words drawn from various curriculum areas. Many of the activities in the *Teacher's Edition* give students the opportunity to practice the words with classmates.

Sample Review Lesson

• The **Review** lesson allows students to practice what they've learned.

• The spelling patterns used in the previous five lessons are reviewed at the beginning of the lesson.

• A variety of activities provide practice and review of selected list words from the previous lessons.

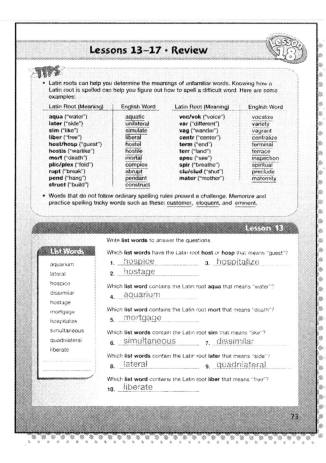

• **Show What You Know** is a cumulative review of the words in the five previous lessons using a standardized-test format.

Spelling Workout in the Classroom

Classroom Management

Spelling Workout is designed as a flexible instructional program. The following plans are two ways the program can be taught.

The 5-day Plan

Day 1 – Pretest/Spelling Strategy
Days 2 and 3 – Spelling Practice
Day 4 – Spelling and Writing
Day 5 – Final Test

The 3-day Plan

Day 1 – Pretest/Spelling Strategy/ Spelling Practice
Day 2 – Spelling Practice/Spelling and Writing
Day 3 – Final Test

Testing

Testing is accomplished in several ways. The **Pretest** is administered before beginning the **Spelling Strategy**, and the **Final Test** at the end of each lesson. Dictation sentences for each **Pretest** and **Final Test** are provided.

Research suggests that students benefit from correcting their own **Pretests**. After the test has been administered, have students self-correct their tests in the following manner. As you read each letter of the list word, ask students to point to each letter and circle any incorrect letters. Then, have students rewrite each misspelled word correctly.

Dictation sentences for the bonus words are also furnished for teachers desiring to include these words in weekly tests.

Tests for review lessons are provided as reproducibles in the back of the Teacher's Edition. These tests provide not only an evaluation tool for teachers, but also added practice in taking standardized tests for students.

Individualizing Instruction

Bonus Words are included in every lesson as a challenge for better spellers and to provide extension and enrichment for all students.

Review lessons reinforce the correct spelling of difficult words from previous lessons.

The **Review** lessons also provide for individual needs. Each has space for students to add words from previous lessons that they found especially difficult.

The **Spelling Notebook** allows each student to analyze spelling errors and practice writing troublesome words independently. Notebook pages appear as reproducibles in the Teacher's Edition and as pages at the back of the student book.

A reproducible individual **Student Record Chart** provided in the Teacher's Edition allows students to record their test scores.

Ideas for meeting the needs of ESL students are provided.

Dictionary

In the back of each student book is a comprehensive dictionary with definitions of all the list words and bonus words. Students will have this resource at their fingertips for any assignment.

The Teacher's Edition
—Everything You Need!

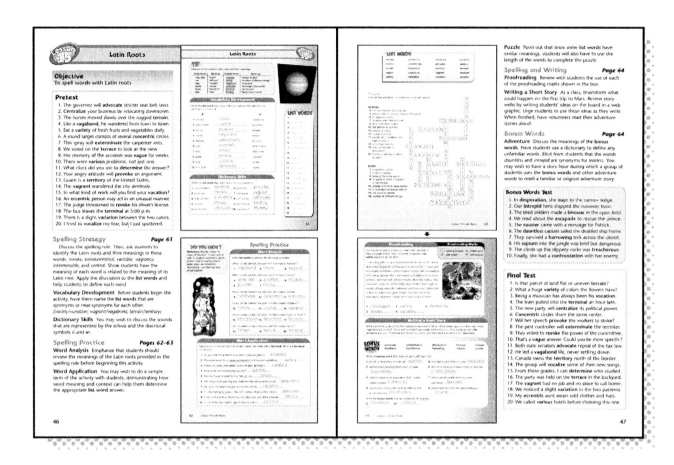

- The **Objective** clearly states the goals of each core lesson.

- A **Pretest** is administered before the start of each lesson. Dictation sentences are provided.

- **Spelling Strategy** provides start-up activities that offer suggestions for introducing the spelling principles.

- Concise teaching notes give guidance for working through the lesson.

- **Spelling Practice** activities provide additional support for reinforcing and analyzing spelling patterns.

- **Spelling and Writing** includes suggestions for helping students use proofreading marks to correct their work. Suggestions for using the writing process to complete the writing activity are also offered.

- Activities for using the bonus words listed in the student books are provided in the **Bonus Words** section.

- Dictation sentences are provided for testing the bonus words.

- A **Final Test** is administered at the end of the lesson. Dictation sentences are provided.

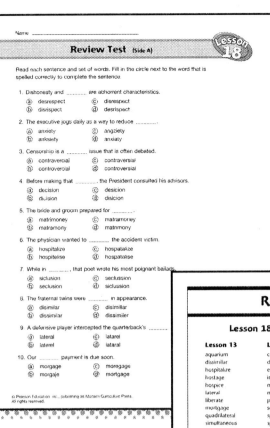

* **Review** lessons review spelling objectives, give guidance for further practice of list words, and provide dictation sentences for a **Final Test**.

* A reproducible two-page standardized test is supplied for assessment purposes for use after each **Review** lesson.

Review Word List

Lesson 18

Lesson 13	Lesson 16
aquarium	conspiracy
dissimilar	disrespect
hospitalize	exclude
hostage	inspiration
hospice	maternal
lateral	matrimony
liberate	perspective
mortgage	seclusion
quadrilateral	spectacle
simultaneous	speculate

Lesson 14	Lesson 17
applicable	anxiety
destruction	controversial
duplicate	courtesy
independently	cruel
inexplicable	customary
instruction	decision
interrupt	defenseless
structural	especially
suspended	excitable
suspense	fallacy

Lesson 15	
advocate	auditor
concentric	documen...
determine	exhilarat...
eccentric	exorbita...
exterminate	juvenile
terrain	molecula...
territory	optician
vague	opulent
variation	ordnance
various	quaranti...

Lesson 24

Lesson 19	Lesson 22
coherent	aeronautics
coincide	analysis
coordinate	archaic
symbolize	architect
symmetry	archive
symphonic	criticize
symptom	democracy
synagogue	economical
synchronize	metropolis
syntax	theology

Lesson 20	Lesson 23
anemia	biological
anesthesia	chronic
anonymous	dialogue
immaculate	enthusiasm
immobilize	geographical
impersonate	parable
inaccurate	parallel
incognito	paralysis
negligent	pharmacy
nonexistent	thermostat

Spelling Enrichment

Group Practice

Crossword Relay First, draw a large grid on the board. Then, divide the class into several teams. Teams compete against each other to form separate crossword puzzles on the board. Individuals on each team take turns racing against members of the other teams to join list words until all possibilities have been exhausted. A list word may appear on each crossword puzzle only once. The winning team is the team whose crossword puzzle contains the greatest number of correctly spelled list words or the team who finishes first.

Proofreading Relay Write two columns of misspelled list words on the board. Although the errors can differ, be sure that each list has the same number of errors. Divide the class into two teams and assign each team to a different column. Teams then compete against each other to correct their assigned lists by team members taking turns erasing and replacing an appropriate letter. Each member may correct only one letter per turn. The team that is first to correct its entire word list wins.

Detective Call on a student to be a detective. The detective must choose a spelling word from the list and think of a structural clue, definition, or synonym that will help classmates identify it. The detective then states the clue using the format, "I spy a word that. . . ." Students are called on to guess and spell the mystery word. Whoever answers correctly gets to take a turn being the detective.

Spelling Tic-Tac-Toe Draw a tic-tac-toe square on the board. Divide the class into X and O teams. Take turns dictating spelling words to members of each team. If the word is spelled correctly, allow the team member to place an X or O on the square. The first team to place three X's or O's in a row wins.

Words of Fortune Have students put their heads down while you write a spelling word on the board in large letters. Then, cover each letter with a sheet of sturdy paper. The paper can be fastened to the board with a magnet. Call on a student to guess any letter of the alphabet they think may be hidden. If that particular letter is hidden, then reveal the letter in every place where it appears in the word by removing the paper.

The student continues to guess letters until an incorrect guess is made or the word is revealed. In the event that an incorrect guess is made, a different student continues the game. Continue the game until every list word has been hidden and then revealed.

Applied Spelling

Journal Allow time each day for students to write in a journal. A spiral bound notebook can be used for this purpose. Encourage students to express their feelings about events that are happening in their lives at home or at school. Alternatively, they could write about what their

plans are for the day. To get them started, you may have to provide starter phrases.

You may wish to collect the journals periodically to write comments that echo what the student has written. For example, a student's entry might read, "My brother is suceptible to infecshuns. He will probable need to see the doctor again today." The teacher's response could be, "People who are susceptible to infections will probably need to visit their doctors regularly to stay well." This method allows students to learn correct spelling and sentence structure without emphasizing their errors in a negative way.

Letter to the Teacher On a regular basis, have students each write a note to the teacher. At first the teacher might suggest topics or provide a starter sentence, including words from the spelling list. The teacher should write a response at the bottom of any spelling or sentence structure that evidences improvement.

Daily Edit Each day provide a brief writing sample on the board that contains errors in spelling, capitalization, or punctuation. Have students rewrite the sample correctly. Provide time later in the day to have the class correct the errors on the board while students self-correct their work.

Spelling Notebook Have students use the Spelling Notebook in the student book, a stenographer's notebook, or pages of the reproducible Spelling Notebook stapled together (see page 111 in the *Teacher's Edition*) to keep a record of words they encounter difficulty spelling. Tabs could be added to some pages to separate a large notebook into sections for each letter of the alphabet. Urge students to use a dictionary or ask the teacher to help them spell words with which they are having trouble. Periodically, allow students to work in pairs to test each other on a set of words taken from their personal word list.

Acrostic Poems Have students write a word from the spelling list vertically. Then, instruct them to join a word horizontally to each letter of the list word. The horizontal words must begin with the letters in the list word. They could be words that are synonyms or that describe or relate feelings about the list word. Encourage students to refer to a dictionary for help in finding appropriate words. Here is a sample acrostic poem:

Evade
Lose
U-turn
Dodge
Escape

Poem Exchange Provide students with copies of a familiar poem. Discuss how some of the words can be exchanged for other words that have similar meanings. Ask the students to rewrite the poem exchanging some of the words for other words.

110

Reproducible study sheets of **Review** lesson words are included in the *Teacher's Edition* to help prepare students for test taking.

Suggested games and group activities make spelling more fun.

Ideas for meeting the needs of ESL students are provided on pages 14–15.

Spelling is the relationship between sounds and letters. Learning to spell words in English is an interesting challenge for English First Language speakers as well as English as a Second Language speakers. You may want to adapt some of the following activities to accommodate the needs of your students—both native and non-English speakers.

Rhymes and Songs
Use rhymes, songs, poems, or chants to introduce new letter sounds and spelling words. Repeat the rhyme or song several times during the day or week, having students listen to you first, then repeat back to you line by line. To enhance learning for visual learners in your classroom and provide opportunities for pointing out letter combinations and their sounds, you may want to write the rhyme, song, poem, or chant on the board. As you examine the words, students can easily see similarities and differences among them. Encourage volunteers to select and recite a rhyme or sing a song for the class.

Student Dictation
To take advantage of individual students' known vocabulary, suggest that students build their own sentences incorporating the list words. For example:

The contestant was agile.

The contestant was agile in gymnastics.

The contestant was agile in gymnastics and acrobatics.

Sentence building can expand students' knowledge of how to spell words and of how to notice language patterns, learn descriptive words, and so on.

Words in Context
Using words in context sentences will aid students' mastery of new vocabulary.

* Say several sentences using the list words in context and have students repeat after you. Encourage more proficient students to make up sentences using list words that you suggest.

* Write cloze sentences on the board and have students help you complete them with the list words.

Point out the spelling patterns in the words, using colored chalk to underline or circle the elements.

Oral Drills
Use oral drills to help students make associations among sounds and the letters that represent them. You might use oral drills at listening stations to reinforce the language, allowing ESL students to listen to the drills their own pace.

Spelling Aloud Say each list word and have students repeat the word. Next, write it on the board as you name each letter, then say the word again as you trace the letters and sound by sweeping your hand under the word. Call attention to spelling changes for words to which endings or suffixes were added. For words with more than one syllable, emphasize each syllable as you write, encouraging students to clap out the syllables. Ask volunteers to repeat the procedure.

Variant Spellings For a group of words that contain the same root, but variant spellings, write an example on the board, say the word, and then present other words in that word family (*district: restrict, constrict*). Point out the root and the letter(s) that make up the root. Then, add words to the list that have similar roots (*conflict, consist, desist*). Say pairs of words (*restrict, consist*) as you point to them, and identify the roots and the different letters that represent the roots (*strict, sist*). Ask volunteers to select a different pair of words and repeat the procedure.

Vary this activity by drawing a chart on the board that shows the variant spellings for different roots. Invite students to add words under the correct spelling pattern. Provide a list of words for students to choose from to help those ESL students with limited vocabularies.

ategorizing To help students discriminate among consonant sounds and spellings, have them help you categorize words with single consonant sounds, consonant blends or digraphs, and prefixes. For example, ask students to close their eyes so that they can focus solely on the sounds in the words, and then pronounce *premier*, *prejudice*, *protrude*, and *protocol*. Next, pronounce the words as you write them on the board. After spelling each word, create two columns—one for *pre*, one for *pro*. Have volunteers pronounce each word, decide which column it fits under, and write the word in the correct column. Encourage students to add to the columns any other words they know that have those sounds.

To focus on initial, medial, or final consonant sounds, point out the position of the consonants, consonant blends, or digraphs in the words. Have students find and list the words under columns labeled *Beginning*, *Middle*, and *End*.

Tape Recording Encourage students to work with a partner or their group to practice their spelling words. If a tape recorder is available, students can practice at their own pace by taking turns recording the words, playing back the tape, and writing each word they hear. Students can then help each other check their spelling against their *Spelling Workout* books. Observe as needed to be sure students are spelling the words correctly.

Comparing/Contrasting To help students focus on word parts, write list words with prefixes or suffixes on the board and have volunteers circle, underline, or draw a line between the prefix or suffix and its base word or root. Review the meaning of each base word/root, then invite students to work with their group to write two sentences: one using just the base word/root; the other using the base word/root with its prefix or suffix. For example: *The weather news you heard yesterday was accurate. The weather news today is inaccurate!* Have students contrast the two sentences, encouraging them to tell how the prefix or suffix changed the meaning of the base word/root.

Questions/Answers Write list words on the board and ask pairs of students to brainstorm questions or answers about the words, such as "Which word means 'not active'? How do you know?" (*inactive*, the prefix *in* means "no") or, "Which word means 'a main station of a railroad or bus line'? How do you know?" (*terminal* comes from the root word *term*, which means "end" or "limit")

Games

You may want to invite students to participate in these activities.

Picture Clues Students can work with a partner to draw pictures or cut pictures out of magazines that represent the list words, then trade papers and label each other's pictures. Encourage students to check each other's spelling against their *Spelling Workout* books.

If desired, you can present magazine cutouts or items that picture the list words. As you display each picture or item, say the word clearly and then write it on the board as you spell it aloud. Non-English speakers may wish to know the translation of the word in their native languages so that they can mentally connect the new word with a familiar one. Students may also find similarities in the spellings of the words.

Letter Cards Have students create letter cards for vowels, vowel digraphs, consonants, consonant blends, consonant digraphs, and so on. Then, say a list word and have students show the card that has the letters representing the sound for the vowels or consonants in that word as they repeat and spell the word after you. Students can use their cards independently as they work with their group.

Charades/Pantomime Students can use gestures and actions to act out the list words. To receive credit for a correctly guessed word, players must spell the word correctly. Such activities can be played in pairs so that beginning English speakers will not feel pressured. If necessary, translate the words into students' native languages so that they understand the meanings of the words before attempting to act them out.

Change or No Change Have students make flash cards for base words/roots and endings/suffixes. One student holds up a base word or root; another holds up an ending or suffix. The class says "Change" or "No Change" to describe what happens when the base word/root and ending/suffix are combined. Encourage students to spell the word with its ending or suffix added.

Scope and Sequence for MCP Spelling Workout

Skills	Level A	Level B	Level C	Level D	Level E	Level F	Level G	Level H
Consonants	1–12	1–2	1–2	1	1	1, 7, 9	RC	3
Short Vowels	14–18	3–5	3	2	RC	RC	RC	RC
Long Vowels	20–23	7–11, 15	4–5, 7–8	3	RC	RC	RC	RC
Consonant Blends/Clusters	26–28	13–14	9–10, 17	5, 7	RC	RC	RC	RC
y as a Vowel	30	16	11–13	RC	RC	RC	27	RC
Consonant Digraphs—**th, ch, sh, wh, ck**	32–33	19–21	14–16	9	RC	RC	RC	RC
Vowel Digraphs		33	6–7, 9	19–21, 23	8–10	11, 14–17	25	RC
Vowel Pairs	29		26	20, 22	7–8, 10	14	25	
r-Controlled Vowels		22, 25	19–20	8	RC	RC	RC	4
Diphthongs	24	32	31	22–23	11	17	RC	RC
Silent Consonants			8	11	4	8–9	RC	RC
Hard and Soft **c** and **g**		21	2	4	2	2	RC	
Plurals			21–22	25–27, 29	33–34	33	RC	RC
Prefixes		34	32–33	31–32	13–17	20–23, 25	7–8, 33	7–11, 19–20
Suffixes/Endings	34–35	26–28	21–23, 25, 33	13–17	25–29, 31–32	26–29, 31–32	5, 9, 13–14, 16, 26	5, 25–27
Contractions		23	34	28	20	RC	RC	RC
Possessives				28–29	20	RC	RC	RC
Compound Words				33	19	RC	34	RC
Synonyms/Antonyms				34	RC	RC	RC	RC
Homonyms		35	35	35	RC	34	RC	RC
Spellings of /f/: **f, ff, ph, gh**				10	3	3	RC	RC
Syllables					21–23	RC	RC	1
Commonly Misspelled Words					35	34	17, 35	17, 29, 35
Abbreviations						35	RC	RC
Latin Roots							11, 15, 31	13–16

Skills	Level A	Level B	Level C	Level D	Level E	Level F	Level G	Level H
Words with French or Spanish Derivations							10, 29	RC 28
Words of Latin/French/Greek Origin								21–23, 28
List Words Related to Specific Curriculum Areas							31–34, 28, 32	
Vocabulary Development	•	•	•	•	•	•	•	•
Dictionary	•	•	•	•	•	•	•	•
Writing	•	•	•	•	•	•	•	•
Proofreading	•	•	•	•	•	•	•	•
Reading Selections	•	•	•	•	•	•	•	•
Bonus Words	•	•	•	•	•	•	•	•
Review Tests in Standardized Format	•	•	•	•	•	•	•	•
Spelling Through Writing								
Poetry	•	•	•	•	•	•	•	•
Narrative Writings	•	•	•	•	•	•	•	•
Descriptive Writings	•	•	•	•	•	•	•	•
Expository Writings	•	•	•	•	•	•	•	•
Persuasive Writings			•	•	•	•	•	•
Notes/Letters	•	•	•		•	•	•	•
Riddles/Jokes	•	•	•					
Recipes/Menus	•	•	•			•	•	
News Stories		•	•	•	•	•	•	•
Conversations/Dialogues	•	•		•	•	•		
Stories	•	•	•		•	•	•	•
Interviews/Surveys		•			•	•	•	•
Logs/Journals	•		•	•	•	•	•	
Ads/Brochures		•	•	•	•	•	•	•
Reports					•	•	•	•
Literary Devices							•	•
Scripts		•					•	•
Speeches					•	•		•
Directions/Instructions	•	•		•				•

Numbers in chart indicate lesson numbers

RC = reinforced in other contexts

• = found throughout

Syllabication

Objective
To spell words using syllabication rules

Pretest

1. Let's **abandon** the ineffective plan and start over.
2. Monuments **commemorate** important events.
3. Fast film needs little **exposure** to light.
4. That decoration is a great **ornament** for the party.
5. Does that dog have a **tendency** to bark very much?
6. Please sign this **affidavit** giving your testimony.
7. We will **consolidate** all departments into one.
8. Sara's warm thanks expressed her **gratitude**.
9. Please don't try to **resurrect** that plan again!
10. In this storm, the train will **undoubtedly** be late.
11. I skipped lunch, so now I have a huge **appetite**.
12. Given her **curiosity**, she'll ask many questions.
13. Is that person the child's parent or **guardian**?
14. Because it is so dry, **saturate** the garden fully.
15. Mr. Koo made a **voluntary** gift to our auction.
16. Can you bring paper plates to the **barbecue**?
17. The tallest building will **dominate** a city's skyline.
18. The **installation** of new club officers is tomorrow.
19. According to the **specifications**, a hall goes here.
20. The doctor can **ascertain** how the injury occurred.

Spelling Strategy   *Page 5*

After students have read the spelling rule, discuss the rules of syllabication and how they aid spelling. Have volunteers read the **list words** aloud, dividing them into syllables. Discuss which rule each word follows. Help students understand the meanings of any unfamiliar words.

Vocabulary Development Write *hunger* on the board and ask students which **list word** means almost the same thing. (*appetite*) Then, point out that in this exercise, students must think about the meaning of each word, as well as its spelling.

Dictionary Skills Write *abandon* on the board and show students how to write it to show syllabication. (*a/ban/don*) Have students read the directions, then work through the first item with them.

Spelling Practice   *Pages 6–7*

Word Analysis Point out to students that analyzing words helps them remember a word's distinctive features and, therefore, its spelling.

Word Application Explain to students that their answers must make sense in the sentences. Encourage them to refer to the **list words** on page 7 if they are unsure about the spelling of a word.

Syllabication

Lesson 1

TIP
Study these rules of syllabication.
Divide words where natural breaks occur between prefixes, roots, and suffixes: un/doubt/ed/ly. When two consonants come between two vowels, divide between the consonants: com/mem/o/rate. When one consonant comes between two vowels, divide before the consonant if the first vowel is long: ex/po/sure. Divide after the consonant if the vowel is short: sat/u/rate. A vowel sounded alone can form a syllable: cur/i/os/i/ty.

Vocabulary Development

Write the **list word** that matches each definition.

1. celebrate something	commemorate
2. eagerness to know	curiosity
3. roast outdoors	barbecue
4. bring back to life	resurrect
5. leave behind	abandon
6. a trinket or decoration	ornament
7. necessary details	specifications
8. to determine	ascertain
9. soak	saturate
10. likely to act a certain way	tendency
11. thankfulness	gratitude
12. desire for food	appetite

LIST WORDS
1. abandon
2. commemorate
3. exposure
4. ornament
5. tendency
6. affidavit
7. consolidate
8. gratitude
9. resurrect
10. undoubtedly
11. appetite
12. curiosity
13. guardian
14. saturate
15. voluntary
16. barbecue
17. dominate
18. installation
19. specifications
20. ascertain

Dictionary Skills

Rewrite each of the following **list words** to show how they are divided into syllables.

1. gratitude   grat/i/tude   6. affidavit   af/fi/da/vit
2. voluntary   vol/un/tar/y   7. undoubtedly un/doubt/ed/ly
3. guardian   guard/i/an   8. consolidate con/sol/i/date
4. exposure   ex/po/sure   9. installation in/stal/la/tion
5. appetite   ap/pe/tite   10. dominate   dom/i/nate

DID YOU KNOW?
Dominate comes from the Latin word for "master," *dominus*, and so do the words *domineer* and *dominion*.

Spelling Practice

Word Analysis

Write the **list words** containing these double consonants:

1. rr   resurrect   4. ll   installation
2. ff   affidavit   5. mm   commemorate
3. pp   appetite

Write the **list words** containing these prefixes:

6. com   commemorate   9. ex   exposure
7. con   consolidate   10. un   undoubtedly
8. re   resurrect

Write the **list words** containing five syllables

11. curiosity   12. specifications

Word Application

Replace the underlined word or words in each sentence with a **list word**. Write the list word on the line.

1. Rain fell so heavily that the water began to soak the dry earth.   saturate
2. We expressed our thankfulness by sending flowers.   gratitude
3. Please do not leave the grocery-store carts in the parking lot.   abandon
4. Tim will head the field of runners in the competition.   dominate
5. On July 4th, the United States will celebrate its birth.   commemorate
6. The committee will place together all of the smaller groups into one.   consolidate
7. Mr. Jackson has been selected as overseer of the club's investments.   guardian
8. You will find the details for building that boat in my book.   specifications
9. For dinner tonight, Dad and I will roast chicken on the grill.   barbecue
10. Too much display of skin to the sun can result in a sunburn.   exposure
11. The salesperson tried to determine what the customer wanted.   ascertain
12. Participation in the clothes drive is your own choice.   voluntary
13. The likelihood of the car to pull to the right on highways is annoying.   tendency
14. The vase of lilacs and tulips on that table is a lovely decoration.   ornament

LIST WORDS

undoubtedly	affidavit	appetite	barbecue
commemorate	tendency	curiosity	dominate
specifications	gratitude	guardian	ornament
installation	resurrect	saturate	exposure
consolidate	abandon	voluntary	ascertain

Puzzle
Use the **list words** to complete the crossword puzzle.

ACROSS
3. the act of letting something be seen
6. strong feelings of wanting to know or learn something
8. done of one's free will; by choice
9. placed in position
12. a person who guards or protects
15. the desire or wish for food
17. thankfulness
18. unite; merge; join together
19. likely to move or act in a certain way
20. a decoration

DOWN
1. to bring back to life
2. to soak through
4. without doubt; certainly
5. to honor or keep alive the memory of
7. a statement of all the necessary details, sizes, materials, etc.
10. to control or rule
11. to find out the facts
13. a statement written by one who swears it is the truth
14. meat roasted over an open fire
16. to give up completely; to leave

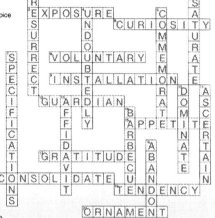

Lesson 1 • Syllabication   7

Proofreading

Use the proofreading marks to correct the mistakes in the biographical sketch. Then, write the misspelled **list words** correctly on the lines.

Robert Frost (1874–1963) is undoutedly one of the greatest american poets of the twentieth century. Born in san francisco, Frost moved with his family to New England after the death of his father in 1885. Frost's exposure to the region's landscapes and speech mannerisms saterate many of his best poems. Yet scenic descriptions donot domminate all of frost's work. The range of moods in his poetry is rich and varied, revealing a curiosity about human nature. Winner of the pulitzer Prize for poetry four times, there are now several books available that comemorate Frost's work.

Proofreading Marks
�circle spelling mistake   ⊙ add period
≡ capital letter   # add space

1. undoubtedly
2. exposure
3. saturate
4. dominate
5. curiosity
6. commemorate

Writing a Persuasive Paragraph

In a Robert Frost poem called "Mending Wall" the poet writes, "Good fences make good neighbors." Write a persuasive paragraph to explain what you think the poet means. Try to persuade the reader that this is a wise—or unwise—statement. Give reasons for your opinion and use as many of the **list words** as you can. Proofread and revise your paragraph, then discuss it with your classmates.

BONUS WORDS

municipality	rural	commune	province	suburb
commonwealth	urban	residential	borough	colony

Write **bonus words** to answer the questions.

Which words describe the character or location of a community?
1. urban
2. suburb
3. residential
4. rural

Which word names a territory distant from its parent country?
5. colony

Which words name political communities that have governments of their own?
6. municipality
7. commonwealth
8. commune
9. province
10. borough

8   Lesson 1 • Syllabication

Puzzle Explain that this crossword puzzle gives two clues: the definition and the number of letters. Urge students to fill in answers they know, as those letters will help them determine other answers. If needed, work through one or two items with students.

Spelling and Writing   *Page 8*
Proofreading Discuss the use of the proofreading marks in the box. Write on the board: *sam's cureosity sometimes gets himin trouble* Have volunteers use the marks to correct the sentence. Tell students they will use these proofreading marks to correct the paragraph.

Writing a Persuasive Paragraph Discuss what students think the quotation means. Encourage a variety of responses. Then, have students write their opinions. Afterward, read the poem aloud and solicit responses.

Bonus Words   *Page 8*
Communities Explain that the **bonus words** name or describe communities. Help students understand the words' meanings, clarifying that a *colony* does not have its own government. Then, have volunteers use the **bonus words** in oral sentences.

Bonus Words Test
1. An **urban** area offers many cultural attractions.
2. The **municipality** will pay for the new school buses.
3. The United States was once an English **colony**.
4. I like the fields in these **rural** areas.
5. In a **commune**, families share the work and the food.
6. The city of Yonkers is not a **borough** of New York.
7. My brother lives in a **suburb** near San Francisco.
8. It's another **province**, but they use the same money.
9. The **Commonwealth** of Australia is a very dry land.
10. This area has **residential** buildings, not businesses.

Final Test
1. I have no **appetite** for hot food in humid weather.
2. Scientists have a great deal of **curiosity**.
3. Only a parent or legal **guardian** can give permission.
4. Will the dye **saturate** the fabric thoroughly?
5. This is a **voluntary** trip, not a mandatory one.
6. Once you **ascertain** the information, write a report.
7. The **specifications** will tell you the car's tire size.
8. Schedule the **installation** of the furnace for Monday.
9. Watch how the older dog will **dominate** the puppy.
10. We have a neighborhood **barbecue** each summer.
11. We need an **affidavit** for the insurance company.
12. Will we **consolidate** the two trips into one long one?
13. I expressed my **gratitude** in a thank-you note.
14. Why do we feel it's valuable to **resurrect** that idea?
15. In February, the weather will **undoubtedly** be cold.
16. **Abandon** the mine immediately; there's a cave-in!
17. The statue will **commemorate** the town's bicentennial.
18. Avoid too much **exposure** to the sun.
19. Kang wore a pretty silver **ornament** on a gold chain.
20. These bushes have a **tendency** to grow very tall.

Objective
To spell words ending with /əl/

Pretest
1. It was purely **accidental**; I didn't mean to do it!
2. After that **dismal** story, she needed cheering up.
3. The film is an **integral** part of a disposable camera.
4. Miguel practiced for the piano **recital** he'll soon give.
5. We must take responsibility for our planet's **survival**.
6. Will these flowers grow well under **artificial** light?
7. This new surgical technique is **experimental**.
8. The **literal** meaning of *blow your top* is "to get mad."
9. Is there a **revival** of clothes from the 1970s?
10. Luckily, my mistake was tiny and not **colossal**.
11. She prefers **cerebral** publications to comic books.
12. Large orders improve our company's **fiscal** health.
13. A person with a **logical** mind can solve this mystery.
14. Won't his experience make a **sensational** novel?
15. Many hurricanes begin as **tropical** storms.
16. Does a **criminal** record stop you from getting a job?
17. The alarm worried us, but no one became **hysterical**.
18. His mouth is in **perpetual** motion; he keeps talking.
19. For extra credit, do the **supplemental** reading.
20. The revolution caused an **upheaval** in the city.

Spelling Strategy   **Page 9**
After students read the spelling rule, point out that *al* creates the adjectival form of words such as *logical* and *experimental*. Have students identify the base words. (*logic*, *experiment*) Then, make sure students understand the **list words'** meanings, encouraging them to use dictionaries to learn unfamiliar words.

Vocabulary Development Ask students which **list word** means "emotionally uncontrolled." (*hysterical*) Point out that in this exercise, students must think about the meanings of words as well as their spellings.

Dictionary Skills Use a dictionary pronunciation key to discuss sound-spellings. Make sure students understand their function and use. Point out, for instance, that *right* and *write* would have the same sound-spelling, *rit*.

Spelling Practice   **Pages 10–11**
Word Analysis Point out any distinctive spelling features of the **list words**, such as *s* as /z/ in *dismal*, *ci* as /sh/ in *artificial*, *ss* in *colossal* and *y* as /i/ in *hysterical*. Encourage students to attempt completing the words before referring to the **list words** on page 11.

Word Application Remind students to look for context clues in each sentence. To extend the activity, have students make up similar sentences for the distractors.

TIP
Many words end with the sound you hear at the end of *dismal*. This sound can be spelled in several different ways, as in *little*, *towel*, and *recital*. Remember that the words in this lesson all end with the same letters: al.

Vocabulary Development
Write the **list word** that matches each definition clue.

1. huge	colossal	
2. reasonable	logical	
3. forever	perpetual	
4. not natural	artificial	
5. dreary	dismal	
6. by chance	accidental	
7. additional	supplemental	
8. lawless	criminal	
9. mental	cerebral	
10. financial	fiscal	
11. hot and steamy	tropical	
12. rebirth	revival	

LIST WORDS
1. accidental
2. dismal
3. integral
4. recital
5. survival
6. artificial
7. experimental
8. literal
9. revival
10. colossal
11. cerebral
12. fiscal
13. logical
14. sensational
15. tropical
16. criminal
17. hysterical
18. perpetual
19. supplemental
20. upheaval

Dictionary Skills
Write the **list word** that matches each sound-spelling.

1. (up hē´ v′l) upheaval
2. (sen sā´shən ′l) sensational
3. (his ter´i k′l) hysterical
4. (träp´i k′l) tropical
5. (ik sper´ə men′t′l) experimental
6. (lit´ər əl) literal
7. (sər vī´v′l) survival
8. (ri sīt´′l) recital
9. (ri vī´v′l) revival
10. (in´tə grəl) integral

9

DID YOU KNOW?
Dismal comes from a Middle English word which meant "unlucky days." Its Latin origins include *dis* or "day" and *mal* or "bad." Today, we use the word when we think something is gloomy, dreary, dreadful, hopeless, or depressing.

Spelling Practice
Word Analysis
Fill in the missing letters to form **list words**. Then, write the completed **list words** on the lines.

1. tropical — tropical
2. fiscal — fiscal
3. cerebral — cerebral
4. artificial — artificial
5. literal — literal
6. colossal — colossal
7. survival — survival
8. integral — integral
9. accidental — accidental
10. dismal — dismal

Word Application
Select a **list word** from the choices in parentheses to complete each sentence. Write the **list word** on the line.

1. That **colossal** stuffed animal is six-feet tall! (colossal, accidental)
2. **Supplemental** vitamins can't replace a meal. (Upheaval, Supplemental)
3. Falling off my bike was **accidental**. (accidental, survival)
4. There is **cerebral** activity even during sleep. (cerebral, tropical)
5. Human beings need food and water for their **survival**. (survival, literal)
6. That **dismal** room is cold, damp, and gray. (accidental, dismal)
7. Take deep breaths to avoid becoming **hysterical**. (perpetual, hysterical)
8. Natural light sources are better than **artificial** ones. (artificial, recital)
9. The **perpetual** noise kept her up all night. (perpetual, logical)
10. The earthquake caused a great **upheaval**. (criminal, upheaval)
11. Stealing from banks is a **criminal** action. (revival, criminal)
12. "Using your head" can be **literal** if you hit the ball with your head while playing soccer. (recital, literal)
13. The quality of the ingredients is **integral** to the recipe. (integral, artificial)
14. Don't forget to memorize the music for your piano **recital**. (experimental, recital)

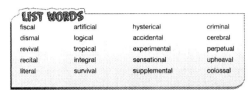

Puzzle

This is a crossword puzzle without clues. Use the length and the spelling of each **list word** to complete the puzzle.

Proofreading

Use the proofreading marks to correct the mistakes in the article below. Then, write the misspelled **list words** correctly on the lines.

The first experimental Concord stagecoach was manufactured in 1827 by the Abbot-Downing Company. It created an upheavel in coach construction. The wheels were an intagral part of the design. Made of oak, they were well-dried to withstand heat and cold, and would not shrink like other coach wheels. The body of the coach was solid, resting on thick leather braces. Even though the braces served to cushion and support the coach, do you think many passengers enjoyed their ride? Most described their travels as dizmal due to the purpetual motion of the coach.

Proofreading Marks

⬭ spelling mistake ⤶ delete word
? add question mark / small letter

1. experimental
2. upheaval
3. integral
4. dismal
5. perpetual

Writing a Description

In his book, *Roughing It*, Mark Twain described the Concord coach as "a cradle on wheels," and added, "It thrills me to think of the life and the wild sense of freedom on those fine overland mornings!" Write a description of what stagecoach travel might have been like, using as many of the **list words** as you can. Proofread and revise your description. Then, discuss your writing with your classmates.

BONUS WORDS

automobile	hydroplane	vessel	schooner	transcontinental
stagecoach	amphibious	gasoline	tributary	propulsion

Write the **bonus word** that matches each clue.

1. driving force	propulsion		6. river feeding another	tributary
2. any boat or ship	vessel		7. one kind of fuel	gasoline
3. horse-drawn carriage	stagecoach		8. ship with two or more masts	schooner
4. from coast to coast	transcontinental		9. this skims along the water's surface	hydroplane
5. adapted for both land or water	amphibious		10. four-wheeled motorized transportation	automobile

12

Puzzle Discuss how students can solve a crossword puzzle without clues. Explain that each answer they write will provide further clues to other answers. If necessary, remind them that all the words end with *al*.

Spelling and Writing   *Page 12*

Proofreading Write *When is is your Sister coming too visit* on the board, and use it to demonstrate the proofreading marks that students will use in this lesson.

Writing a Description Remind students that descriptive language adds flavor to writing. Have the class brainstorm adjectives and adverbs describing a stagecoach journey and list them on the board. Urge students to be creative, giving them the option to write in the first-person narrative form.

Bonus Words   *Page 12*

Transportation Explain that the **bonus words** relate to transportation. Through discussion and dictionary use, help students understand the words' meanings. Encourage them to share their own knowledge on the subject.

Bonus Words Test

1. Your **vessel** carries ten inflatable lifeboats.
2. This isn't the Red River, but only a **tributary**.
3. My great-grandmother rode in a **stagecoach**.
4. An **amphibious** vehicle drives and floats.
5. One early **automobile** was called a Stanley Steamer.
6. The first **transcontinental** flight was in 1911.
7. Jet fuel provided the necessary **propulsion**.
8. A **schooner** may have two or more masts.
9. **Gasoline** is very flammable, so handle it carefully.
10. A **hydroplane** skims quickly across the channel.

Final Test

1. The brain is divided into two **cerebral** hemispheres.
2. The treasurer is in charge of **fiscal** matters.
3. Holmes solved the case by asking **logical** questions.
4. What a **sensational** party this has been!
5. In many **tropical** countries, rain falls daily.
6. Each pyramid is a **colossal** stone structure.
7. Isn't this song a **revival** of an earlier version?
8. The **literal** translation of that poem is very awkward.
9. Only test pilots fly this **experimental** plane.
10. These **artificial** plants actually look very real.
11. After the political **upheaval**, order was restored.
12. Are **supplemental** vitamins good for a poor diet?
13. Chan's **perpetual** complaints became very tiresome.
14. I know you're frightened, but don't get **hysterical**.
15. Not every wrong act is a **criminal** act.
16. This discovery was **accidental**, not planned.
17. Bright lights will make the room look less **dismal**.
18. The antenna is an **integral** part of the radio.
19. Olivia made a quick **recital** of the facts she learned.
20. My **survival** was assured by the life jacket I wore.

Double Consonants

Objective
To spell words with double consonants

Pretest

1. The new mayor gave a short **acceptance** speech.
2. The **corrupt** leader was accused of embezzlement.
3. They became citizens after their **immigration**.
4. We'll **boycott** that store because of its high prices.
5. She will **summon** the delegates for the meeting.
6. Can you lend us your **assistance** with this project?
7. After a brief bout of **depression**, he was his cheery self.
8. Which is the most important **necessity**, food or shelter?
9. In spring, **pollen** from flowers causes hay fever.
10. She tried to quietly **suppress** her sneeze.
11. Did low ticket sales cause the play's **cancellation**?
12. A cool **drizzle** fell before it really started to rain.
13. Our car is our most prized **possession**.
14. The dinner guests enjoyed the **succulent** lobster.
15. Do the jurors agree **wholly** that the man is not guilty?
16. With arms outstretched, they greeted us **cordially**.
17. That small puppy will one day be an **immense** dog.
18. Linh doesn't let her problems **oppress** her.
19. They've been the winners for six **successive** years!
20. The frightened witness is **withholding** evidence.

Spelling Strategy   Page 13

Ask students to identify the double consonants in each **list word**. Work with them to syllabicate each word and lead them to notice the pronunciation of the consonants in the individual syllables. Elicit from students that in *acceptance* and *successive*, the first c has the hard sound while the second c has the soft sound. You may also wish to discuss the meanings of the **list words**.

Vocabulary Development To review synonyms, have students identify the **list words** that are synonyms for the following words: *gloominess* (depression), *aid* (assistance).

Dictionary Skills Remind students to use alphabetical order to determine which **list word** comes between each pair of dictionary guide words.

Spelling Practice   Pages 14–15

Word Analysis You may wish to have students review the **list words** before completing this activity.

Analogies Review analogies by writing on the board: *sock, coat, hat*. Have students select the word that completes this analogy: *Shoelace is to boot* as *button is to _____*. (*coat*)

Lesson 3

Double Consonants

You may find it easier to spell a word that contains double consonants if you first divide the word into syllables. Pronounce each syllable of the following words, and listen for the sounds of the consonants.

ne/ces/si/ty   with/hold/ing

Vocabulary Development
Write the **list word** that matches each synonym.

1. restraining	withholding	7. agreement	acceptance
2. ruin	corrupt	8. juicy	succulent
3. graciously	cordially	9. squash	suppress
4. enormous	immense	10. call	summon
5. need	necessity	11. ownership	possession
6. sprinkle	drizzle	12. despair	depression

Dictionary Skills
Write the **list word** that comes between each pair of dictionary guide words.

1. succeed/succinct   successive
2. immerse/immortal   immigration
3. denounce/drain   depression
4. access/assurance   assistance
5. breeze/coral   cancellation
6. detour/drum   drizzle
7. polka/position   pollen
8. neck/policy   oppress
9. white/width   wholly
10. astute/canary   boycott
11. window/worry   withholding
12. suppose/supreme   suppress

LIST WORDS
1. acceptance
2. corrupt
3. immigration
4. boycott
5. summon
6. assistance
7. depression
8. necessity
9. pollen
10. suppress
11. cancellation
12. drizzle
13. possession
14. succulent
15. wholly
16. cordially
17. immense
18. oppress
19. successive
20. withholding

13

DID YOU KNOW?
Around 1880, a man named Captain Charles Boycott acted as a rent collector for wealthy landowners in Ireland. Captain Boycott charged farmers extremely high rent for the land they worked. As a result, the farmers got together and refused to pay. Their tactics worked, and the rents were lowered. Soon, the term **boycott** became part of our language, meaning "a strike against unfair practices."

Spelling Practice
Word Analysis
Write **list words** to answer the following questions.

Which words contain the following suffixes?

ance	sion	ly
1. acceptance	3. depression	5. wholly
2. assistance	4. possession	6. cordially

Which words contain the prefix **im**?
7. immigration   8. immense

Analogies
Write a **list word** to complete each analogy.

1. Hurricane is to breeze as downpour is to   drizzle
2. Spending is to saving as giving is to   withholding
3. Small is to tiny as large is to   immense
4. Resist is to resistance as assist is to   assistance
5. Enemy is to cruelly as friend is to   cordially
6. Something is to everything as partly is to   wholly
7. Accept is to recruit as refuse is to   boycott
8. Going out is to emigration as coming in is to   immigration
9. Squirrel is to acorn as bee is to   pollen
10. Show is to express as hide is to   suppress
11. Accept is to renewal as reject is to   cancellation
12. Last is to previous as next is to   successive
13. Tasty is to savory as juicy is to   succulent
14. Send away is to expel as call forth is to   summon
15. Clean is to pure as dirty is to   corrupt
16. Encourage is to uplift as burden is to   oppress
17. Disapproval is to rejection as approval is to   acceptance
18. Happy is to elation as despondent is to   depression
19. Want is to desire as need is to   necessity

14   Lesson 3 • Double Consonants

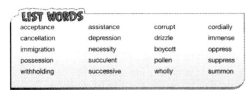

LIST WORDS

acceptance	assistance	corrupt	cordially
cancellation	depression	drizzle	immense
immigration	necessity	boycott	oppress
possession	succulent	pollen	suppress
withholding	successive	wholly	summon

Puzzle
Use the **list words** to complete the crossword puzzle.

ACROSS

2. holding something by ownership
6. very large
8. the act of doing away with
9. deeply felt; sincere
10. the entire amount or degree
11. to refuse to buy, sell, or use
13. change from good to bad
14. yellow powder found on the stamen of flowers
15. coming in regular order without a break
16. help; aid
17. to put down by force; crush

DOWN

1. to rain lightly in fine drops
3. to call together
4. something necessary or needed
5. sadness; gloominess
6. the act of moving to a foreign country
7. taking willingly; responding in the affirmative
10. to keep from giving or granting
12. to burden; weigh down; worry
15. full of juice; juicy

Proofreading

Use the proofreading marks to correct the mistakes in the article below. Then, write the misspelled **list words** correctly on the lines.

Proofreading Marks
- ⊙ spelling mistake
- ≡ capital letter
- ⌄ add apostrophe
- ⌃ add comma

Between 1881 and 1920, imigration to the United States skyrocketed. An imennse number of people—over 23 million—came to americas shores in succesive waves most of them from europe. They came for various reasons. Some wanted to escape from corupt political regimes, while others were fleeing economic depresion. All of them saw the United States as a land in which theyd be able to find new opportunities.

1. immigration
2. immense
3. successive
4. corrupt
5. depression

Writing Interview Questions

Imagine you are a reporter working for a big-city newspaper early in the twentieth century. What kind of questions would you want to ask a new immigrant to the United States? Write a list of interview questions, using as many **list words** as possible. Proofread and revise your questions, then use them to stage a question-and-answer session with another classmate.

BONUS WORDS

commissioner	magistrate	coroner	attorney general	supervisor
superintendent	treasurer	secretary	vice-president	ambassador

Write the **bonus word** that matches each clue.

1. title of some members of the president's cabinet — secretary
2. representative of one country to another country — ambassador
3. minor official, such as a justice of the peace — magistrate
4. country's top law official — attorney general
5. official next in rank to a company's president — vice-president
6. officer in charge of funds or finances — treasurer
7. official who determines causes of death — coroner
8. official who heads a government department, such as fire or police — commisioner
9. manager or director of a department or group — supervisor
10. person in charge of a department or institution, such as a school — superintendent

---

Puzzle Urge students to think about the meanings of the **list words** as they complete the puzzle. Tell students to use capital letters and to print clearly.

Spelling and Writing   *Page 16*

Proofreading Discuss the use of the proofreading marks in the box. Then, write on the board: *patsys allergies to polen bees and grass are severe.* Have volunteers use the marks to correct the mistakes.

Writing Interview Questions Discuss how the question words *Who? What? When? Where?* and *Why?* help newswriters gather information for stories. Ask students to use the words to suggest questions they might ask a new immigrant to the United States.

Bonus Words   *Page 16*

Government Offices Point out that many of the **bonus words** have similar meanings. For example, *secretary, supervisor, commissioner,* and *superintendent* are names for officials that head government departments. A *commissioner* is the head of the police in a state; a *superintendent* is the head of a school system.

Bonus Words Test

1. Gerald Ford was a **vice-president** and a president.
2. He knows finances and was once state **treasurer**.
3. Kennedy appointed his brother as **attorney general**.
4. The police **commissioner** promised us a safe city.
5. She is the **superintendent** of our school district.
6. The **coroner** said the man died of natural causes.
7. The senator was appointed **ambassador** to Italy.
8. The President is often referred to as chief **magistrate**.
9. The **Secretary** of State addressed Congress.
10. Mr. Liggett is **supervisor** of a government agency.

Final Test

1. The **immense** ocean liner has ten decks.
2. Rain is a **necessity** to vegetable farmers.
3. You are **cordially** invited to my graduation party.
4. Rulers who want power often **oppress** people.
5. Yellow **pollen** dust settled on and coated the car.
6. It may continue to **drizzle** or it may pour.
7. Applicants for **immigration** must obtain a visa.
8. We tried to cheer her out of her **depression**.
9. The menu says the steak is **succulent** and tender.
10. What amount will you be **withholding** for taxes?
11. Rudy has **possession** of a valuable baseball card.
12. The students will **boycott** all Saturday classes.
13. Mr. Lee will **summon** the students to the auditorium.
14. Does the cough syrup help **suppress** your cough?
15. The game's **cancellation** disappointed everyone.
16. Nora's final exams lasted for five **successive** days.
17. Kele offered his **assistance** to the furniture movers.
18. Julie received an **acceptance** letter from the college.
19. The settlers **wholly** objected to the unfair tax laws.
20. The evil wizard could not **corrupt** the good prince.

Lesson 4

Words with the Sound of ər

Objective
To spell words with /ər/

Pretest
1. An **alligator** is a large reptile with powerful jaws.
2. My little sister is my **junior** by eight years.
3. Will the premature baby be put in the **incubator**?
4. Outside, I heard the soft **murmur** of far-off voices.
5. Mount a red **reflector** on your back bike fender.
6. Our family album shows photos of our **ancestors**.
7. Many icebergs have broken off the **glacier**.
8. A good **investor** will invest your money wisely.
9. Which butterfly is attracted to this **particular** plant?
10. We can sail as soon as we haul up the **anchor**.
11. He has sharp features and an **angular** face.
12. The **gladiator** entertained the Roman audience.
13. A river curves, but a canal is more **linear**.
14. The two lines should be **perpendicular**, not parallel.
15. Can you remove this splinter without **tweezers**?
16. Each victory in battle pleased the **conqueror**.
17. That isn't the real prince; it must be an **impostor**.
18. The **moderator** of the debate timed each team.
19. Dr. Chávez is a Spanish **professor** at the university.
20. Did she ever wince when she tasted the **vinegar**!

Spelling Strategy   Page 17
Have students read the spelling rule and tell how /ər/ is spelled in each example word. After each word is read, have them find other **list words** with the same pattern. Make sure students know the meanings of unfamiliar words, encouraging them to use dictionaries if needed.

Vocabulary Development Write *beach* and *shore* on the board, and point out that the words are synonyms. Discuss what synonyms are, and have students give other examples of synonym pairs.

Dictionary Skills Encourage students to first try to complete this exercise without referring to a pronunciation key. When they have finished, have them check their answers in dictionaries.

Spelling Practice   Pages 18–19
Word Analysis Encourage students to refer to the **list words** on page 19 if they are unsure of spellings.

Word Application Point out that in these exercises, the meanings of the **list words** are as important as the spellings, and that each word must make sense in the context of the sentence.

Words with the Sound of ər

Lesson 4

 TIP
The **ər** sound that you hear at the end of *murmur, linear, alligator,* and *glacier* can be spelled many different ways. When you hear this sound in a word, pay close attention to how it is spelled. Remember, when the sound comes at the end of a word that names a person who does something, the sound is often spelled with **or**, as in *conqueror.*

Vocabulary Development
Write the **list word** that matches each synonym.

1. straight	linear	
2. crocodile	alligator	
3. winner	conqueror	
4. faker	impostor	
5. younger	junior	
6. whisper	murmur	
7. forebears	ancestors	
8. warrior	gladiator	
9. pincers	tweezers	
10. teacher	professor	
11. vertical	perpendicular	
12. specific	particular	

LIST WORDS
1. alligator
2. junior
3. incubator
4. murmur
5. reflector
6. ancestors
7. glacier
8. investor
9. particular
10. anchor
11. angular
12. gladiator
13. linear
14. perpendicular
15. tweezers
16. conqueror
17. impostor
18. moderator
19. professor
20. vinegar

Dictionary Skills
Write the **list word** that matches each sound-spelling.

1. (käŋ′kər ər) conqueror
2. (an′ses tərs) ancestors
3. (mäd′ə rāt′ər) moderator
4. (iŋ′kyə bāt′ər) incubator
5. (aŋ′gyə lər) angular
6. (im päs′tər) impostor
7. (ri flek′tər) reflector
8. (vin′i gər) vinegar
9. (in vest′ər) investor
10. (glā′shər) glacier
11. (aŋ′kər) anchor
12. (jōōn′yər) junior

17

DID YOU KNOW?
Tweezers comes from an obsolete English word, *tweeses,* that meant "a case for small surgical instruments." That word came in turn from *etuis,* plural of a French word for a small case used to hold needles or other small implements.

Spelling Practice
Word Analysis
Write the **list words** in which the sound of /ər/ is spelled **ar**.
1. particular   4. perpendicular
2. angular   5. vinegar
3. linear

Write the **list words** in which the sound of /ər/ is spelled **er**.
6. glacier   8. tweezers
7. perpendicular   9. conqueror

Write the **list word** in which the sound of /ər/ is spelled **ur**.
10. murmur

Write the **list words** containing these double letters.
11. ee tweezers   13. ll alligator
12. ss professor

Word Application
Replace the underlined word or words in each sentence with a **list word**. Write the **list word** on the line.
1. The two lines are at right angles to each other. perpendicular
2. The recipe calls for just a dash of a sour liquid. vinegar
3. We are looking for a specific kind of mustard. particular
4. The trek will begin at the base of the mountain of ice. glacier
5. Although the artist's drawings of people were rounded, the buildings had a narrow, uniform appearance. linear
6. Mrs. Greenbaum, a wealthy stockbroker, discussed the methods she used to become a successful person who uses money or capital to gain a financial return. investor
7. Mr. Olson moved the hen's eggs into the place that is kept warm for hatching eggs. incubator
8. Captain Martinez ordered the sailors to drop the heavy object that is put in water to keep a ship from drifting. anchor

18   Lesson 4 • Words with the Sound of ər

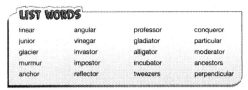

LIST WORDS

linear	angular	professor	conqueror
junior	vinegar	gladiator	particular
glacier	investor	alligator	moderator
murmur	impostor	incubator	ancestors
anchor	reflector	tweezers	perpendicular

Puzzle
Use the **list words** to complete the crossword puzzle.

ACROSS
1. at right angles
6. a sour liquid
7. person in charge of conducting a debate
9. surface that reflects
11. large mass of snow and ice
12. in a line
14. small pincers for holding small items
16. having sharp corners
18. warm container for hatching eggs

DOWN
2. person who invests
3. distinct; not general
4. one who cheats or tricks people
5. one who overcomes another
8. teacher at college
10. people who come before others in a family line
11. ancient Roman fighter
13. large, lizard-like animal
15. low, steady sound
17. a younger person
19. heavy object that holds a boat in place

Crossword answers: PERPENDICULAR, VINEGAR, MODERATOR, REFLECTOR, GLACIER, LINEAR, ANGULAR, TWEEZERS, INCUBATOR

Proofreading

Use the proofreading marks to correct the mistakes in the article below. Then, write the misspelled **list words** correctly on the lines.

Proofreading Marks
∧ add comma   ⌐ delete word
◯ spelling mistake
! add exclamation mark

Norway is known for its its scenery and a particuler glacier that is one of the largest in the world. A cruise along the Norwegian coast can be truly spectacular As your ship drops anchor perpindiculer to the steep mountain walls of a long narrow bay known as a fjord listen for the murmer of a a distant waterfall. Many of these fjords have incredible vistas, with lush, green mountainsides that plunge straight into the water.

1. particular
2. glacier
3. anchor
4. perpendicular
5. murmur

Writing a Description

Write a description of what you might see from the deck of a ship that is traveling along the Norwegian coast. Use as many of the **list words** as you can. Proofread and revise your description, then read it aloud to your classmates.

BONUS WORDS

petition	indictment	warrant	trespass	mandate
judicial	misdemeanor	property	subpoena	judgment

Write the **bonus word** that matches each clue given.

1. legal decision   judgment
2. order to appear in court   subpoena
3. a formal accusation from a grand jury   indictment
4. written order to arrest   warrant
5. order from higher court   mandate
6. something that is owned   property
7. to enter illegally   trespass
8. formal written request   petition
9. related to court   judicial
10. minor offense   misdemeanor

Puzzle Ask students what two clues help them with each answer. (*the definition; the number of letters in a word*) Point out that each answer helps find the next one, reminding students to first fill in known answers.

Spelling and Writing   *Page 20*
Proofreading Write the following sentence on the board, and then ask volunteers to correct it using the proofreading marks for this lesson.
Damon hurry up or or we'll be latte

Writing a Description Ask students to compare the following sentences: *The leaf fell from the tree.* and *The withered, brown leaf fell from the ancient oak, spiraling slowly downward.* Remind students that description uses verbs, adverbs, and adjectives to convey images. If possible, bring in books or articles containing photographs to help students visualize the Norwegian coast.

Bonus Words   *Page 20*
Law Discuss the meanings of the **bonus words**. Some words, such as *subpoena, mandate,* and *indictment,* relate to the judicial process. Other words, such as *property, trespass,* and *misdemeanor* refer to crimes.

Bonus Words Test
1. Each witness received a **subpoena** on Thursday.
2. A **misdemeanor** is less serious than a felony.
3. The Kangas family made a **petition** to adopt Laurie.
4. As I expected, the **judgment** was in my favor.
5. Dr. Juarez read many materials on **judicial** matters.
6. The **mandate** came directly from Superior Court.
7. We do not **trespass** on our neighbor's property.
8. The grand jury handed down an **indictment**.
9. You will need a search **warrant** to enter that room.
10. Some stolen **property** is easy to identify.

Final Test
1. My **ancestors** came from Portugal and Russia.
2. The **glacier** looks like a river of ice.
3. Of course, no **investor** wanted that company to fail!
4. Arlene had one **particular** song she wanted to hear.
5. Use the spikes to **anchor** the tent to the ground.
6. An **alligator** can weigh as much as 550 pounds.
7. She will be a **junior** partner only one more year.
8. Gently turn the eggs that are in the **incubator**.
9. A faint **murmur** of approval rose from the audience.
10. Did her bike have a **reflector** on its wheels?
11. Tien added too much **vinegar** to the salad.
12. Which **professor** will be teaching that course?
13. The **moderator** helped the meeting run smoothly.
14. What a surprise to learn the man was an **impostor**!
15. Almost at once, the **conqueror** wrote new laws.
16. Do you prefer the **angular** shape of those roofs?
17. The **gladiator** carried a large bronze shield.
18. Use a yardstick to record the **linear** measurement.
19. That avenue runs **perpendicular** to this street.
20. Use a pair of **tweezers** to remove the splinter.

Lesson 5

Doubling Final Consonants

Objective
To spell words that double the final consonant when adding an ending or suffix

Pretest

1. The **controller** of that machine needs training.
2. A fleet of Coast Guard boats **patrolled** the harbor.
3. Swimming is strictly **forbidden** in the river.
4. Mr. Chan **conferred** with Kendra about her grades.
5. She **preferred** eating fish rather than meat.
6. What an **unforgettable** vacation in Bermuda!
7. She **deferred** passing judgment until Tuesday.
8. Will he be **expelled** from school for his behavior?
9. The radio tower is **transmitting** sound waves.
10. Snow is **deterring** climbers from reaching the peak.
11. Do you **occasionally** visit your relatives in Mexico?
12. These events were **occurring** as we slept.
13. He **incurred** a lot of debt by using his credit card.
14. The antique plane's **propeller** spun around.
15. I'm **admitting** that I was your secret admirer.
16. Was your name mistakenly **omitted** from the list?
17. The director **permitted** us to watch the rehearsal.
18. The defendant was **acquitted** and released from jail.
19. The roof shingles are **overlapping** one another.
20. We felt **handicapped** without a map to guide us.

Spelling Strategy **Page 21**

Discuss the two spelling rules for adding endings or suffixes. Point out the words *occasionally*, *occurring*, and *acquitted* as examples, as well as *conferred*, *preferred*, and *deferred*. To reinforce the spelling rules, write the following words on the board and ask volunteers to add either *ed* or *ing* to *refer*, *equip*, *cram*; *er* to *thin*, *call*; *ly* to *final*, *total*; *able* to *regret*.

Vocabulary Development Before students begin this activity, discuss the definitions of the **list words**. Urge students to consult a dictionary for any unfamiliar words.

Dictionary Skills Point out to students that it may be helpful to pronounce each word slowly and carefully to themselves, listening for the sound of each syllable.

Spelling Practice **Pages 22–23**

Word Analysis Explain to students that they will make **list words** by adding one of the endings or suffixes listed in the directions to each word. Remind students that the spelling rules apply to these words.

Word Application Point out that each sentence contains context clues that will help students identify the missing **list word**. To extend the activity, have students create sentences with the other **list words** to exchange with partners.

TIP

When a short-vowel word or syllable ends in a single consonant, usually double the final consonant before adding an ending or suffix that begins with a vowel.

unforget + able = unforgettable
overlap + ing = overlapping
defer + ed = deferred
propel + er = propeller

When adding ly to a word that ends in l, keep both l's.

usual + ly = usually

Vocabulary Development

Write the **list word** from column B that matches the clue in column A.

A		B
1. stopping	deterring	permitted
2. came together	conferred	omitted
3. memorable	unforgettable	deferred
4. cast out	expelled	deterring
5. cleared one's name	acquitted	conferred
6. chose a certain one	preferred	unforgettable
7. postponed	deferred	expelled
8. once in a while	occasionally	acquitted
9. allowed to act	permitted	occasionally
10. left out	omitted	preferred

Dictionary Skills

Rewrite the following **list words** to show how they are divided into syllables.

1. handicapped hand/i/capped
2. patrolled pa/trolled
3. forbidden for/bid/den
4. transmitting trans/mit/ting
5. overlapping o/ver/lap/ping
6. controller con/trol/ler
7. occurring oc/cur/ring
8. incurred in/curred
9. propeller pro/pel/ler
10. admitting ad/mit/ting

21

Spelling Practice

DID YOU KNOW?

There was a form of bartering in the 1660s in which two people wishing to exchange items would get together with an umpire. All three parties would put a small amount of money into a hat. Eventually, the owners would insert a hand into the hat, or *hand in cap*. Depending on whether the owners withdrew their hands with money determined the outcome of the deal. The term *handicap* was used in rules for horse racing in the late 1600s. Today, it applies to a disadvantage in a sporting event, like golf, or it describes something that holds a person back or that makes things harder for him or her.

Word Analysis

Write the **list word** formed by adding one of the following endings or suffixes to each of the words given: **er, ed, en, ing, ly.**

1. admit admitting
2. confer conferred
3. omit omitted
4. forbid forbidden
5. permit permitted
6. defer deferred
7. patrol patrolled
8. control controller
9. occur occurring
10. occasional occasionally
11. propel propeller
12. handicap handicapped
13. incur incurred
14. overlap overlapping
15. prefer preferred
16. acquit acquitted
17. expel expelled
18. deter deterring

Word Application

Write a **list word** to complete each sentence.

1. The directors of the manufacturing firm ___conferred___ about how to increase production.
2. Unfortunately, Ian ___omitted___ his name from his project.
3. Lisa was ___expelled___ from the program because she broke the rules.
4. The breathtaking view from the top of Mt. Washington was ___unforgettable___
5. A new local television station will begin ___transmitting___ programs next week.
6. Mrs. Chase is the air-traffic ___controller___ who will be guiding the disabled jet through the landing.
7. The guard dogs are doing a fine job of ___deterring___ trespassers.
8. After weeks of testimony, the jury ___acquitted___ the defendant.
9. A solar eclipse will be ___occurring___ at the beginning of next month.
10. Any bills that have been ___incurred___ during your stay will be paid by the company.
11. Although Jon enjoyed snowboarding, he really ___preferred___ summer sports.
12. Since their vacations are ___overlapping___, they plan to spend some time together at the beach.
13. State troopers ___patrolled___ the highway in unmarked cars.

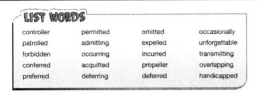

LIST WORDS

controller	permitted	omitted	occasionally
patrolled	admitting	expelled	unforgettable
forbidden	occurring	incurred	transmitting
conferred	acquitted	propeller	overlapping
preferred	deterring	deferred	handicapped

Puzzle

Write the **list word** that is a synonym for each word given to complete the crossword puzzle.

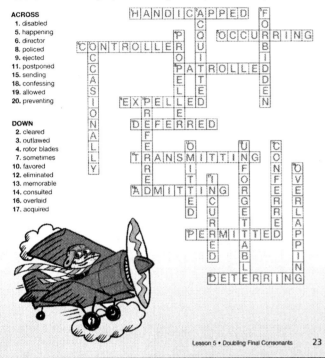

ACROSS

1. disabled
5. happening
6. director
8. policed
9. ejected
11. postponed
15. sending
18. confessing
19. allowed
20. preventing

DOWN

2. cleared
3. outlawed
4. rotor blades
7. sometimes
10. favored
12. eliminated
13. memorable
14. consulted
16. overlaid
17. acquired

Lesson 5 • Doubling Final Consonants   23

Proofreading

Use the proofreading marks to correct the mistakes in the article below. Then, write the misspelled **list words** correctly on the lines.

On July 26,2000,the americans with Disabilities Act celebrated its tenth anniversary.This historic law conferred on handicaped people throughout america the right to greater access, admiting them to buildings nationwide. Before 1990, for example, many people in wheelchairs found that the stairs in most museums were deterring them from seeing exhibits. Now, all public buildings must provide easy access for wheelchairs. Some businesses have incurred fines for not following the law, but many people share retired Attorney General Janet reno's feeling that Americans with disabilities are well on their way to experiencing all that society has to offer.

Proofreading Marks

⌒ spelling mistake   ⊙ add period
≡ capital letter   ⋀ add comma

1. conferred
2. handicapped
3. admitting
4. deterring
5. incurred

Writing a Persuasive Paragraph

Write a persuasive paragraph in which you explain why the Americans with Disabilities Act is an important law for all Americans. Give reasons for your opinion, and try to use as many of the **list words** as you can. Then, proofread and revise your paragraph, and share it with your classmates.

BONUS WORDS

adverb	interjection	nominative	singular	auxiliary verb
clause	possessive	objective	adjective	interrogative

Write the **bonus word** that the underlined word or words exemplify.

1. They arrived in time to see the opening ceremonies. nominative
2. We read in the paper that Raymond's brother joined the Peace Corps. possessive
3. Tina drove cautiously on the icy road. adverb
4. Wow! What a surprise it is to see you again! interjection
5. Because it was raining, the game was postponed. clause
6. We will help Mom fix dinner. auxiliary verb
7. You have to read this marvelous book. adjective
8. Are you listening carefully to the directions? interrogative
9. Miss Lewis assigned him the role of Caesar in the play. objective
10. In the box, there were magazines, postcards, stamps, and one pencil. singular

24   Lesson 5 • Doubling Final Consonants

Puzzle Elicit the definition of *synonym* from students. (*"words with the same or nearly the same meaning"*) Point out that to complete this puzzle they will have to recognize synonyms for all of the **list words**.

Spelling and Writing   *Page 24*

Proofreading Review the proofreading marks in this lesson, emphasizing when to add a comma.

Writing a Persuasive Paragraph Facilitate a class discussion on what it would be like to live with a disability and why the Americans with Disabilities Act is important. Urge students to incorporate ideas from the discussion into their writing. Remind them to make their position clear and support it with three convincing arguments. When finished, provide time for volunteers to read their paragraphs aloud.

Bonus Words   *Page 24*

Grammar Discuss the definition of each **bonus word**, eliciting from students examples of each word. If they are unfamiliar with any term, provide an example. You may also wish to have students find examples of these terms in current reading assignments.

Bonus Words Test

1. *Him* is the **objective** case form of the pronoun *he*.
2. An **interrogative** sentence asks a question.
3. An **adverb** is a word used to modify a verb.
4. An **interjection** is a word showing strong emotion.
5. An **auxiliary verb** is also called a helping verb.
6. *Josh*, *Chicago*, and *cat* are all **singular** nouns.
7. An **adjective** modifies a noun or pronoun.
8. Nouns in the subject are in the **nominative** case.
9. A dependent **clause** cannot function as a sentence.
10. A **possessive** noun shows ownership.

Final Test

1. The dictator **expelled** the rebels from his country.
2. Television often reports the news as it is **occurring**.
3. The lawyer is confident her client will be **acquitted**.
4. No one is **permitted** to enter without a ticket.
5. What is your most **unforgettable** experience?
6. Soldiers **patrolled** the area after the battle.
7. Our **overlapping** lunch hours are great.
8. **Admitting** she was wrong took a lot of courage.
9. Which document is he **transmitting** by modem?
10. This company designs cars for **handicapped** drivers.
11. A **propeller** helps put a ship or plane in motion.
12. He liked to go out, but she **preferred** to stay home.
13. The **controller** switched the train to another track.
14. Fear of water is **deterring** Ann from swimming.
15. The call was **deferred** while I answered the door.
16. **Occasionally**, I'll see a hummingbird outside.
17. The news story **omitted** an important fact.
18. The president **conferred** with his top advisor.
19. How were the injuries **incurred** in the accident?
20. Smoking here is **forbidden**.

Lessons 1–5 · Review

Objectives
To review syllabication, spelling words with double consonants and words that end with /əl/ and /ər/

Spelling Strategy — Page 25
This lesson helps students review the spelling patterns of words they studied in Lessons 1–5. Have students read and discuss each of the spelling rules separately. After each spelling rule, have them apply what they learned to example words of their own choice.

Spelling Practice — Pages 25–27
Lesson 1 Write *abandon, exposure, consolidate,* and *curiosity* on the board. Use the words to review syllabication. (*a/ban/don; ex/po/sure; con/sol/i/date; cur/i/os/i/ty*) Discuss with students how this helps them spell words. Point out the additional write-on lines, and encourage students to add two words from Lesson 1 that they found especially difficult, or assign words that seemed difficult for everyone. (Repeat this procedure for each lesson in the Review.)

Lesson 2 Write *upheaval, survival,* and *recital* on the board. Have students identify the ending sound by circling the letters standing for that sound. Then, discuss analogies, asking what relationship *huge* and *small* have. (*antonyms*) Lead students through the first example, asking what **list word** is an antonym for *tiny*. (*colossal*) Point out that *colossal* completes the analogy. Discuss the relationship between the pair of words in item 6 (*synonyms*) before having students complete the exercise.

Lesson 3 Write *pollen, wholly,* and *succulent* on the board. Discuss how to divide the words into syllables between the double consonants. Have students identify double consonants in the **list words**.

Lesson 4 Review the different ways /ər/ can be spelled, using *runner, sailor, linear, murmur*. Have students identify the letters that spell /ər/ in each **list word**, pointing out that the *ur* spelling is the least common.

Lesson 5 Review the doubling rule with students. Then, write these words on the board and discuss why each final consonant was doubled: *casually, admitting, beginner, committed*. Remind students that the number of letters in each word is a clue.

Show What You Know — Page 28
Point out that this review will help students know if they have mastered the words in Lessons 1–5. Have a volunteer restate the directions and tell which word in the first item should be marked as incorrect. (*cancelation*) When finished, have students write their misspelled words correctly.

28

Lessons 1–5 · Review

TIPS
- Dividing words into syllables can help you spell them. Usually, you can divide between a root or base word and a prefix or suffix, as in re/act. You can divide between two consonants that come between two vowels, as in col/lect. When only one consonant comes between two vowels, divide after the first vowel if it is long, as in pro/tect, and after the consonant if the vowel is short, as in sat/is/fy. A vowel can also form its own syllable, as in vi/o/lent.
- Pay particular attention to the spelling of word endings. Words ending with **al**, such as fiscal, may sound as if they end with **le** or **el**. The /ər/ sound you hear at the end of junior can be spelled many ways, as in murmur, grammar, humor, and super.
- Pay attention to words that have endings beginning with vowels. These may have had their final consonants doubled if the vowel before the consonant is short, as in trotting and permitted.

Lesson 1
List Words
affidavit
appetite
commemorate
tendency
voluntary
resurrect
dominate
guardian
saturate
installation

Write a **list word** to complete each sentence.

1. Tomatoes have a __tendency__ to grow best during hot, sunny weather.
2. The __affidavit__ the witness signed was given to the judge.
3. Your idea didn't work last year, but let's __resurrect__ it and see if we have better luck this year.
4. A sprinkler is the easiest way to __saturate__ a lawn with an inch of water.
5. A child's __guardian__ is an adult who is authorized to make decisions for the child.
6. A contribution of $10.00 is __voluntary__, not required.
7. The __installation__ of an antenna can improve TV reception.
8. A water tower that is as large as a skyscraper will __dominate__ the landscape.
9. My parents will plant a cherry tree to __commemorate__ my sister's birth.
10. After a workout, it takes a lot more than one sandwich to satisfy my __appetite__.

25

Lesson 2
List Words
artificial
criminal
experimental
hysterical
revival
tropical
logical
perpetual
colossal
accidental

Write a **list word** to complete each analogy.

1. Huge is to small as __colossal__ is to tiny.
2. Cold is to hot as arctic is to __tropical__.
3. Careful is to thoughtless as __logical__ is to irrational.
4. Death is to burial as rebirth is to __revival__.
5. Serenity is to disorganization as tranquil is to __hysterical__.
6. Genuine is to authentic as __artificial__ is to unnatural.
7. Eternity is to momentary as __perpetual__ is to temporary.
8. Honorable is to dishonorable as legal is to __criminal__.
9. Purposeful is to scheduled as __accidental__ is to unscheduled.
10. Photography is to artistic as chemistry is to __experimental__.

Lesson 3
List Words
possession
summon
cancellation
successive
acceptance
assistance
depression
immense
necessity
immigration

Write **list words** to answer the questions. Some words are used more than once.

Which words contain double **m**?
1. summon
2. immense
3. immigration

Which words contain double **s**?
4. possession
5. successive
6. assistance
7. depression
8. necessity

Which words end in **ance**?
9. acceptance
10. assistance

Which words end in **ation**?
11. cancellation
12. immigration

Which words end in **sion**?
13. possession
14. depression

26   Lesson 6 • Review

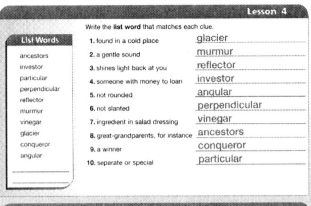

Lesson 4

Write the **list word** that matches each clue.

List Words

ancestors
investor
particular
perpendicular
reflector
murmur
vinegar
glacier
conqueror
angular

1. found in a cold place — glacier
2. a gentle sound — murmur
3. shines light back at you — reflector
4. someone with money to loan — investor
5. not rounded — angular
6. not slanted — perpendicular
7. ingredient in salad dressing — vinegar
8. great-grandparents, for instance — ancestors
9. a winner — conqueror
10. separate or special — particular

Lesson 5

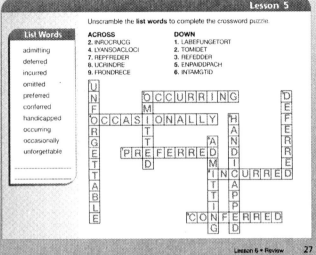

Unscramble the **list words** to complete the crossword puzzle.

List Words

admitting
deferred
incurred
omitted
preferred
conferred
handicapped
occurring
occasionally
unforgettable

ACROSS
2. INROCRUCG
4. LYANSOACLOCI
7. REPFREDER
8. UCRINDRE
9. FRONDRECE

DOWN
1. LABEFUNGETORT
2. TOMIDET
3. REFEDDER
5. ENPAIDDPACH
6. INTAMGTID

Show What You Know

Lessons 1–5 • Review

One word is misspelled in each set of **list words**. Fill in the circle next to the **list word** that is spelled incorrectly.

1. ○ artificial   ○ abandon   ○ conqueror   ● cancelation
2. ● drizle   ○ impostor   ○ wholly   ○ experimental
3. ○ exposure   ○ possession   ○ literal   ● moderater
4. ● succulant   ○ revival   ○ professor   ○ ornament
5. ○ vinegar   ○ tendency   ○ colossal   ● comemorate
6. ● affidavet   ○ cordially   ○ cerebral   ○ controller
7. ○ patrolled   ● fiscall   ○ consolidate   ○ immense
8. ● graditure   ○ oppress   ○ logical   ○ forbidden
9. ○ resurrect   ○ sensational   ○ conferred   ● succesive
10. ○ tropical   ○ undoubtedly   ● prefered   ○ withholding
11. ○ criminal   ○ appetite   ● alligater   ○ unforgettable
12. ● hystericle   ○ junior   ○ curiosity   ○ deferred
13. ○ incubator   ● perpetuel   ○ expelled   ○ guardian
14. ● murmer   ○ saturate   ○ transmitting   ○ supplemental
15. ○ voluntary   ○ reflector   ● upheeval   ○ occasionally
16. ○ deterring   ○ ancestors   ● barbaque   ○ acceptance
17. ○ dominate   ○ corrupt   ○ glacier   ● occuring
18. ○ investor   ● imigration   ○ incurred   ○ installation
19. ○ boycott   ● propellor   ○ particular   ○ specifications
20. ○ anchor   ○ ascertain   ● admiting   ○ summon
21. ○ accidental   ● anguler   ○ assistance   ○ omitted
22. ○ gladiator   ○ permitted   ● dizmal   ○ depression
23. ● nescessity   ○ integral   ○ linear   ○ acquitted
24. ○ recital   ○ overlapping   ○ pollen   ● perpendiculer
25. ○ survival   ● supress   ○ tweezers   ○ handicapped

Final Test

1. No one would dare **resurrect** last year's plan!
2. Won't the tall evergreen **dominate** your landscape?
3. The wall should be **perpendicular** to the floor.
4. Make sure the water doesn't **saturate** the carpets!
5. **Immigration** brings diverse people to our country.
6. The plant looks real, but it's **artificial**.
7. Was she looking for a **particular** kind of raincoat?
8. The doctors may try an **experimental** treatment.
9. Most of my **ancestors** are from Italy.
10. This play is a **revival** of one from 1940.
11. Please **summon** the guests to the dinner table.
12. The house is on the edge of an **immense** cornfield.
13. People were crying, but no one became **hysterical**.
14. Eliza's **acceptance** into the college pleased her.
15. Did you have an opening after their **cancellation**?
16. The cable **installation** will be at 2:00 p.m.
17. Each **investor** will provide ten thousand dollars.
18. She wants to specialize in **criminal** law.
19. A legal **guardian** must grant permission in writing.
20. I'll be safer riding at night with a bicycle **reflector**.
21. Every mystery has a **logical** explanation.
22. This parking space is for **handicapped** people.
23. Erosion is always **occurring** along the seashore.
24. By mistake, the newspaper **omitted** the author's name.
25. That **colossal** pumpkin weighs ninety pounds!
26. The witness provided a sworn **affidavit**.
27. Will jogging each day increase my **appetite**?
28. This statue will **commemorate** the first settlers.
29. These trees have a **tendency** to grow very slowly.
30. Enlistment in the United States Army is **voluntary**.
31. Many orchids grow in **tropical** climates.
32. The team **conferred** awhile and then decided.
33. The new movie has **perpetual** lines for tickets.
34. Everyone raved about his **unforgettable** meal.
35. Our meeting was **accidental**, so I was surprised.
36. Sprinkle a little **vinegar** on your fish and chips.
37. Each **successive** day Carla ran faster and faster.
38. We **deferred** our decision until after the debates.
39. Water collected in each **depression** after the storm.
40. Our little general store can supply every **necessity**.
41. Suddenly, the **murmur** of voices became a roar.
42. This portrait is my most treasured **possession**.
43. After many years, the **glacier** melted into the valley.
44. After the war, the **conqueror** renamed the city.
45. I like modern houses with high, **angular** rooflines.
46. He is **admitting** that he is responsible for the thefts.
47. If you need **assistance**, a salesperson will help you.
48. Last year's class **incurred** several long-term debts.
49. Do you cook frequently but eat out **occasionally**?
50. The Chu family **preferred** driving to flying.

Prefixes for Numbers

Objective
To spell words with prefixes indicating amount or degree

Pretest

1. A **centigrade** scale measures temperature.
2. The metric system is **decimal**, that is, based on tens.
3. Is a **kiloliter** the equivalent of one thousand liters?
4. A **monolith** is a large, single block of stone.
5. King Juan Carlos is the **monarch** who rules Spain.
6. A **centimeter** is one hundredth of a meter.
7. A **deciliter** is one tenth of a liter.
8. Isn't electricity use measured in **kilowatt** hours?
9. A store with a **monopoly** has no competition.
10. A **myriad** of colors burst forth in the sunset.
11. A **decade** is a period of ten years.
12. A **duet** on the piano requires four hands.
13. A **milligram** is one thousandth of a gram.
14. Don't speak in a **monotone** while you give a speech!
15. When is the store's **semiannual** clearance sale?
16. A **decimeter** is one tenth of a meter.
17. A **duplex** house contains two residences.
18. A **milliliter** is one thousandth of a liter.
19. The leading man ends the play with a **monologue**.
20. The garnet is a **semiprecious** gem.

Spelling Strategy   *Page 29*

Discuss the spelling rule. If necessary, review the metric system and the measuring function of grams (*weight*), liters (*volume* or *capacity*), watts (*electric power*), and meters (*length*). Have students use the prefixes *milli, centi, deci, deca,* and *kilo* with *liter, meter,* and *gram* to form and define new words. For more words with the prefixes *mono, duo, semi,* and *myria,* use: *monogram, duplicate, semiconscious,* and *myriapod.* Then, discuss each **list word**.

Vocabulary Development If needed, review the decimal system, making sure that students understand the values of *0.1, 0.01,* and *0.001.*

Dictionary Skills Before the exercise, have students use dictionaries to find and pronounce the sound-spellings of *duet, semiprecious,* and *monopoly.*

Spelling Practice   *Pages 30–31*

Word Analysis Point out how the structure and the definition of each Greek or Latin root are clues.

Syllabication To review syllabication skills, have students identify the number of syllables in *signature, machine,* and *rectangle.*

Word Application Explain that the **list words** are in the wrong sentences and need to be moved to other sentences to make sense.

TIP

Prefixes with Greek or Latin roots can indicate "how much." Here are some examples.

Prefix	Origin	Meaning	Prefix	Origin	Meaning
milli	Latin	"one-thousandth"	duo	Latin	"two"
centi	Latin	"one-hundredth"	deca	Greek	"ten"
deci	Latin	"one-tenth"	kilo	Greek	"one thousand"
semi	Latin	"half"	myria	Greek	"countless"
mono	Greek	"one"			

Vocabulary Development

Write the **list word** that matches each clue.

1. music for two people — duet
2. speech by one person — monologue
3. on one tone — monotone
4. 1,000 watts — kilowatt
5. not of high value — semiprecious
6. total control — monopoly
7. 0.1 liter — deciliter
8. 0.01 meter — centimeter
9. 0.001 liter — milliliter
10. large stone block — monolith
11. ten years — decade
12. king or queen — monarch

Dictionary Skills

Write the **list word** that matches each sound-spelling.

1. (sem'i an'yōō wəl) — semiannual
2. (des'ə met'ər) — decimeter
3. (sen'tə grad) — centigrade
4. (män'ə lôg) — monologue
5. (mil'ə gram) — milligram
6. (kil'ə lēt'ər) — kiloliter
7. (des'ə məl) — decimal
8. (mir'ē əd) — myriad
9. (dōō'pleks) — duplex
10. (män'ərk) — monarch

LIST WORDS

1. centigrade
2. decimal
3. kiloliter
4. monolith
5. monarch
6. centimeter
7. deciliter
8. kilowatt
9. monopoly
10. myriad
11. decade
12. duet
13. milligram
14. monotone
15. semiannual
16. decimeter
17. duplex
18. milliliter
19. monologue
20. semiprecious

29

DID YOU KNOW?
Kilowatt means "1,000 watts." A watt is a unit of electric power that was named for Scottish inventor James Watt, best known for his contributions to the development of the steam engine in the late 1700s.

Spelling Practice

Word Analysis

Write the **list word** derived from the Greek or Latin root given.

1. Greek *polein* ("to sell") — monopoly
2. Greek *plax* ("surface") — duplex
3. Greek *lithos* ("stone") — monolith
4. Latin *annus* ("year") — semiannual
5. Greek *tonos* ("tone") — monotone
6. Greek *archein* ("to rule") — monarch
7. Latin *gradus* ("degree") — centigrade
8. Greek *legein* ("to speak") — monologue
9. Latin *gramma* ("small weight") — milligram
10. Latin *pretium* ("price") — semiprecious

Syllabication

Write each **list word** under the correct heading.

Words with Two Syllables
1. monarch
2. decade
3. duet
4. duplex

Words with Five Syllables
5. semiannual

Words with Three Syllables
6. myriad
7. centigrade
8. decimal
9. monolith
10. kilowatt
11. milligram
12. monotone
13. monologue

Words with Four Syllables
14. kiloliter
15. centimeter
16. deciliter
17. monopoly
18. decimeter
19. milliliter
20. semiprecious

Word Application

Underline the **list word** that is used incorrectly in each sentence. Write the correct **list word** on the line.

1. The library has a monopoly of books to choose from. — myriad
2. That person speaks in an uninteresting myriad. — monotone
3. Does the company have a monotone on cable-TV service? — monopoly

30   Lesson 7 • Prefixes for Numbers

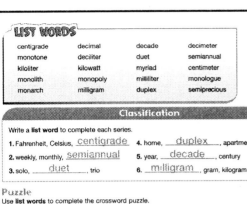

LIST WORDS

centigrade	decimal	decade	decimeter
monotone	deciliter	duet	semiannual
kiloliter	kilowatt	myriad	centimeter
monolith	monopoly	milliliter	monologue
monarch	milligram	duplex	semiprecious

Classification

Write a **list word** to complete each series.

1. Fahrenheit, Celsius, _centigrade_
2. weekly, monthly, _semiannual_
3. solo, _duet_, trio
4. home, _duplex_, apartment
5. year, _decade_, century
6. _milligram_, gram, kilogram

Puzzle

Use **list words** to complete the crossword puzzle.

ACROSS
1. period of ten years
3. large block of stone
7. owned or controlled by one person or group
8. maintaining the same tone or pitch
9. one-thousandth of a gram
10. having two units or parts
14. thermometer based on 0° as the freezing point of water
16. one-tenth of a meter
17. large, indefinite number or variety
18. 1,000 liters
19. one-thousandth of a liter

DOWN
1. counted by tens
2. long speech by one person
4. king, queen, or emperor
5. happening twice a year
6. not highly valuable
11. one-tenth of a liter
12. one-hundredth of a meter
13. 1,000 watts
15. music for two voices

(Crossword grid with answers: DECADE, MONOLITH, MONOPOLY, MONOTONE, MILLIGRAM, DUPLEX, SEMIPRECIOUS, DECILITER, CENTIGRADE, DECIMETER, MYRIAD, KILOLITER, KILOWATT, MILLILITER, SOLO, MONOLOGUE, MONARCH, CENTIMETER)

Proofreading

Use the proofreading marks to correct the mistakes in the article below. Then, write the misspelled **list words** correctly on the lines.

Proofreading Marks
- ◯ spelling mistake
- ⊙ add period
- ? add question mark
- ∧ add comma

Have you ever seen a picture of Stonehenge? A *miriad* of giant stones form this ruin in southern England. It is not a single edifice, but a circular stone structure that was built beginning around 3,100 B.C. Each *monnolith* that makes up Stonehenge weighs several tons. Over a *dekade* ago, scientists proposed the theory that the structure was an early observatory. In England, some people believe that Queen Boudicca a *monarck* of the Celtic people built Stonehenge as her monument. Today many people come on a *semiannual* basis to celebrate the summer and winter solstices at Stonehenge.

1. _myriad_
2. _monolith_
3. _decade_
4. _monarch_
5. _semiannual_

Writing Interview Questions

What kind of questions would you like to ask scientists about their work at Stonehenge? Write a set of interview questions, using as many **list words** as possible. Proofread and revise your questions. Then, use your questions to stage a question-and-answer session with another classmate.

BONUS WORDS

genetics	reproduction	pregnancy	fetus	identical
heredity	umbilical cord	fertilization	embryo	fraternal

Write the **bonus word** to complete each sentence.

1. Twins from the same egg are _identical_
2. _Fraternal_ twins come from two different eggs and do not look identical.
3. The branch of biology that deals with heredity and variation in living things is _genetics_
4. The _umbilical cord_ is the source of nourishment for a fetal mammal.
5. The transmission of traits from parent to offspring is called _heredity_
6. Animals create new members of the species through the process of _reproduction_
7. _Pregnancy_ is the state of a female animal as she carries her unborn child.
8. Through _fertilization_, the female's egg begins to develop into offspring.
9. An _embryo_ is an animal's fertilized egg in the earliest stage of development.
10. In its later stages of development, the unborn offspring is called the _fetus_

Classification To start, have students complete this series: *president, premier, _____ . (monarch)*

Puzzle Urge students to use as clues not only the definitions, but also the number of spaces in each answer.

Spelling and Writing   Page 32

Proofreading Give examples or ask students to give examples illustrating the proofreading marks.

Writing Interview Questions Remind students to consider *Who?, What?, Where?, When?,* and *Why?* when writing their questions. Provide encyclopedias, books, or periodical articles on Stonehenge for background information. Point out that doing research helps a writer formulate in-depth questions. When finished, allow time for students to interview partners.

Bonus Words   Page 32

Biology Use reference books to discuss the **bonus words**. Have students compare and contrast the gestation periods and the different birth processes (hatching of eggs versus live births) of reptiles, birds, and mammals.

Bonus Words Test

1. An **embryo** slowly develops a distinct shape.
2. An **umbilical cord** carries food and oxygen.
3. Nutrition is important during **pregnancy**.
4. The **fetus** grows inside the womb.
5. **Identical** twins are often difficult to tell apart.
6. **Fraternal** twins may be of different sexes.
7. After **fertilization**, an egg begins to grow.
8. Through **heredity**, you may resemble your parents.
9. **Genetics** is the science of heredity.
10. Life continues through **reproduction** of the species.

Final Test

1. Viking symbols had been carved on the **monolith**.
2. This hospital has a **monopoly** on health care.
3. The speaker droned on in a boring **monotone**.
4. This stand-up comedian has a funny **monologue**.
5. There are ten millimeters in a **centimeter**.
6. A **decimeter** is ten times as long as a centimeter.
7. The queen ruled for more than a **decade**.
8. At 100 degrees **centigrade**, water will boil.
9. We saw a **myriad** of colorful birds at the aviary.
10. Queen Victoria is a famous British **monarch**.
11. Turquoise is a **semiprecious** stone used in jewelry.
12. The club sends out a **semiannual** newsletter.
13. The chemist added one **milligram** of sodium chloride.
14. A **milliliter** of water is such a tiny amount!
15. The oil company measures oil by the **kiloliter**.
16. The electric meter measures **kilowatt** hours.
17. Will the soprano and the tenor sing a **duet**?
18. Maria and Ray live in a **duplex** apartment.
19. One **deciliter** equals about a third of a cup.
20. The **decimal** figure 0.1 equals one tenth.

Lesson 8

Prefixes <u>ante</u>, <u>epi</u>, <u>pre</u>, <u>pro</u>

Objective
To spell words with the prefixes *ante, epi, pre,* or *pro*

Pretest

1. A flat tire occurred **antecedent** to the blowout.
2. The author put her comments in the book's **epilogue**.
3. This is my favorite **episode** of this television show.
4. This is the **premier** brand; that's why it's expensive.
5. Will braces straighten the teeth that **protrude**?
6. I wore braces only on my **anterior** eight teeth.
7. Leona had a **premonition** of trouble on this journey.
8. The **preamble** to the Constitution tells its purpose.
9. A mind free from **prejudice** is an open mind.
10. A long **procession** of graduates entered the hall.
11. An **epitaph** is an inscription on a tombstone.
12. Leave your muddy boots in the **anteroom**.
13. Does he **presuppose** that I know that already?
14. Until the votes are in, a statement is **premature**.
15. The **prophet** warned the people of danger.
16. Each **epistle** was signed and then sealed with wax.
17. **Epidermis** refers to the outer layer of skin.
18. This tune is a **prelude** to the main theme.
19. You must submit a written **proposal** for the loan.
20. Each country's legal system has its own **protocol**.

Spelling Strategy   **Page 33**

Have students read the spelling rule, pointing out that the prefix *ante* is different from the prefix *anti,* meaning "against." Then, have students read the **list words** and discuss their meanings. If necessary, have students use dictionaries to learn the meanings of unfamiliar words.

Vocabulary Development Ask students what synonyms are (*words having the same or almost the same meaning*), and have them give examples.

Dictionary Skills Review the rules of syllabication with students, having them refer to Lesson 1, if needed. As an example, you may wish to write *pro/trude* on the board. If needed, work through the first few items with students.

Spelling Practice   **Pages 34–35**

Word Analysis Encourage students to first try to complete this exercise without looking at the **list words** on page 35. Later, you may wish to discuss how each prefix relates to the word's meaning.

Word Application Point out that each sentence needs two **list word** replacements. Remind students to pay attention to both the spelling and the meaning of each **list word**.

32

Prefixes <u>ante</u>, <u>epi</u>, <u>pre</u>, <u>pro</u>   Lesson 8

TIP

Some prefixes give "when" or "where" clues. The prefixes **ante, epi, pre,** and **pro** can refer to time or place. An understanding of these prefixes can help you spell many words. Look at the chart below.

Prefix	Meaning	Example	Meaning
ante	"before," "in front of"	anteroom	"entrance room"
epi	"on the outside," "over"	epidermis	"outer skin layer"
pre	"in front," "earlier"	premature	"happening early"
pro	"forward," "ahead"	protrude	"to stick out"

Vocabulary Development

Write the **list word** that matches each synonym.

1. event   episode
2. first   premier
3. letter   epistle
4. assume   presuppose
5. early   premature
6. overhang   protrude
7. foreseer   prophet
8. parade   procession
9. skin   epidermis
10. forerunner   antecedent
11. forward   anterior
12. forewarning   premonition

LIST WORDS

1. antecedent
2. epilogue
3. episode
4. premier
5. protrude
6. anterior
7. premonition
8. preamble
9. prejudice
10. procession
11. epitaph
12. anteroom
13. presuppose
14. premature
15. prophet
16. epistle
17. epidermis
18. prelude
19. proposal
20. protocol

Dictionary Skills

Rewrite each of the following **list words** to show how they are divided into syllables.

1. protocol   pro/to/col
2. presuppose   pre/sup/pose
3. prelude   pre/lude
4. epitaph   ep/i/taph
5. anteroom   an/te/room
6. proposal   pro/po/sal
7. premonition   pre/mo/ni/tion
8. epilogue   ep/i/logue
9. anterior   an/te/ri/or
10. prejudice   prej/u/dice

33

DID YOU KNOW?

Premonition comes from the Latin word *monere*, meaning "to warn." This word is, in turn, related to the Latin word *memini*, meaning "I remember." Thus, a premonition could be considered a reminder that occurs beforehand, or a forewarning.

Spelling Practice

Word Analysis

Write the missing prefixes to form **list words** that complete the definitions.

1. ..epi.. **dermis,** the outer layer of skin
2. ..pre.. **monition,** a preconceived notion
3. ..pro.. **trude,** to stick out
4. ..pre.. **suppose,** to suppose beforehand
5. ..pro.. **tocol,** a code of proper behavior
6. ..ante.. **room,** an outside chamber
7. ..pro.. **posal,** a suggestion
8. ..pre.. **judice,** judging beforehand
9. ..epi.. **logue,** a speech at the end of a play
10. ..epi.. **taph,** words engraved on a tombstone
11. ..pre.. **mature,** before the proper or usual time
12. ..pre.. **lude,** a preliminary part

Word Application

Replace the underlined words in each sentence with **list words**. Write the **list words** on the lines.

1. As we entered the <u>front part</u> of the park, we saw a long <u>parade</u> of musicians marching in formation. ..anterior.. ..procession..
2. During his life, he was considered a great <u>seer</u>, which is why the <u>inscription on his gravestone</u> refers to him as a man of wisdom and faith. ..prophet.. ..epitaph..
3. If it weren't for the unpleasant <u>event</u> with the doorman, no one would have known that our arrival was <u>too early</u>. ..episode.. ..premature..
4. <u>Correct behavior</u> dictates that we must wait in the <u>front room</u> before all the elders have taken their seats. ..protocol.. ..anteroom..
5. The <u>beginning</u>, or opening paragraph, of the Constitution is a kind of <u>introduction</u> for the rest of the document. ..preamble.. ..prelude..
6. It is of the <u>first</u> importance that this <u>letter</u> be sent immediately! ..premier.. ..epistle..

34   Lesson 8 • Prefixes ante, epi, pre, pro

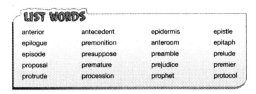

LIST WORDS

anterior	antecedent	epidermis	epistle
epilogue	premonition	anteroom	epitaph
episode	presuppose	preamble	prelude
proposal	premature	prejudice	premier
protrude	procession	prophet	protocol

Puzzle

This is a crossword puzzle without clues. Use the length and the spelling of each **list word** to complete the puzzle.

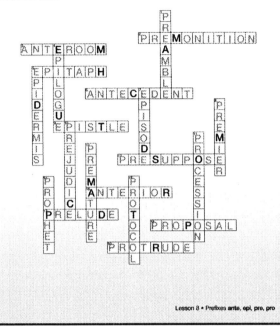

Proofreading

Proofreading Marks
- ◯ spelling mistake
- ⌐ delete word
- # add space
- / small letter

Use the proofreading marks to correct the mistakes in the article below. Then, write the misspelled **list words** correctly on the lines.

The Great Circus Parade was first presented in Milwaukee, Wisconsin, in 1963, but it has its antecedent in the circus parades of Europe. In fact, the circus as an American Amusement Institution was born in 1793 when John Ricketts, who had worked in a circus in London, England, presented a performance in Philadelphia, Pennsylvania. It was a a preloode to the big-top shows people enjoy today. The proposel for the Great Circus Parade came from the director of a circus museum, and the procesion now includes 60 historic circus wagons from around the world. Each year, the Parade is is the most exciting epesode ofa week-long festival of circus activities in Milwaukee.

1. antecedent
2. prelude
3. proposal
4. procession
5. episode

Writing a Description

Think of an interesting job in a circus, such as an animal trainer or keeper, a high-wire performer, or a clown. Write a brief description of the job, including what you might like about it, and what might be unpleasant or dangerous. Use some **list words** in your description. Proofread and revise your writing, then share it with classmates. Discuss which jobs seem the most interesting.

 BONUS WORDS

musician	horticulturist	psychiatrist	meteorologist	dental hygienist
dietitian	chiropractor	metallurgist	mathematician	physical therapist

Write the **bonus word** to complete each series.

1. ores, smelting, mines, metallurgist
2. weather, clouds, winds, meteorologist
3. nerves, spinal column, joints, chiropractor
4. songs, performances, instruments, musician
5. trees, shrubs, gardens, horticulturist
6. food, nutrition, vitamins, dietitian
7. teeth, dentist, X-rays, dental hygienist
8. numbers, formulas, equations, mathematician
9. psychoses, neuroses, depression, psychiatrist
10. hydrotherapy, exercises, massage, physical therapist

Puzzle Have volunteers describe how to solve a puzzle without clues. Remind them, if necessary, to use both the length and the letters provided as clues.

Spelling and Writing   *Page 36*

Proofreading Use this sentence to demonstrate the proofreading marks: *Nikki's favorete Foodis is Spaghetti.*

Writing a Description Invite students to brainstorm and discuss qualifications that a job in the circus might require. For example, a high-wire performer would need to be flexible, athletic, and not be afraid of heights. Then, have students write their descriptions independently.

Bonus Words   *Page 36*

Occupations Explain that the **bonus words** all name occupations. Discuss those that students are familiar with, and then help them understand those that are new. You may need to help them distinguish between a *chiropractor* and a *physical therapist*, since both deal with the human body.

Bonus Words Test
1. Our band needs one more **musician**.
2. A **metallurgist** can tell us how to mine this gold.
3. The school **dietitian** planned the month's menus.
4. A **psychiatrist** diagnosed the patient as sane.
5. The back clinic was given by a local **chiropractor**.
6. My teeth were cleaned by the **dental hygienist**.
7. A local **horticulturist** arranged these plants.
8. On the news, the **meteorologist** predicted rain.
9. The **physical therapist** retrained my muscles.
10. A **mathematician** explained the equation.

Final Test
1. Can you still read the **epitaph** on the old tombstone?
2. Please wait in the **anteroom** until you are called.
3. Don't **presuppose** anything until you know the facts.
4. It is **premature** to announce the winner now.
5. Either you're a **prophet** or a lucky guesser!
6. The **epistle** was read as part of the service.
7. Below the **epidermis**, there are other skin layers.
8. Is this meeting a **prelude** to a longer one?
9. Every **proposal** the architect made was accepted.
10. In court, you must follow accepted **protocol**.
11. This is an original idea that has no **antecedent**.
12. The **epilogue** told the fate of each character.
13. What do you predict will happen in the final **episode**?
14. She is the **premier** candidate for the position.
15. Don't let that stick **protrude** or someone will trip.
16. The wedding **procession** was long and stately.
17. A jury must consider the case without **prejudice**.
18. The beginning of the by-laws is the **preamble**.
19. Before the accident, I had a **premonition** of trouble.
20. Put it in the closet's **anterior** part for easy access.

Prefixes ab, af, ag, an, anti

Objective
To spell words with the prefixes *ab, af, ag, an,* or *anti*

Pretest
1. I truly **abhor** that ugly building across the street!
2. To avoid cholesterol, **abstain** from high-fat foods.
3. We'd like an **affirmative**, not negative, response.
4. Will the **announcement** be made on the radio?
5. This amendment will **annul** and replace the old law.
6. We all need to do our part to **abolish** discrimination.
7. Will the evidence **absolve** the defendant from guilt?
8. Our local group is an **affiliate** of that organization.
9. To revise, **annotate** your draft with corrections.
10. The doctor gave me a prescription for an **antibiotic**.
11. I found the comedy too **absurd** and unrealistic.
12. An **affable**, cooperative partner makes a job easier.
13. Scratching will only **aggravate** your poison ivy.
14. Farmers want to **annihilate** the insect pests.
15. Will this **antihistamine** clear my sinuses?
16. Your idea is too **abstract** and needs more detail.
17. The **affluent** family gave money to medical research.
18. Defensive players must be quick and **aggressive**.
19. The overflow of mail will go to the post office **annex**.
20. His shy behavior was misconstrued as **antisocial**.

Spelling Strategy   *Page 37*
Discuss the spelling rule with students. For further examples of words with the prefixes *ab, af, ag, an,* and *anti,* use: *abrupt, absent; affix, affect; aggrieve, aggrandize; announce, annunciate; antidote,* and *antifreeze.* Have students find these examples in dictionaries, and explain the meanings of each prefix and root. Then, discuss the **list words**.

Vocabulary Development Before the exercise, have students select a **list word** to match this synonym: *nonspecific.* (abstract)

Dictionary Skills If necessary, review alphabetical order with these words: *antifreeze, antibody, antinuclear, antithesis,* and *antidote.*

Spelling Practice   *Pages 38–39*
Word Analysis Encourage students to use as clues both the structure and the definition of each root. If necessary, use the spelling rule examples to illustrate.

Analogies Before the exercise, have students select a **list word** to complete this analogy: *Colorful is to sunset as _____ is to joke.* (absurd)

Word Application To extend the activity, have students make up similar context clue sentences for the distractors. Call on volunteers to challenge their classmates for the correct answers.

34

Prefixes ab, af, ag, an, anti

TIP
When added to base words or roots derived from Latin roots, the prefix **ab** usually means "away," "from," or "down." The prefixes **af, ag,** and **an** usually mean "to," "at," or "toward." The prefix **anti** means "against."

Latin Root	Meaning	Example	Meaning
horrere	"to shudder"	abhor (verb)	"to dislike intently"
filius	"son"	affiliate (verb)	"to connect with"
gravis	"heavy"	aggravate (verb)	"to make something worse"
nihil	"nothing"	annihilate (verb)	"to destroy completely"
socius	"companion"	antisocial (adj.)	"unfriendly"

Vocabulary Development
Write the **list word** that matches each synonym or definition.
1. friendly — affable
2. positive — affirmative
3. to refrain willingly — abstain
4. to free from guilt — absolve
5. pushy; assertive — aggressive

Dictionary Skills
Write the **list words** beginning with ab in alphabetical order.
1. abhor   4. abstain
2. abolish   5. abstract
3. absolve   6. absurd

Write the **list words** beginning with af and ag in alphabetical order.
7. affable   10. affluent
8. affiliate   11. aggravate
9. affirmative 12. aggressive

Write the **list words** beginning with an in alphabetical order.
13. annex   17. annul
14. annihilate 18. antibiotic
15. annotate   19. antihistamine
16. announcement 20. antisocial

LIST WORDS
1. abhor
2. abstain
3. affirmative
4. announcement
5. annul
6. abolish
7. absolve
8. affiliate
9. annotate
10. antibiotic
11. absurd
12. affable
13. aggravate
14. annihilate
15. antihistamine
16. abstract
17. affluent
18. aggressive
19. annex
20. antisocial

37

DID YOU KNOW?
Aggravate comes from a Latin word which means "to make heavier" and is related to the word *gravity.* When a problem is aggravated, it is made heavier or greater than it was.

Spelling Practice
Word Analysis
Write the **list word** derived from the Latin root given.
1. notare ("to mark") — annotate
2. fluere ("to flow") — affluent
3. nectere ("to bind") — annex
4. nullum ("nothing") — annul
5. biosis ("life") — antibiotic
6. solvere ("to release") — absolve
7. firmare ("to make firm") — affirmative
8. abolere ("to destroy") — abolish
9. nuntiare ("to report") — announcement
10. surdus ("dull; insensible") — absurd

Analogies
Write a **list word** to complete each analogy.
1. Dessert is to meal as _____annex_____ is to building.
2. Artistic is to painter as _____affable_____ is to companion.
3. Feed is to hunger as _____absolve_____ is to guilt.
4. Fast is to slow as specific is to _____abstract_____
5. "Yes, please" is to accept as "No, thank you" is to _____abstain_____

Word Application
Select a **list word** from the choices in parentheses to complete each sentence. Write the **list word** on the line.
1. Many nations _____affiliate_____ with the United Nations. (affiliate, annul, aggravate)
2. People on low-fat diets _____abstain_____ from rich foods. (absolve, abstain, aggravate)
3. This storm will _____aggravate_____ the river's flooding. (abhor, aggravate, annul)
4. I don't mean to be _____antisocial_____ but I'd like to be alone. (affluent, affable, antisocial)
5. We _____annihilate_____ termites before they ruin a house! (absolve, annihilate, annex)
6. Both parties voted to _____annul_____ the bad agreement. (annul, absolve, abstract)
7. An _____affluent_____ family donated funds for the hospital wing. (antibiotic, affluent)

LIST WORDS

aggressive	aggravate	absurd	annul
antisocial	absolve	affluent	affable
affirmative	annihilate	abolish	abhor
announcement	annotate	affiliate	annex
antihistamine	antibiotic	abstract	abstain

Puzzle

Use the **list words** to complete the crossword puzzle.

ACROSS
1. to put in notes
5. something that is announced
6. to put an end to or cancel
8. friendly or easy to talk to
11. medicine used to fight hay fever or colds
12. saying "yes"
14. to make worse
15. disliking company
16. ridiculous
17. to free of guilt
18. to get rid of

DOWN
2. wealthy or rich
3. to destroy completely
4. addition to a building
7. eager to fight
8. unlike real things
9. to become associated with
10. detest or hate
11. to hold oneself back
13. something used to kill germs

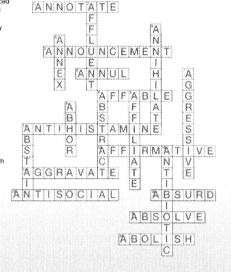

Lesson 9 • Prefixes ab, af, ag, an, anti   39

Proofreading

Proofreading Marks
- ◯ spelling mistake ⊙ add period
- ⌄ add apostrophe ¶ new paragraph

Use the proofreading marks to correct the mistakes in the article. Write the misspelled **list words** correctly on the lines.

The aptly named common cold is the most frequent infection in the United States, and one that most people abhore. Its hard to remain afable when you dont feel well. Cold symptoms begin when an aggresive virus attaches itself to the lining of your nasal passages or throat. Your immune system then attacks the germs with white blood cells, which is what causes the symptoms of a cold.

Millions eagerly await the anouncement of a cure. In the meantime, an antihistamene may temporarily relieve symptoms, but an antebiotic will have no effect on a cold, since it doesnt kill viruses.

1. abhor
2. affable
3. aggressive
4. announcement
5. antihistamine
6. antibiotic

Writing a List

Write a list of steps people can take to both prevent catching a cold, and to feel better if they do catch one. Use as many **list words** as you can. When finished, proofread and revise your list, then share it with others. Use the lists to create a group poster entitled "The Common Cold—Prevention and Cures."

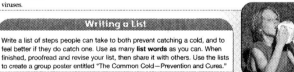

BONUS WORDS

cliché	obsolete	slang	superfluous	verbose
jargon	colloquial	trite	redundant	vernacular

Write a **bonus word** to match each etymology.

1. Greek **tryein** ("to wear away")   trite
2. Latin **ob** ("toward") + **exolescere** ("out of use")   obsolete
3. Latin **super** ("above") + **fluctus** ("wave")   superfluous
4. Latin **verna** ("native population")   vernacular
5. German **klitsch** ("clump of clay")   cliché
6. Latin **com** ("together") + **loqui** ("to speak")   colloquial
7. Latin **verbum** ("word")   verbose
8. Latin **re** ("again") + **undare** ("to swell")   redundant

Write a **bonus word** to define each example.

9. Path noise disrupted the radio transmission.   jargon
10. Those wheels will run you about ten grand.   slang

40   Lesson 9 • Prefixes ab, af, ag, an, anti

Spelling and Writing   *Page 40*

Proofreading   Review the use of all of the proofreading marks shown in the box, emphasizing the use of the apostrophe and the paragraph indent marks.

Writing a List   Point out to students that even though they are writing lists rather than paragraphs, they must write complete sentences and use proper grammar, spelling, and punctuation.

Bonus Words   *Page 40*

Language   Elicit volunteers to define and give examples of the **bonus words**, using dictionaries when necessary. Discuss how *slang*, *colloquialisms*, and *vernacular* are sometimes appropriate in spoken English, but should be avoided in compositions.

Bonus Words Test

1. *Skip it* is a **colloquial** phrase meaning "Never mind."
2. *Chill out* is **slang** for "Relax."
3. Avoid such **trite** words as *good, bad,* and *nice.*
4. *Soda* and *pop* are **vernacular** terms for *soft drinks.*
5. To say something is *big and huge* is **redundant.**
6. *As bright as the sun* is a tired **cliché.**
7. *I struck out* is an example of baseball **jargon.**
8. A **verbose** speaker uses too many words.
9. *Vermeil* is an **obsolete** word that meant "bright red."
10. Revise your drafts to remove **superfluous** words.

Final Test

1. What a shocking **announcement** he made today!
2. Farmers fear locusts may **annihilate** the crops.
3. **Annotate** your partner's answers to show any errors.
4. The exhibit is displayed in the museum's **annex.**
5. Will this law finally **abolish** the high sales tax?
6. Good directions are specific rather than **abstract.**
7. Gina arrived at the party in an **absurd** gorilla suit.
8. I **abhor** the fact that my cat scratches the furniture.
9. My new neighbors are **affable,** interesting people.
10. Please **abstain** from talking in the library.
11. Her testimony will **absolve** him of the charges.
12. An **affluent** woman left her fortune to the college.
13. Won't the icy, harsh wind **aggravate** my cold?
14. Be careful, sharks are often extremely **aggressive!**
15. Vote in the **affirmative** to approve the amendment.
16. Ali likes to **affiliate** with different groups.
17. We'll **annul** the contract and dissolve the business.
18. Dad forgot to take his **antihistamine** this morning.
19. Penicillin is an important **antibiotic.**
20. A hermit is an extremely **antisocial** individual.

Lesson 10

Prefixes bene, beni, coll, com, contra, eu

Objective
To spell words with the prefixes *bene, beni, coll, com, contra,* or *eu*

Pretest
1. A **benefactor** may give money to a charity.
2. Chang is a **colleague** of mine from the office.
3. Do you **commute** by train to work?
4. A **communal** fountain provided water for everyone.
5. He will **contradict** the truth by telling a lie.
6. She was relieved when the results were **benign**.
7. Mr. Cooper has a fine **collection** of silver spoons.
8. Did anyone **comment** on your new haircut?
9. We wore caps and gowns at our **commencement**.
10. If you **contrast** our heights, we differ by two inches.
11. Everyone will **benefit** from a cure for cancer.
12. Six classmates will **collaborate** on that project.
13. She made a **commitment** to exercise every day.
14. Cuban cigars are **contraband** in the States.
15. One mourner said he found the **eulogy** comforting.
16. Those cars came very close to having a **collision**.
17. A **commodity** is anything that is bought or sold.
18. Nations trade products via international **commerce**.
19. A surprise ending is **contrary** to your expectations.
20. What **euphoria** Rita felt when she won the race!

Spelling Strategy   *Page 41*
After students have read the spelling rule, have them read the **list words** and identify each prefix. Discuss which words have doubled consonants and where they occur in the words. Help students understand the words' meanings, asking them to use the words in oral sentences.

Vocabulary Development Remind students to think carefully about each word's spelling as well as its meaning.

Dictionary Skills Write *käm'ent* (comment) on the board, and use it to review the letters and symbols used in sound-spellings. Suggest that students use dictionaries to check any answers they are unsure of.

Spelling Practice   *Pages 42–43*
Word Analysis To extend the activity, discuss the meanings of the following words with the prefixes *bene, coll, com, contra,* and *eu: beneficial, collective, commiserate, contradiction,* and *euphony.*

Classification Write on the board: *gathering, assembly, _____.* Ask which **list word** belongs in the series. (*collection*)

Word Application Discuss with students how to let sentence context help them choose each answer. Remind them to pay attention to word spelling as well as word meaning.

36

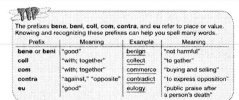
TIP
The prefixes **bene, beni, coll, com, contra,** and **eu** refer to place or value. Knowing and recognizing these prefixes can help you spell many words.

Prefix	Meaning	Example	Meaning
bene or **beni**	"good"	benign	"not harmful"
coll	"with; together"	collect	"to gather"
com	"with; together"	commerce	"buying and selling"
contra	"against," "opposite"	contradict	"to express opposition"
eu	"good"	eulogy	"public praise after a person's death"

Vocabulary Development
Write the **list word** that matches each definition clue.

1. something sold — commodity
2. public or shared — communal
3. beginning — commencement
4. happiness; giddiness — euphoria
5. to compare — contrast
6. different; opposed — contrary
7. smuggled goods — contraband
8. a crash — collision
9. remark — comment
10. a promise or pledge — commitment
11. not harmful — benign
12. fellow worker — colleague

Dictionary Skills
Write the **list word** that matches each sound-spelling.

1. (kə lab'ə rāt) — collaborate
2. (käm'ərs) — commerce
3. (ben'ə fak'tər) — benefactor
4. (kə lek'shən) — collection
5. (yōō'lə jē) — eulogy
6. (ben'ə fit) — benefit
7. (kän trə dikt') — contradict
8. (bi nīn') — benign
9. (käl'ēg) — colleague
10. (kə myōōt') — commute

LIST WORDS
1. benefactor
2. colleague
3. commute
4. communal
5. contradict
6. benign
7. collection
8. comment
9. commencement
10. contrast
11. benefit
12. collaborate
13. commitment
14. contraband
15. eulogy
16. collision
17. commodity
18. commerce
19. contrary
20. euphoria

41

Spelling Practice

DID YOU KNOW?
Euphoria once meant "relief that comes from a medical procedure." This meaning, in turn, came from a Greek word meaning "power of bearing children easily." Today, euphoria no longer refers to medical procedures, but is used to describe an extreme feeling of well-being.

Word Analysis
Write each **list word** under its prefix.

bene, beni
1. benefactor   3. benefit
2. benign

coll
4. colleague   6. collaborate
5. collection   7. collision

eu
8. eulogy   9. euphoria

contra
10. contradict   12. contraband
11. contrast   13. contrary

com
14. commute   18. commitment
15. communal   19. commodity
16. comment   20. commerce
17. commencement

Classification
Write a **list word** to complete each series.
1. accident, crash, collision   2. harmless, favorable, benign

Word Application
Write a **list word** to complete each sentence.
1. This new gymnasium will benefit everyone in the entire city!
2. Professor Katz and Dr. Sanchez will collaborate on a new book.
3. At the funeral, the minister gave a beautiful eulogy.
4. If we receive funds, we will make a commitment to this new project.
5. All the animals, both horses and cattle, drank from one communal trough.

LIST WORDS

benefactor	benign	commencement	comment
colleague	contrary	collaborate	collision
commute	eulogy	commitment	commerce
communal	contrast	contraband	collection
contradict	benefit	commodity	euphoria

Puzzle
Use the **list words** to complete the crossword puzzle.

ACROSS
2. a crash or clash
5. a person who works in the same office or field as another
6. anything that is bought or sold
7. a person who helps those in need
10. to travel to a particular place on a regular basis
11. kindly, good-natured
13. smuggled goods
15. a feeling of high spirits
16. a remark expressing an opinion
17. in opposition
18. something gathered

DOWN
1. to work together in preparing something
2. a promise; a pledge
3. anything that helps
4. buying or selling; trade
8. belonging to the community; public
9. to say the opposite of
10. a beginning or a start; a graduation ceremony
12. to compare in a way that shows differences
14. a speech or writing praising a person who has died

Crossword answers: COLLISION, BENEFACTOR, COLLEAGUE, COMMODITY, BENEFACTOR, COMMUTE, COMMITMENT, BENIGN, COLLABORATE, CONTRADICT, COMMUNAL, CONTRABAND, EUPHORIA, COMMENT, EULOGY, CONTRARY, COLLECTION

Lesson 10 • Prefixes bene, beni, coll, com, contra, eu   43

Proofreading

Use the proofreading marks to correct the mistakes in the following article. Then, write the misspelled **list words** correctly on the lines.

Proofreading Marks
○ spelling mistake ≡ capital letter
✓ add quotation marks
! add exclamation mark

The College of philadelphia was one of the first American colleges to grant degrees. The school held its first comencment in 1757. In contrast with other schools, the program was conducted with prayers and sermons. In 1783, an early benefactor of the school, george washington, received an honorary degree. Imagine the students' excitement in 1823, the ceremony was moved to Masonic Hall, which was the work of architect William Strickland. Architectural historians have made the comment that the Hall is "one of the earliest important American buildings in the Gothic style." Now known as the university of pennsylvania, the college offers degrees in everything from comerce to art history.

1. commencement
2. contrast
3. benefactor
4. comment
5. commerce

Writing a Graduation Speech

Imagine that you have been chosen to speak at your school's graduation ceremony. Write a short speech that tells your hopes for the future and your feelings about your school. Include as many **list words** as you can. Then, proofread and revise your speech, and read it aloud to your classmates.

philharmonic	classical	virtuoso	a cappella	crescendo
conservatory	soloist	vibrato	cadence	decrescendo

Write the **bonus word** that matches each definition clue.

1. highly skilled performer virtuoso
2. one who performs alone soloist
3. society of music lovers philharmonic
4. music in the European tradition classical
5. voices without instrumental accompaniment a cappella
6. pulsating musical effect vibrato
7. beat or rhythm cadence
8. getting louder and louder crescendo
9. getting less and less loud decrescendo
10. place where musicians study and learn conservatory

Puzzle Remind students to print neatly and to first fill in known answers.

Spelling and Writing   *Page 44*
Proofreading Use this sentence to review the proofreading marks: *Ouch My sunbern hurts said josh.*

Writing a Graduation Speech Point out that a speech contains an introduction, a body, and a conclusion. Urge students to outline at least three main points to make in their speeches. Remind them that they are writing a formal speech and should avoid using slang. When finished, you may wish to have volunteers present their speeches to the class.

Bonus Words   *Page 44*
Music Explain that the **bonus words** are related to music. You may wish to relate each **bonus word** to the musical qualities of a recorded vocal or instrumental selection. Then, elicit the meanings of words students know, and through discussion and dictionary use, help them learn the meanings of unfamiliar words.

Bonus Words Test
1. A **crescendo** is an increase in loudness.
2. A **decrescendo** is a decrease in loudness.
3. **Philharmonic** members sold symphony tickets.
4. The verses had music but the chorus was **a cappella**.
5. Only a true **virtuoso** can play that melody quickly.
6. Sara won a scholarship to the **conservatory**.
7. True **vibrato** is more subtle than a quiver.
8. At the end of the concert, the **soloist** bowed.
9. A popular song includes this **classical** musical theme.
10. People's heads rocked to the **cadence** of the march.

Final Test
1. At Grandpa's funeral, a friend gave a warm **eulogy**.
2. The police dogs sniffed out the **contraband**.
3. Volunteers make a year's **commitment** to serve.
4. With whom did he **collaborate** on the book?
5. The major **benefit** to my plan is its simplicity.
6. Stay to the right to avoid a **collision**.
7. Brazil's leading exported **commodity** is coffee.
8. Many businesses join local chambers of **commerce**.
9. Isn't that statement **contrary** to what you just said?
10. I felt **euphoria** when my recital concluded.
11. Sam Red Sky is the park's greatest **benefactor**.
12. Linda, a **colleague** from work, lives near me.
13. Many employees **commute** to work in carpools.
14. At camp, we cooked in a **communal** kitchen.
15. The witness will **contradict** what the suspect said.
16. Although the dog looks fierce, it is quite **benign**.
17. How many pieces does she have in the **collection**?
18. Each candidate took time to **comment** on the issues.
19. At **commencement**, my sister got her diploma.
20. How does the movie **contrast** with the novel?

Lesson 11 — Prefixes mal, meta, de, dis

Objective
To spell words with the prefixes *mal, meta, de,* or *dis*

Pretest
1. If washers **malfunction**, soapy puddles may occur.
2. The **detour** on Route 2 took us miles out of our way.
3. *You are my sunshine* is such a cheery **metaphor**!
4. Her sore knee put her at a **disadvantage** in the race.
5. The dead leaves will **decompose** into rich soil.
6. People who wish others harm are **malevolent**.
7. Her **dissatisfaction** led her to ask for a refund.
8. Caterpillars turn into moths by **metamorphosis**.
9. To be fair, don't **distort** facts to support an opinion.
10. What kind of juice is in the crystal **decanter**?
11. A body's **metabolism** changes food into energy.
12. How long does it take ice to **dissolve** into water?
13. The disease has caused a **decline** in his health.
14. His negative attitude made him seem **maladjusted**.
15. The judge attempted to settle the **dispute** fairly.
16. He claims to be a **descendant** of Genghis Khan.
17. A well-meaning person's actions show no **malice**.
18. **Deception** means anything that deceives.
19. The store hopes to **deplete** its stock during the sale.
20. Is that character still alive or is he **deceased**?

Spelling Strategy — Page 45
Discuss the spelling rule with students. For further examples of words with the prefixes *mal, meta, de,* and *dis,* use: *malicious, malady; metaphysics, metacarpus; decide, decrease; discover, displeasure.*

Vocabulary Development Before beginning the exercise, have students select a **list word** to match this definition clue: *use up; exhaust.* (*deplete*)

Dictionary Skills If necessary, review alphabetical order with these words: *discover, disease, discount, disassemble, disharmony, discredit,* and *disarm.*

Spelling Practice — Pages 46–47
Word Analysis Encourage students to use as clues both the structure and the definition of each root. If necessary, use the examples in the spelling rule for illustration.

Antonyms Before the exercise, have students select a **list word** as an antonym for the phrase *work properly.* (*malfunction*)

Word Application To extend the activity, have students make up similar context clue sentences for the distractors. Call on volunteers to challenge their classmates for the correct answers.

 TIP

The prefixes **mal, de,** and **dis** have Latin roots. The prefix **mal** usually means "bad." The prefix **de** often means "away from" or "undo." The prefix **dis** often means "not" or "apart." The prefix **meta** has Greek roots. It can mean "with, after, behind, beyond, among, about."

Root	Meaning	English Word	Meaning
functio	"to perform"	malfunction	"to function incorrectly"
morphe	"form; shape"	metamorphosis	"a change in form"
cedere	"to go forward"	deceased	"dead"
solvere	"to free"	dissolve	"to break apart in liquid"

Vocabulary Development
Write the list word that matches each definition clue.

1. argument — dispute
2. twist; deform — distort
3. displeasure — dissatisfaction
4. drawback; minus — disadvantage
5. ill will — malice
6. complete change — metamorphosis
7. break apart in liquid — dissolve

Dictionary Skills
Under each heading, write the list words in alphabetical order.

Words with Prefix de
1. decanter
2. deceased
3. deception
4. decline
5. decompose
6. deplete
7. descendant
8. detour

Words with Prefix mal
9. maladjusted
10. malevolent
11. malfunction
12. malice

Words with Prefix meta
13. metabolism
14. metamorphosis
15. metaphor

LIST WORDS
1. malfunction
2. detour
3. metaphor
4. disadvantage
5. decompose
6. malevolent
7. dissatisfaction
8. metamorphosis
9. distort
10. decanter
11. metabolism
12. dissolve
13. decline
14. maladjusted
15. dispute
16. descendant
17. malice
18. deception
19. deplete
20. deceased

DID YOU KNOW?
We often use the word **metamorphosis** to describe the transformation of a caterpillar into a butterfly. *Metamorphosis* literally means "a change." It is based on the Greek word *metamorphoun*, which includes the prefix *meta* and the word *morphe* ("form").

Spelling Practice
Word Analysis
Write the list word derived from the Latin root given.

1. clinare ("to bend") — decline
2. deplere ("to empty") — deplete
3. satis ("enough") — dissatisfaction
4. torquere ("to twist") — distort
5. volens ("to wish") — malevolent
6. functio ("to perform") — malfunction
7. componer ("to put together") — decompose
8. scandere ("to climb") — descendant
9. cedere ("to go forward") — deceased
10. justus ("just") — maladjusted

Antonyms
Write the list word that matches each antonym.

1. satisfaction — dissatisfaction
2. truth — deception
3. accept — decline
4. agreement — dispute
5. ancestor — descendant
6. kind — malevolent
7. goodwill — malice
8. alive — deceased
9. permanent form — metamorphosis
10. benefit — disadvantage

Word Application
Select a list word from the choices in parentheses to complete each sentence. Write the list word on the line.

1. Through metabolism, the body regulates its flow of energy. (metaphor, metabolism, malice)
2. The crystal decanter was filled with cold water. (decanter, deplete, maladjusted)
3. Fallen trees will eventually decompose and enrich the forest soil. (dispute, decompose, distort)
4. The detour around the construction is clearly marked. (dispute, deplete, detour)
5. "Life is just a bowl of cherries" is a metaphor. (decanter, metaphor, malice)

LIST WORDS

malice	malevolent	deplete	descendant
detour	dissatisfaction	metaphor	malfunction
dispute	metamorphosis	deception	decompose
distort	disadvantage	decanter	metabolism
decline	maladjusted	dissolve	deceased

Puzzle

Each of the following clues is an example, or illustration, of a **list word**. Write the associated **list words** in the answer spaces. Then, transfer the numbered letters to the spaces below to answer the riddle.

1. "No, thank you." d e c l i n e
   ₇ ₂₃

2. Traffic is diverted. d e t o u r
   ₁₄ ₅

3. grandchild d e s c e n d a n t
   ₂₄ ₂

4. "Truth is beauty." m e t a p h o r
   ₁ ₂₀

5. Flowers wither. d e c o m p o s e
   ₁₂ ₁₉

6. "I'm not pleased." d i s s a t i s f a c t i o n
   ₈ ₄

7. false advertising claims d e c e p t i o n
   ₁₇ ₆

8. Stir sugar in water. d i s s o l v e
   ₂₂ ₃

9. revenge m a l i c e
   ₁₆ ₉

10. Exaggerate the facts. d i s t o r t
    ₁₀ ₁₈

11. cemetery occupants d e c e a s e d
    ₁₃ ₁₅

12. fairy-tale dragon m a l e v o l e n t
    ₂₁ ₁₁

RIDDLE: How did the caterpillar turn into an elephant?

ANSWER: through a m a l f u n c t i o n of
1 2 3 4 5 6 7 8 9 10 11

m e t a m o r p h o s i s
12 13 14 15 16 17 18 19 20 21 22 23 24

Proofreading

Use the proofreading marks to correct the mistakes in the following paragraphs. Then, write the misspelled **list words** correctly on the lines.

Monarch butterflies go through many stages in their metamorphisis from egg to adult. First, the female lays her eggs on a Milkweed plant. When the caterpillar has grown, it forms a cocoon called a chrysalis. The Monarch has a fast metabolizm and can sometimes change into a butterfly in about a week. Even so, due to habitat loss, their numbers are in decline around the world.

Did you know that birds avoid Monarchs? When monarchs feed on milkweed, they collect a poison that makes them distasteful to birds, putting other insects at a disatvantage. Birds learn to spot the monarch's pattern and avoid it. Viceroy butterflies share similar markings, a deseption that keeps birds from eating them, too.

Proofreading Marks
- ◯ spelling mistake
- / small letter
- ? add question mark
- ∧ add comma

1. metamorphosis
2. metabolism
3. decline
4. disadvantage
5. deception

Writing a Descriptive Paragraph

Migratory groups of monarch butterflies gather each winter at places in California and central Mexico. Write a description of what it might be like to stumble upon these gatherings. Use as many **list words** as you can. Proofread and revise your description, then read it aloud to your classmates.

BONUS WORDS

arcade	façade	geodesic	Doric	colonnade
buttress	frieze	Corinthian	Ionic	gargoyle

Write the **bonus word** that matches each definition clue.

1. ornamental "creature" gargoyle
2. with a gridlike frame geodesic
3. projecting support structure buttress
4. row of columns colonnade
5. band of sculpture frieze
6. front of building façade
7. arched, covered passageway arcade

Write the **bonus words** that name types of columns.

8. Doric   9. Ionic   10. Corinthian

Puzzle Urge students to use as clues not only the examples or illustrations, but also the number of spaces.

Spelling and Writing   *Page 48*

Proofreading Review the proofreading marks that students will be using in this lesson.

Writing a Descriptive Paragraph Have students research the migration of monarch butterflies. For students interested in doing independent research, suggest they visit these two Web sites, www.learner.org/jnorth and www.monarchwatch.org, which have information on how to raise monarch butterflies, as well as an opportunity for students to engage in a national global study of wildlife migration.

Bonus Words   *Page 48*

Architecture Define each **bonus word** and display pictures showing examples of the architectural features. Have students find photos or illustrations of *Doric*, *Ionic*, and *Corinthian* columns in books on architecture or classical civilizations. Point out the polygons created by the grid work in *geodesic* domes.

Bonus Words Test

1. A **Doric** column has an unadorned top.
2. An **Ionic** column is topped by symmetrical coils.
3. Leaves decorate the top of a **Corinthian** column.
4. An ugly **gargoyle** peered at me from the roof.
5. A flying **buttress** of oak supported the old roof.
6. Aluminum siding covers the store's **façade**.
7. The Greek gods appear on a **frieze** at the museum.
8. Buckminster Fuller created the **geodesic** dome.
9. That arch marks the entrance to the **arcade** shops.
10. The **colonnade** at Tintern Abbey lies in ruins.

Final Test

1. A sore throat is a great **disadvantage** to a singer.
2. At first, I was **maladjusted** to living in the city.
3. Large expenses can **deplete** your account quickly.
4. A carnival mirror will **distort** your appearance.
5. Her **dissatisfaction** made her try another idea.
6. The highway **detour** took us along a back road.
7. The soap powder will **dissolve** in hot water.
8. There is no place for **malice** in a scholarly debate.
9. My great aunt, now **deceased**, was an inventor.
10. Pouring juice from the heavy **decanter** was difficult.
11. How relieved we are that their **dispute** is settled!
12. Seaweed on the beach will **decompose** in the sun.
13. I learned that I was a **descendant** of Mark Twain.
14. Do enzymes play a role in your body's **metabolism**?
15. A **malfunction** in the engine caused the car to stall.
16. Did a **malevolent** wolf threaten the three pigs?
17. *He's a tower of strength* is a **metaphor**.
18. I've decided to **decline** the job you offered me.
19. Is this advertising claim bordering on **deception**?
20. Tadpoles turn into frogs through **metamorphosis**.

Lessons 7–11 · Review

Objective
To review spelling words with Greek and Latin prefixes

Spelling Strategy
Page 49

Read and discuss the spelling rules with students. Ask them to name other words containing the various prefixes. You may wish to have students review each spelling rule separately in Lessons 7–11, applying the rule to its full selection of **list words**.

Spelling Practice
Pages 49–51

Lesson 7 Review the numerical prefixes and cite examples from the metric system when appropriate. Then, review the **list words**. Point out the additional write-on lines to students. Have them add two words from Lesson 7 that they found especially difficult, or assign certain words that seemed to be difficult for everyone. (Repeat this procedure for each lesson in the Review.) Before the exercise, point out that in some words the prefix is shortened slightly. Use *duo/duet* and *mono/monarch* as examples.

Lesson 8 Use these words to review the meanings of the prefixes *ante, epi, pre,* and *pro: anteroom, episode, premature,* and *proposal.* Then, review the **list words**, having students use them in oral sentences. To extend the exercise, have students make up similar context clue sentences for their additional words.

Lesson 9 To review the meanings of prefixes *ab, af, ag, an,* and *anti,* discuss these examples: *abstain, affluent, aggressive, annex,* and *antibiotic.* Then, apply the discussion to the **list words**.

Lesson 10 To review the meanings of prefixes *bene, coll, com, contra,* and *eu,* discuss: *benefit, collection, communal, contraband,* and *euphemism.* Then, apply the discussion to the **list words**. Urge students to use context clues to find the correct words. To extend the exercise, have them challenge each other with similar "wrong word" sentences, using the **list words** they added to their lists.

Lesson 11 To review the meanings of *mal, meta, de,* and *dis,* discuss: *malfunction, metabolism, deceased,* and *disadvantage.* Apply the discussion to other **list words**. Have students use each word in oral sentences.

Show What You Know
Page 52

Point out to students that this review will help them know if they have mastered the words in Lessons 7–11. Have a volunteer restate the directions and tell which word in the first item should be marked as incorrect. *(colision)* When students have finished the exercise, have them write their misspelled words correctly.

40

Lessons 7–11 · Review

TIPS
- Some Greek and Latin prefixes can be added to roots and base words to indicate time, place, direction, or value. Here are some examples.

Prefix	Meaning	English Word	Meaning
ab	"away; from; down"	abhor	"to dislike intensely"
af, ag, an	"to; at; toward"	affiliate	"to join with"
ante	"before; in front"	anterior	"toward the front"
anti	"against"	antisocial	"unfriendly"
bene, beni	"good"	benefit	"advantage"
coll, com	"with; together"	commerce	"business; trade"
contra	"against"	contradict	"disagree; dispute"
de	"apart; undo"	detour	"alternative route"
dis	"apart; not"	dissatisfied	"not satisfied"
epi	"outside; over"	epidermis	"outside skin layer"
eu	"good"	eulogy	"funeral tribute"
mal	"bad"	malevolent	"evil"
meta	"with; beyond"	metaphor	"exaggerated comparison"
pre	"infront; earlier"	preview	"glimpse of future event"
pro	"forward; ahead"	protrude	"stick out in front"

- Other Greek and Latin prefixes, such as **duo** and **deca**, indicate number. A <u>duet</u> is music for two voices. A <u>decade</u> is ten years.

Lesson 7

Write prefixes and **list words** to complete this chart.

List Words
centimeter
monologue
semiprecious
decade
myriad
kilowatt
semiannual
deciliter
milligram
duplex

	Prefix	English Word	Meaning
1.	deca	decade	ten years
2.	deci	deciliter	one-tenth of a liter
3.	myria	myriad	an extreme amount
4.	milli	milligram	one-thousandth of a gram
5.	kilo	kilowatt	1,000 watts
6.	semi	semiannual	occurring twice a year
7.	centi	centimeter	one-hundredth of a meter
8.	duo	duplex	having two units
9.	mono	monologue	speech by one person
10.	semi	semiprecious	not of the highest value

49

Lesson 8

Write a **list word** to complete each sentence.

List Words
antecedent
epilogue
epidermis
prejudice
procession
preamble
premier
epistle
anterior
epitaph

1. In the _epilogue_ the author explained what happened to the explorers following their discovery.
2. The humorous poet Dorothy Parker once suggested this _epitaph_ for her own tombstone: "Excuse My Dust."
3. As the maid of honor, I was next to last in the bridal _procession_
4. The _preamble_ of the U.S. Constitution begins, "We the People of the United States. . . ."
5. In an _epistle_ to his editor, the author F. Scott Fitzgerald introduced a writer named Ernest Hemingway.
6. A pronoun must agree in number with its _antecedent_
7. The _anterior_ lobe is in the front part of the brain.
8. _Prejudice_ can cause people to dislike strangers.
9. Sunburn is an inflammation of the _epidermis_
10. Wheat and corn are two of the _premier_ agricultural products of America's midwestern states.

Lesson 9

Write a **list word** to answer each definition clue.

List Words
abhor
affiliate
absurd
antisocial
annihilate
antihistamine
affirmative
aggressive
announcement
aggravate

1. medicine to relieve allergy symptoms _antihistamine_
2. silly or foolish _absurd_
3. unfriendly _antisocial_
4. ready to argue or fight _aggressive_
5. to become a member _affiliate_
6. to destroy completely _annihilate_
7. a public message _announcement_
8. positive or bold _affirmative_
9. dislike intently _abhor_
10. to make worse or to annoy _aggravate_

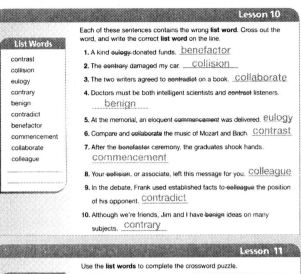

Lesson 10

List Words

contrast
collision
eulogy
contrary
benign
contradict
benefactor
commencement
collaborate
colleague

Each of these sentences contains the wrong **list word**. Cross out the word, and write the correct **list word** on the line.

1. A kind ~~eulogy~~ donated funds. benefactor
2. The ~~contrary~~ damaged my car. collision
3. The two writers agreed to ~~contradict~~ on a book. collaborate
4. Doctors must be both intelligent scientists and ~~contrast~~ listeners. benign
5. At the memorial, an eloquent ~~commencement~~ was delivered. eulogy
6. Compare and ~~collaborate~~ the music of Mozart and Bach. contrast
7. After the ~~benefactor~~ ceremony, the graduates shook hands. commencement
8. Your ~~collision~~, or associate, left this message for you. colleague
9. In the debate, Frank used established facts to ~~colleague~~ the position of his opponent. contradict
10. Although we're friends, Jim and I have ~~benign~~ ideas on many subjects. contrary

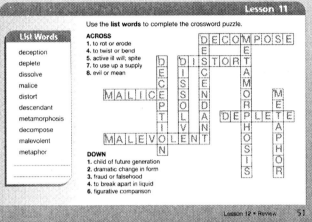

Lesson 11

List Words

deception
deplete
dissolve
malice
distort
descendant
metamorphosis
decompose
malevolent
metaphor

Use the **list words** to complete the crossword puzzle.

ACROSS
1. to rot or erode
4. to twist or bend
5. active ill will; spite
7. to use up a supply
8. evil or mean

DOWN
1. child of future generation
2. dramatic change in form
3. fraud or falsehood
4. to break apart in liquid
6. figurative comparison

Lesson 12 • Review   51

Show What You Know

Lessons 7–11 • Review

One word is misspelled in each set of **list words**. Fill in the circle next to the **list word** that is spelled incorrectly.

1. ○ centigrade	● colision	○ absurd	○ anterior
2. ● agravate	○ premonition	○ decimal	○ commodity
3. ○ preamble	○ commerce	○ affable	● kilolitre
4. ○ contrary	● monolithe	○ prejudice	○ annihilate
5. ○ monarch	○ procession	○ euphoria	● antihystamine
6. ○ centimeter	● epitaphe	○ abstract	○ malfunction
7. ● antiroom	○ metaphor	○ affluent	○ deciliter
8. ○ aggressive	● killowatt	○ detour	○ presuppose
9. ○ monopoly	○ premature	○ annex	● disadvantige
10. ● myried	○ decompose	○ prophet	○ antisocial
11. ○ milligram	● benefacter	○ decade	○ malevolent
12. ○ colleague	● epidimmis	○ epistle	○ dissatisfaction
13. ○ prelude	○ commute	○ duet	● metamorfosis
14. ○ communal	○ monotone	○ distort	● proposel
15. ○ decanter	○ semiannual	● protocal	○ contradict
16. ○ decimeter	○ maladjusted	○ benign	● metabolizm
17. ● dessolve	○ collection	○ duplex	○ abstain
18. ○ comment	○ affirmative	○ decline	● mililiter
19. ● monologe	○ semiprecious	○ abhor	○ commencement
20. ○ contrast	● anouncement	○ annul	○ dispute
21. ● anticedent	○ descendant	○ benefit	○ abolish
22. ● malise	○ collaborate	○ absolve	○ epilogue
23. ○ episode	○ commitment	● afiliate	○ deception
24. ○ premier	○ contraband	○ deplete	● anotate
25. ○ antibiotic	○ deceased	○ protrude	● uelogy

52   Lesson 12 • Review

Final Test

1. The actress is studying lines for her **monologue**.
2. The popular musician received a **myriad** of fan mail.
3. The play ended with the hero delivering an **epilogue**.
4. You'll carry the flag at the head of the **procession**.
5. Careful review is an **antecedent** to taking a test.
6. I appreciate humor, but I **abhor** slapstick comedy.
7. Carol gave an **affirmative** answer to my question.
8. Can you **annihilate** cockroaches with insecticide?
9. Icy roads caused a minor traffic **collision** today.
10. Lourdes welcomed her **colleague** to the law firm.
11. The professor seemed strict but had a **benign** smile.
12. Unfortunately, he was fooled by her **deception**.
13. Are things that **dissolve** in water called solutes?
14. *Let a smile be your umbrella* is a **metaphor**.
15. The use of aerosols will **deplete** the ozone layer.
16. Alice was the victim of the Red Queen's **malice**.
17. On the map, one **centimeter** equals ten miles.
18. The chart will **contrast** the two programs' features.
19. Poison ivy causes the **epidermis** to erupt in a rash.
20. The Matrano family moved to a new **duplex** home.
21. Our family has a **semiannual** reunion.
22. Was the **anterior** portion of the train totally full?
23. In a **preamble**, the chemist outlined his procedure.
24. We received a formal **epistle** from the embassy.
25. Keiko made an **announcement** about her new job.
26. The comedian stressed the **absurd** qualities of life.
27. Becky wanted to **affiliate** with other musicians.
28. After **commencement**, he'll go to Colby College.
29. The composer will **collaborate** with a lyricist.
30. The editor delivered a **eulogy** praising the writer.
31. A **semiprecious** gem costs less than a precious one.
32. I can't believe they've been gone for a **decade**!
33. The chemist added one **milligram** of bicarbonate.
34. Do you have a **prejudice** against technology?
35. Copper is among the **premier** products of Chile.
36. An **epitaph** is a verse or tribute on a tombstone.
37. A soccer goalie must be quick and **aggressive**.
38. To prevent hay fever, Lian takes an **antihistamine**.
39. **Antisocial** people miss much of the fun of life.
40. Who's the **benefactor** who funded the new school?
41. Jo's a **descendant** of George Washington Carver.
42. By **metamorphosis**, a tadpole becomes a frog.
43. The compost will **decompose** into fertilizer.
44. There are one thousand watts in a **kilowatt**.
45. The chemist measured one **deciliter** of sulfuric acid.
46. Spicy foods can **aggravate** an ulcer.
47. These test results **contradict** earlier reports.
48. The hero set out to conquer the **malevolent** dragon.
49. A cheap tape player will **distort** the music's sound.
50. The nations will negotiate their **contrary** views.

Latin Roots

Objective
To spell words with Latin roots

Pretest

1. We enjoyed the dolphin show at the **aquarium**.
2. A **hostel** is a boarding house or inexpensive hotel.
3. Move your arm to the side in a **lateral** motion.
4. Dead bodies are kept in a **mortuary** before burial.
5. The two **simultaneous** noises sounded like one.
6. The cats looked alike but had **dissimilar** natures.
7. Those people were held **hostage** by a gunman!
8. Swimming and boardsailing are **aquatic** sports.
9. That bank holds the **mortgage** loan on my house.
10. Does this machine **simulate** weightlessness?
11. We need to **hospitalize** you for the surgery.
12. The otherwise friendly man acted **hostile**.
13. Are your political views **liberal** or conservative?
14. A **mortician** is sometimes called an undertaker.
15. The **unilateral** decision echoed only one opinion.
16. A **hospice** provides care for terminally ill patients.
17. Every living creature is **mortal** and will die.
18. **Aquamarine** water surrounded the tropical island.
19. A **quadrilateral** has four sides and four angles.
20. The dictator agreed to **liberate** the prisoners of war.

Spelling Strategy *Page 53*

Discuss the spelling rule with students. Then, ask students to identify the Latin roots in these words: *aquanaut, collateral, mortify, similar, hospitality,* and *liberation.* Help students understand how the meaning of each word is related to the meaning of the Latin root. Apply the discussion to the **list words** and help students to define each word. Caution students about the similar pronunciation and spelling of *hostile* and *hostel.*

Vocabulary Development Encourage students to review the spelling rule before beginning this activity.

Dictionary Skills Elicit the function of dictionary guide words. Point out guide words on a dictionary page. Review that all the words on the page are arranged alphabetically between the two guide words.

Spelling Practice *Pages 54–55*

Word Analysis Encourage students to refer to the **list words** to determine the words with the same roots.

Word Application Remind students that each sentence contains context clues that will help them determine the missing **list word**. To extend, students can use other **list words** to create sentences to exchange with partners.

TIP
A root is a word part that gives the word its basic meaning. Here are some English words that are based on Latin roots.

Latin Roots	Meaning	English Word	Meaning
aqua	"water"	aquatic	"growing or living in water"
hosp, host	"guest; visitor"	hostel	"inn; inexpensive lodging"
hostis	"stranger; enemy"	hostile	"warlike; unfriendly"
later	"side"	lateral	"toward the side"
mort	"death"	mortal	"that which will die"
sim	"like; same"	simultaneous	"occurring at once"
liber	"free"	liberate	"to set free"

Vocabulary Development

Write **list words** with the same Latin root as the word given.

latitude
1. lateral
2. unilateral
3. quadrilateral

mortality
4. mortuary
5. mortgage
6. mortician
7. mortal

simile
8. simultaneous
9. dissimilar
10. simulate

liberty
11. liberal
12. liberate

hospital
13. hospitalize
14. hospice

hostess
15. hostel
16. hostage

Dictionary Skills

Write the **list words** that come between each pair of dictionary guide words. Write the words in alphabetical order.

apt/arid
1. aquamarine
2. aquarium
3. aquatic

hose/hot
4. hospice
5. hospitalize
6. hostage
7. hostel
8. hostile

LIST WORDS
1. aquarium
2. hostel
3. lateral
4. mortuary
5. simultaneous
6. dissimilar
7. hostage
8. aquatic
9. mortgage
10. simulate
11. hospitalize
12. hostile
13. liberal
14. mortician
15. unilateral
16. hospice
17. mortal
18. aquamarine
19. quadrilateral
20. liberate

53

DID YOU KNOW?
Mortgage comes from two words in Old French, *mort* and *gage,* that meant "dead" and "pledge." The pledge would be "dead" to the lender if the borrower paid the debt and kept the property that had been pledged. The pledge would also be "dead" to the borrower if he or she failed to pay the debt and lost the property.

Spelling Practice
Word Analysis

Write **list words** to answer the following questions.
Which words contain the Latin root that means "free"?
1. liberal
2. liberate

Which words contain the Latin root that means "death"?
3. mortuary
5. mortician
4. mortgage
6. mortal

Which words contain the Latin root that means "like" or "same"?
10. simultaneous
12. simulate
11. dissimilar

Which word contains the Latin root that means "stranger"?
13. hostile

Which words have the Latin root hosp that means "guest"?
14. hospitalize
15. hospice

Which words contain the Latin root that means "water"?
16. aquarium
18. aquamarine
17. aquatic

Word Application

Write a **list word** to complete each sentence.

1. Have you seen every fish in the ___aquarium___?
2. An ordinary sheet of paper has a ___quadrilateral___ shape.
3. It will take 20 more years to pay the ___mortgage___ on the house.
4. We should ___liberate___ all the enslaved people in the world.
5. The ___mortician___ will help us take care of the funeral proceedings.
6. I am afraid of my neighbor's ___hostile___ dogs, so I try to avoid passing his house.
7. Amanda turned on a fan indoors to ___simulate___ the wind for her science project.
8. He and his sister are very ___dissimilar___; they enjoy none of the same things!
9. In skiing, ___lateral___ movement helps to avoid going forward too fast.
10. He can afford ___liberal___ contributions to charity because he is very wealthy.

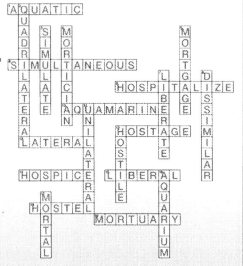

LIST WORDS

aquarium	hospice	hostel	mortgage
hospitalize	hostage	hostile	unilateral
aquamarine	aquatic	liberal	mortician
quadrilateral	liberate	lateral	mortuary
simultaneous	simulate	mortal	dissimilar

Puzzle
Use the **list words** to complete the crossword puzzle.

ACROSS
1. growing or living in water
6. happening at the same time
9. to admit to a medical care facility
10. bluish-green color
12. a prisoner taken by an enemy
13. in a sideward direction
14. a health-care facility with a home-like feeling
15. free-thinking; generous
18. an overnight shelter used by hikers and other travelers
19. place where corpses are kept before funeral

DOWN
2. a figure with four sides and four angles
3. to pretend; to act like
4. a person who prepares bodies for burial
5. a long-term loan on a piece of property
7. to set free
8. not alike; different
11. one-sided
12. warlike; unfriendly
16. a place where fish are exhibited
17. that which will die

Lesson 13 • Latin Roots 55

Proofreading

Use the proofreading marks to correct the mistakes in the article below. Then, write the misspelled **list words** correctly on the lines.

The newly remodeled aquarium recently hired an agency to handle their advertising campaign. The campaign was designed to release simultainous print and media ads.

The newspaper and magazine ads were not dissimilar—both featured full-color photos of the diverse aquatic life that can be seen in the many tanks on display. The television ad was able to simmulate an underwater dive where viewers were treated to the beauty of a coral reef. The advertising agency's production department outdid itself and created a great campaign, which generated increased ticket sales in a matter of weeks.

Proofreading Marks
- ◯ spelling mistake
- ⌄ add apostrophe
- ⌗ add space
- ¶ new paragraph

1. aquarium
2. simultaneous
3. dissimilar
4. aquatic
5. simulate

Writing a Commercial

Write a script for a radio commercial advertising a new aquarium. You may wish to write a dialogue between two people who visited the aquarium and who were very impressed with what they saw. Include dialogue for an announcer and use as many **list words** in your ad as you can. After proofreading and revising your script, work with a small group to present your ad to the class. Later, discuss what made each ad effective.

BONUS WORDS

| telecast | ad-libbed | production | technological | frequencies |
| audition | videotape | amplifier | closed circuit | broadcasting |

Write the bonus word that matches each clue given.

1. cable-TV program — closed circuit
2. TV transmission — broadcasting
3. technical progress — technological
4. transmitted TV signals — frequencies
5. a TV presentation — production
6. spoken without preparation — ad-libbed
7. to broadcast by TV — telecast
8. device to increase sound — amplifier
9. a prerecorded TV program — videotape
10. to try out for a TV show — audition

Puzzle Remind students that the puzzle will not work if the answers are not spelled correctly.

Spelling and Writing   Page 56
Proofreading Demonstrate the proofreading marks by writing on the board: *Isnt it thyme forthe bus to leave?* Ask volunteers to demonstrate the use of the paragraph mark.

Writing a Commercial Discuss what students liked or disliked about radio commercials they've heard, and how such commercials differ from TV commercials. You may wish to point out that the average thirty-second radio spot is only about seventy words long. Remind students to include any information a tourist would need to know to visit the aquarium.

Bonus Words   Page 56
Television Have students tell what they know about television broadcasting as you discuss the meaning of the **bonus words**. You may wish to have students broadcast a live television talk show from the classroom, adapting their radio commercials for television.

Bonus Words Test
1. The actor will **audition** for a role in a new series.
2. The series will go into **production** this spring.
3. They **videotape** the show on location in Atlanta.
4. Next week, we'll be **broadcasting** live from Hawaii.
5. Radio stations broadcast on different **frequencies**.
6. The royal wedding was **telecast** around the world.
7. The class viewed the **closed circuit** science program.
8. The comedian **ad-libbed** with the talk show host.
9. In 1941, television was a **technological** wonder.
10. An **amplifier** is a device that increases sound.

Final Test
1. We have **dissimilar** tastes and disagree often.
2. When she's feeling **hostile**, we can't get along.
3. Is this **aquarium** large enough to house these fish?
4. It will take thirty years to pay off the **mortgage**.
5. **Hospice** care involves a patient's whole family.
6. The funeral director works at the **mortuary**.
7. Mr. Lu, the **mortician**, spoke to the grieving family.
8. Dolphins, seals, and turtles are **aquatic** animals.
9. A **liberal** education is rich in many fields of study.
10. Didn't her **aquamarine** eyes remind you of the sea?
11. **Unilateral** disarmament is one step toward peace.
12. The **hostage** was held for a million-dollar ransom.
13. The cyclists stayed at an inexpensive youth **hostel**.
14. This whistle will **simulate** the call of a screech owl.
15. The knight inflicted a **mortal** wound on his enemy.
16. A square is an example of a **quadrilateral**.
17. The army fought to **liberate** the prisoners.
18. We all waved in one **simultaneous** gesture.
19. Do you have to **hospitalize** her if the pain worsens?
20. The quarterback made a **lateral** pass to his left.

Lesson 14 — Latin Roots

Objective
To spell words with Latin roots

Pretest

1. The **abrupt** drop in temperature forced us indoors.
2. There is no easy solution to the **complex** problem.
3. His confession may **implicate** his accomplice as well.
4. His strange, **inexplicable** behavior confused us all.
5. The earthquake caused major **structural** damage.
6. Those facts are in no way **applicable** in this case!
7. Will a railway strike **disrupt** commuters' schedules?
8. We all worked **independently** on separate projects.
9. The clock's **pendulum** swung back and forth.
10. The trapeze artist is **suspended** from the swing.
11. A **bankrupt** person lacks the funds to pay bills.
12. Is this contract a **duplicate** of the original one?
13. I prefer hands-on **instruction** to reading a manual.
14. A diamond **pendant** hung from her gold necklace.
15. The film's **suspense** glued me to my seat.
16. A technical **complication** delayed the plane.
17. I stayed inside due to the **impending** storm.
18. It's rude to **interrupt** her when she is speaking.
19. The tornado caused major **destruction** in the town.
20. Ed's **perplexing** statement left me puzzled.

Spelling Strategy   **Page 57**

To reinforce the spelling rule, ask students to identify the Latin roots in these words: *corruption, construction, implicit,* and *dependable.* Have students consult a dictionary to define the words. Relate each definition to the meaning of the word's Latin root. Apply the discussion to the **list words** and help students to define them. Discuss the similar pronunciation and spelling of *pendant* and *pendent.*

Vocabulary Development Before students begin the activity, you may wish to have them name synonyms for as many **list words** as possible.

Dictionary Skills Remind students to pronounce each word slowly and carefully, listening for the sounds in the word.

Spelling Practice   **Pages 58–59**

Word Analysis Have students review the meanings of the Latin roots in the spelling rule before beginning this activity. Encourage them to think of other words that contain the Latin roots in this lesson.

Word Application Remind students to find the answer by using the context clues in each sentence. To extend the activity, have students use the **list word** answers in new sentences.

Latin Roots

TIP

Recognizing Latin roots in words can help you determine the meanings of unfamiliar words. Here are some examples.

Latin Roots	Meaning	English Word	Meaning
plic, plex	"fold"	complication	"something that confuses"
rupt	"break"	interrupt	"break in on"
pend	"hang"	suspended	"hanging down"
struct	"build"	structural	"suitable for building"

Look for the Latin roots in the **list words**.

Vocabulary Development

Write the **list word** from column B that matches the synonym in column A.

	A		B
1.	puzzling	perplexing	implicate
2.	disturb	disrupt	bankrupt
3.	individually	independently	impending
4.	involve	implicate	duplicate
5.	unexplainable	inexplicable	destruction
6.	sudden	abrupt	perplexing
7.	impoverished	bankrupt	independently
8.	threatening	impending	inexplicable
9.	copy	duplicate	disrupt
10.	wreckage	destruction	abrupt

Dictionary Skills

Write the **list word** that matches each sound-spelling.

1. (pen'jən ləm) pendulum
2. (sə spend'ed) suspended
3. (in struk'shən) instruction
4. (ap'li kə b'l) applicable
5. (käm'plə kā'shən) complication
6. (struk'chər əl) structural
7. (sə spens') suspense
8. (pen'dənt) pendant
9. (kəm pleks') complex
10. (in tə rupt') interrupt

LIST WORDS

1. abrupt
2. complex
3. implicate
4. inexplicable
5. structural
6. applicable
7. disrupt
8. independently
9. pendulum
10. suspended
11. bankrupt
12. duplicate
13. instruction
14. pendant
15. suspense
16. complication
17. impending
18. interrupt
19. destruction
20. perplexing

57

DID YOU KNOW?

Bankrupt comes from two Italian words meaning "broken bench." Moneylenders used to carry on their business at a bench or table. They would be put out of business if the bench were broken, just as nowadays people are put out of business if they cannot pay their debts.

Spelling Practice

Word Analysis

Write **list words** to answer the following questions.

Which words contain the Latin root that means "hang"?

1. independently
2. pendulum
3. suspended
4. pendant
5. suspense
6. impending

Which words contain the Latin root that means "build"?

7. structural
8. instruction
9. destruction

Which words contain the Latin root that means "break"?

10. abrupt
11. disrupt
12. bankrupt
13. interrupt

Which words contain the Latin root that means "fold"?

14. complex
15. implicate
16. inexplicable
17. applicable
18. duplicate
19. complication
20. perplexing

Word Application

Replace each underlined word or words in the sentences with a **list word**. Write the **list word** on the line.

1. The confusing page design suffers from unnecessary intricacy.
   perplexing   complication

2. He said he saw a UFO hanging in midair, but when asked how it could be flying, he said that it was unexplainable. suspended   inexplicable

3. When we tried to repeat the experiment, the weather was no longer suitable.
   duplicate   applicable

4. They didn't want their phones to cause a break in the experiment, so they turned them off. interrupt

5. Since the president didn't want the weather to disturb the meeting, she called it off until the threatening storm passed by. disrupt   impending

58   Lesson 14 • Latin Roots

44

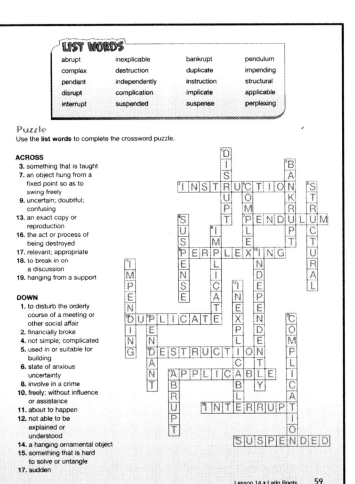

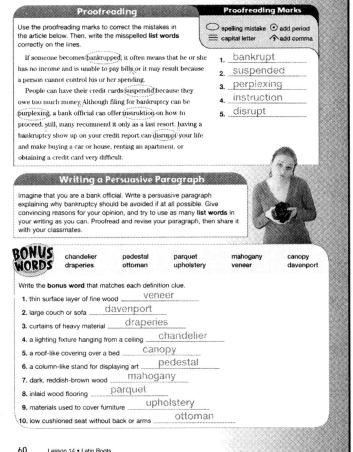

Puzzle
Tell students to print clearly and to use capital letters as they fill in the puzzle.

Spelling and Writing *Page 60*
Proofreading Review the use of the proofreading marks in the box.

Writing a Persuasive Paragraph Talk about the process and causes of declaring bankruptcy. If possible, bring in brochures about bankruptcy from a local bank to distribute and discuss with students. When students are sharing their work, urge them to proofread their peer's writing for any spelling or grammatical errors.

Bonus Words *Page 60*
Interior Decorating Have a volunteer define *interior decorating*. Then, discuss the meaning of each **bonus word**, having students consult a dictionary as needed. To extend the activity, divide students into small groups and have them choose a room in the school that they would like to redecorate. Have them prepare a list of furnishings and sketches for the new room.

Bonus Words Test
1. Lady Diane sat primly on the edge of the **davenport**.
2. That **mahogany** end table is an antique.
3. A statue of Zeus stood on the **pedestal** in the hall.
4. A crystal **chandelier** hung in the dining room.
5. Dark velvet **draperies** covered the library windows.
6. She looked up at the white lace **canopy** over her bed.
7. Dad rested his feet on the brown leather **ottoman**.
8. The carpenter installed a **parquet** floor in the foyer.
9. The nail polish stained the desk's oak **veneer**.
10. The sofa's **upholstery** was worn and tattered.

Final Test
1. We **interrupt** this program for a weather alert.
2. The cause of the freak accident was **inexplicable**.
3. I was stunned by her **abrupt** departure.
4. Tanya's solution was **applicable** to the problem.
5. Can you **duplicate** this tape so I can have a copy?
6. As **suspense** built, the audience clung to their seats.
7. The movement of the **pendulum** was hypnotizing.
8. The student protest will **disrupt** the meeting.
9. Businesses went **bankrupt** during the Depression.
10. Pollution causes the **destruction** of habitats.
11. We studied long hours for the **impending** exam.
12. Sue inspected the bridge's **structural** stability.
13. The flag hung **suspended** from the ceiling.
14. Why did she **implicate** my client in the crime?
15. Everyone was confused by the **perplexing** facts.
16. What an exquisite jeweled **pendant** for that chain!
17. Kim made her decision **independently**.
18. Was the idea too **complex** for me to understand?
19. Luis received **instruction** in fine furniture making.
20. She cleared up the **complication** in our schedule.

Latin Roots

Objective
To spell words with Latin roots

Pretest
1. The governor will **advocate** stricter seat belt laws.
2. **Centralize** your business by relocating downtown.
3. The horses moved slowly over the rugged **terrain**.
4. Like a **vagabond**, he wandered from town to town.
5. Eat a **variety** of fresh fruits and vegetables daily.
6. A round target consists of several **concentric** circles.
7. This spray will **exterminate** the carpenter ants.
8. We stood on the **terrace** to look at the view.
9. Her memory of the accident was **vague** for weeks.
10. There were **various** problems, not just one.
11. What clues did you use to **determine** the answer?
12. Your angry attitude will **provoke** an argument.
13. Guam is a **territory** of the United States.
14. The **vagrant** wandered the city aimlessly.
15. In what kind of work will you find your **vocation**?
16. An **eccentric** person may act in an unusual manner.
17. The judge threatened to **revoke** his driver's license.
18. The bus leaves the **terminal** at 5:00 p.m.
19. There is a slight **variation** between the two colors.
20. I tried to **vocalize** my fear, but I just sputtered.

Spelling Strategy   Page 61
Discuss the spelling rule. Then, ask students to identify the Latin roots and their meanings in these words: *invoke, extraterrestrial, variable, vagrancy, interminable,* and *central.* Show students how the meaning of each word is related to the meaning of its Latin root. Apply the discussion to the **list words** and help students to define each word.

Vocabulary Development Before students begin the activity, have them name the **list words** that are synonyms or near-synonyms for each other.
(variety/variation; vagrant/vagabond; terrain/territory)

Dictionary Skills You may wish to discuss the sounds that are represented by the schwa and the diacritical symbols *ä* and *ʉr.*

Spelling Practice   Pages 62–63
Word Analysis Emphasize that students should review the meanings of the Latin roots provided in the spelling rule before beginning this activity.

Word Application You may wish to do a sample item of the activity with students, demonstrating how word meaning and context can help them determine the appropriate **list word** answer.

Latin Roots

TIP
Here are some common Latin roots and their meanings.

Latin Roots	Meaning	English Word	Meaning
voc, vok	"voice"	vocalize	"speak or sing"
var	"different"	variety	"number of different things"
vag	"wander"	vagabond	"wanderer"
centr	"center"	centralize	"to bring to the center"
term	"end; limit"	terminal	"at the end"
terr	"land"	territory	"large tract of land"

Vocabulary Development
Write the **list word** from column **B** that matches the definition or synonym in column **A**.

	A		B
1.	unclear	vague	vagabond
2.	assortment	variety	eccentric
3.	annoy	provoke	terrace
4.	tramp	vagabond	terrain
5.	destroy	exterminate	provoke
6.	odd	eccentric	exterminate
7.	land	terrain	determine
8.	patio	terrace	vocalize
9.	sing	vocalize	variety
10.	conclude	determine	vague

Dictionary Skills
Write the **list word** that matches each sound-spelling.

1. (ver′ē ā′shən) variation
2. (ver′ē əs) various
3. (kən sen′trik) concentric
4. (ri vōk′) revoke
5. (sen′trə līz) centralize
6. (prə vōk′) provoke
7. (vā′grənt) vagrant
8. (ad′və kāt) advocate
9. (ter′ə tôr′ē) territory
10. (tur′mə n'l) terminal

LIST WORDS
1. _____
2. _____
3. _____
4. _____
5. _____
6. _____
7. _____
8. _____
9. _____
10. _____
11. _____
12. _____
13. _____
14. _____
15. _____
16. _____
17. _____
18. _____
19. _____
20. _____

61

DID YOU KNOW?
Determine literally means "to mark off the end." It was used to refer to verdicts reached in courts of law. That is exactly what is done when we determine something—we reach an end or conclusion.

Spelling Practice
Word Analysis
Write **list words** to answer the following questions.

Which words contain the Latin root that means "wander"?
1. vagabond 2. vague 3. vagrant

Which words contain the Latin root that means "voice"?
4. advocate 6. vocation 8. vocalize
5. provoke 7. revoke

Which words contain the Latin root that means "center"?
9. centralize 10. concentric 11. eccentric

Which words contain the Latin root that means "different"?
12. variety 13. various 14. variation

Which words contain the Latin root that means "end" or "limit"?
15. exterminate 16. determine 17. terminal

Which words contain the Latin root that means "land"?
18. terrain 19. terrace 20. territory

Word Application
Replace the underlined word or words in each sentence with a **list word**. Write the **list word** on the line.

1. Do you think Uncle Harold is an <u>odd or unusual</u> person? eccentric
2. The supermarket has a <u>generous selection</u> of fruits and vegetables. variety
3. Priests, ministers, and rabbis have a religious <u>profession</u>. vocation
4. What is the northwest <u>border country</u>? territory
5. The new house is being built on hilly <u>ground</u>. terrain
6. The design in the painting was made with the <u>same center</u> circles. concentric
7. His music included a <u>change</u> of a familiar theme. variation
8. A consumer rights <u>speaker</u> met with a group of concerned citizens. advocate
9. If you drink and drive, the police may <u>take back</u> your driver's license. revoke
10. Go left at the next block to get to the bus <u>station</u>. terminal

LIST WORDS

terrace	concentric	advocate	eccentric
revoke	exterminate	provoke	various
terrain	determine	territory	terminal
vague	vagabond	vagrant	variation
variety	centralize	vocation	vocalize

Puzzle

Use the **list words** to complete the crossword puzzle.

ACROSS
2. the main station of a railroad
5. person with no obvious means of support
6. to anger or irritate
7. a paved area near a house
8. ground or area of land
12. not definite or distinct
13. several or many
14. to speak or sing
17. person who wanders from place to place
18. to find out exactly
19. one's profession or occupation
20. the land ruled by a nation or state

DOWN
1. to gather together
3. to kill or destroy
4. sharing the same center
9. to speak or write in support of something
10. change in form or appearance
11. to take back or put an end to
15. not usual or normal
16. number of different things

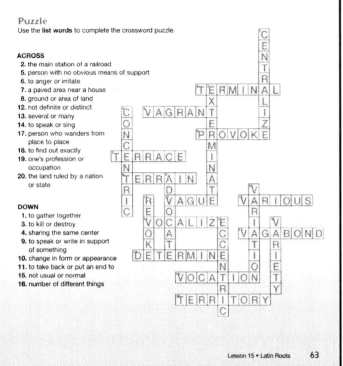

Proofreading

Use the proofreading marks to correct the mistakes in the paragraph below. Then, write the misspelled **list words** correctly on the lines.

Proofreading Marks
- ◯ spelling mistake
- ⊙ add period
- ⌐ delete word
- ⋀ add comma

On July 4 1997, the spacecraft Pathfinder landed on the planet Mars to investigate the terrian and collect a variety of rocks and soil samples. Pathfinder carried a digital camera, and a a complete meteorology package that could measure variation in temperature, pressure, and wind at at different heights above the surface. This would help scientists on Earth ditermine whether Mars might be capable of supporting life. Pathfinder sent back over 2 billion bits of data, including over 16000 images. Scientists will be be studying the data from Pathfinder for many years to come.

1. investigate   3. variety   5. determine
2. terrain   4. variation

Writing a Short Story

Write a short story about the first astronauts to travel to Mars. What could happen on their trip? What might they encounter? Use a web to record your ideas, then write your story, using as many **list words** as you can. Proofread and revise your story, and then read it aloud to your classmates.

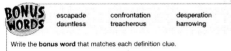

| escapade | confrontation | desperation | bivouac | intrepid |
| dauntless | treacherous | harrowing | sojourn | courier |

Write the **bonus word** that matches each definition clue.

1. a brief or temporary stay or visit   sojourn
2. recklessness resulting from a loss of hope   desperation
3. used to describe an experience that causes mental distress   harrowing
4. used to describe someone or something that is untrustworthy   treacherous
5. a reckless adventure or prank   escapade
6. the act of facing someone boldly or defiantly   confrontation
7. temporary encampment in the open with tents   bivouac
8. messenger sent with an urgent message   courier

Write the **bonus words** that are synonyms for fearless.

9. dauntless   10. intrepid

Puzzle Point out that since some **list words** have similar meanings, students will also have to use the length of the words to complete the puzzle.

Spelling and Writing   Page 64

Proofreading Review with students the use of each of the proofreading marks shown in the box.

Writing a Short Story As a class, brainstorm what could happen on the first trip to Mars. Review story webs by writing students' ideas on the board in a web graphic. Urge students to use these ideas as they write. When finished, have volunteers read their adventure stories aloud.

Bonus Words   Page 64

Adventure Discuss the meanings of the **bonus words**. Have students use a dictionary to define any unfamiliar words. Elicit from students that the words *dauntless* and *intrepid* are synonyms for *fearless*. You may wish to have a story hour during which a group of students uses the **bonus words** and other adventure words to retell a familiar or original adventure story.

Bonus Words Test

1. In **desperation**, she leapt to the narrow ledge.
2. Our **intrepid** hero stopped the runaway train.
3. The tired soldiers made a **bivouac** in the open field.
4. We read about the **escapade** to rescue the prince.
5. The **courier** came with a message for Patrick.
6. The **dauntless** captain sailed the disabled ship home.
7. They survived a **harrowing** trek across the desert.
8. His **sojourn** into the jungle was brief but dangerous.
9. The climb up the slippery rocks was **treacherous**.
10. Finally, she had a **confrontation** with her enemy.

Final Test

1. Is that parcel of land flat or uneven **terrain**?
2. What a huge **variety** of colors the flowers have!
3. Being a musician has always been his **vocation**.
4. The train pulled into the **terminal** an hour late.
5. The new party will **centralize** its political power.
6. **Concentric** circles share the same center.
7. Will her speech **provoke** the workers to strike?
8. The pest controller will **exterminate** the termites.
9. They voted to **revoke** the power of the committee.
10. That's a **vague** answer. Could you be more specific?
11. Both state senators **advocate** repeal of the tax law.
12. He led a **vagabond** life, never settling down.
13. Canada owns the **territory** north of the border.
14. The group will **vocalize** some of their new songs.
15. From these grades, I can **determine** who studied.
16. The party was held on the **terrace** in the backyard.
17. The **vagrant** had no job and no place to call home.
18. We noticed a slight **variation** in the two patterns.
19. My **eccentric** aunt wears odd clothes and hats.
20. We called **various** hotels before choosing this one.

Latin Roots

Objective
To spell words with Latin roots

Pretest

1. The group had a **conspiracy** to rob the store.
2. Your library card will **expire** if you don't renew it.
3. His accomplishments were an **inspiration** to us all.
4. A synonym for *marriage* is **matrimony**.
5. The circus is such a colorful and exciting **spectacle**!
6. He's very polite and would never show **disrespect**.
7. In **expectation** of a busy day, she woke at dawn.
8. Chang and her baby are in the **maternity** ward.
9. His **perspective** on life changed after the accident.
10. The police can only **speculate** about the cause.
11. They own **exclusive** rights; it's not open publicly.
12. I washed the windows, **including** the skylights.
13. The dorm **matron** called the students to lunch.
14. The traffic jam will **preclude** our arriving on time.
15. Religion focuses on the **spiritual** needs of people.
16. The contest rules **exclude** employees from winning.
17. The **inspection** revealed a faulty wiring system.
18. The baby's crying awoke her **maternal** instincts.
19. She wished to be alone so she went into **seclusion**.
20. It finally **transpired** that the item had been stolen.

Spelling Strategy
Page 65

Have students identify the Latin roots and their meanings in these words: *inspector, spectacular, inspire, recluse,* and *matriarch.* Elicit from students that the meaning of each word relates to the meaning of its Latin root. Have students identify the Latin roots in the **list words**. Point out that the *s* is dropped from the Latin roots *spir* and *spec* in *expire* and *expectation*.

Vocabulary Development Emphasize to students that the meaning of the Latin roots can help them determine the definition of the **list words**.

Dictionary Skills Elicit that guide words can help students find words in a dictionary. To extend, you may wish to have them alphabetize all the **list words**.

Spelling Practice
Pages 66–67
Word Analysis Before students begin, review the meanings of the Latin roots in the spelling rule.

Analogies To review, have students complete this analogy: *Politeness is to courtesy as rudeness is to* _____ . *(disrespect)*

Word Application When finished, have volunteers read the sentences with the **list words** in place of the underlined words.

48

Latin Roots

TIP

These common Latin roots can help you determine the meanings of many English words.

Latin Roots	Meaning	English Word	Meaning
spec	"see; look at"	perspective	"a particular view"
spir	"breathe"	expire	"to come to an end"
clu, clud	"shut"	exclude	"keep out"
mater, matri	"mother"	maternal	"motherly"

Study the Latin roots to determine the meanings of the **list words**.

Vocabulary Development

Write the **list word** that matches each definition clue.

1. to make impossible — preclude
2. a grand event — spectacle
3. privacy; isolation — seclusion
4. critical examination — inspection
5. a stimulation to do something creative — inspiration
6. an unlawful plot — conspiracy
7. of the soul rather than the body — spiritual
8. to think about — speculate
9. happened — transpired
10. making a part of a whole — including

Dictionary Skills

Identify the **list words** that come between each pair of dictionary guide words. Write the words in alphabetical order.

conspire/external
1. disrespect
2. exclude
3. exclusive
4. expectation
5. expire

mate/precious
6. maternal
7. maternity
8. matrimony
9. matron
10. perspective

LIST WORDS
1. conspiracy
2. expire
3. inspiration
4. matrimony
5. spectacle
6. disrespect
7. expectation
8. maternity
9. perspective
10. speculate
11. exclusive
12. including
13. matron
14. perspective
15. spiritual
16. include
17. inspection
18. maternal
19. seclusion
20. transpired

65

DID YOU KNOW?

Spectacle, spectacular, spectator, spectroscope. and **spectrum** all come from the Latin word *spectare,* meaning "to behold" or "to watch." All of these words have to do with someone seeing or with something seen or used in seeing.

Spelling Practice
Word Analysis

Write **list words** to answer the following questions.

Which words contain the Latin root that means "breathe"?
1. conspiracy 3. inspiration 5. transpired
2. expire 4. spiritual

Which words contain the Latin root that means "see"?
6. spectacle 8. expectation 10. speculate
7. disrespect 9. perspective 11. inspection

Which words contain the Latin root that means "shut"?
12. exclusive 14. preclude 16. seclusion
13. including 15. exclude

Which words contain the Latin root that means "mother"?
17. matrimony 19. matron 20. maternal
18. maternity

Analogies

Write a **list word** to complete each analogy.
1. Fatherhood is to paternity as motherhood is to maternity
2. Guess is to predict as think is to speculate
3. Allow is to forbid as permit is to preclude
4. Body is to soul as physical is to spiritual
5. Ordinary is to common as unique is to exclusive

Word Application

Replace each underlined word or words in the sentences with **list words**. Write the **list words** on the lines.

1. The privacy of the hillside cabin allowed Martin to change his view on life.
   seclusion   perspective

2. He found that the solitude of the mountains gave him the uplifting experience he needed to reaffirm his religious beliefs. inspiration   spiritual

3. A dramatic change had occurred within him. transpired

LIST WORDS

conspiracy	disrespect	exclusive	exclude
expectation	inspection	including	matron
inspiration	maternity	seclusion	expire
matrimony	spectacle	preclude	maternal
perspective	speculate	transpired	spiritual

Puzzle

Unscramble the **list words** to complete the crossword puzzle.

ACROSS
1. NPRTADEISR
6. CSUVIEELX
8. PCUSALETE
9. OYISCPNARC
12. REUEPCLD
15. LANEMTRA
16. ESLSUNCIO
17. NIEPSNCITO
18. IEDTRSEPSC
19. NLIDCGUIN

DOWN
2. UPIRLSTA
3. RXIEPE
4. ECPTSLEAC
5. RPPVEECSETI
6. EEUXLCD
7. TNRPNISIAIO
10. YENAMTRIT
11. PECXTENTAIO
13. RNAMTO
14. ROYTAIMMN

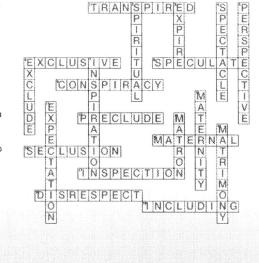

Lesson 16 • Latin Roots   67

Proofreading

Use the proofreading marks to correct the mistakes in the article below. Then, write the misspelled **list words** correctly on the lines.

Proofreading Marks
- ◯ spelling mistake
- ? add question mark
- ∨ add apostrophe
- / small letter

Matrimmony during the Middle Ages was considered a family affair, and weddings themselves were not often lavish. From our purspective, they offered little in the way of spectackle for members of the community. In Italy, for example, a couple exchanged gifts, such as a piece of fruit, in the exklusion of the Bride's house. The "vows" could be as simple as "Will you marry me "I will." The presence of a state or religious official, includeing a priest or rabbi, was not even necessary. The role of a religious leader at a medieval Wedding was simply to bless the couple after the ceremony.

1. Matrimony   4. seclusion
2. perspective   5. including
3. spectacle

Writing a Friendly Letter

Imagine that you have a relative in medieval Italy who is going to be married. Write a letter to a friend in which you describe the preparations for the ceremony. Use as many of the **list words** as you can. Include all the parts of a friendly letter, such as the date, greeting, and closing. When finished, proofread and revise your letter, then read it to your classmates.

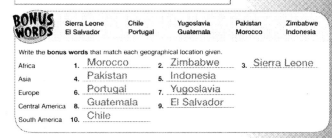

BONUS WORDS

Sierra Leone	Chile	Yugoslavia	Pakistan	Zimbabwe
El Salvador	Portugal	Guatemala	Morocco	Indonesia

Write the **bonus words** that match each geographical location given.

Africa	1. Morocco 2. Zimbabwe	3. Sierra Leone
Asia	4. Pakistan 5. Indonesia	
Europe	6. Portugal 7. Yugoslavia	
Central America	8. Guatemala 9. El Salvador	
South America	10. Chile	

Puzzle Elicit from students that they are to unscramble the **list words** to find the answers to this puzzle.

Spelling and Writing   *Page 68*

Proofreading Show examples on the board to illustrate the proofreading marks.

Writing a Friendly Letter Have students compare these two sentences:
> They will serve a delicious dinner.
> The bride's parents will serve a succulent stuffed quail and shrimp scampi for dinner.

Urge students to use details appealing to the five senses (taste, touch, smell, sight, sound) when describing the wedding preparations. Remind students to use correct spelling and grammar.

Bonus Words   *Page 68*

Countries Invite partners to research three or four interesting facts about each country, including the country's geography. Then, have students report their facts to the class.

Bonus Words Test
1. Fishing is an important industry in **Portugal.**
2. The Republic of **Sierra Leone** is in West Africa.
3. **Guatemala** is a country in Central America.
4. Santiago is the capital of **Chile.**
5. **Pakistan** is located on the Arabian Sea.
6. Gold is a chief export of **Zimbabwe.**
7. Alvarado explored **El Salvador** in 1524.
8. More than 13,000 islands make up **Indonesia.**
9. Before 1929, **Yugoslavia** had a different name.
10. **Morocco** is a monarchy and is ruled by a king.

Final Test
1. Her bold statement was not meant in **disrespect.**
2. He won't **speculate** on who will win the race.
3. When will our car registration **expire**?
4. The minister wrote a book about **spiritual** growth.
5. He bought some furniture, **including** a new bed.
6. After a careful **inspection**, we bought the car.
7. My **maternal** grandparents visit every summer.
8. The memo tells what **transpired** at the meeting.
9. His illness will **preclude** his attending soccer camp.
10. The law does **exclude** noncitizens from voting.
11. Her courageous deed served as **inspiration** for us.
12. The town looks tiny from this **perspective.**
13. Mr. Ross is in **seclusion** and will not see anyone.
14. She led the **conspiracy** against the tyrant.
15. **Maternity** clothes are designed for pregnancy.
16. Do you think it's right to have an **exclusive** club?
17. The school **matron** checks our rooms for neatness.
18. Our **expectation** is that we will win the game.
19. What a grand **spectacle** the holiday fireworks were!
20. The couple will celebrate fifty years of **matrimony.**

Challenging Words

Objective
To spell difficult words with unusual spelling patterns

Pretest
1. Darnell's lateness filled us with **anxiety**.
2. Brad is a regular **customer** at the Olympia Diner.
3. The danger of fire will **diminish** with this rain.
4. Wow, was I **entirely** exhausted after the race!
5. The scholarship will cover Beth's college **expenses**.
6. It's a **controversial** issue, meaning it's debatable.
7. Tipping food servers 15% of the bill is **customary**.
8. His **eloquent** speech moved each of us to tears.
9. Do you agree that coaches treat all players **equally**?
10. The **fallacy** that the Earth is flat was once popular.
11. As a **courtesy**, thank each clerk for his or her help.
12. When did she make the **decision** to move?
13. She is an **eminent** biologist, well-known in the field.
14. Speak in soothing tones to the **excitable** puppy.
15. Hamid used that book as a **source** for research.
16. Jack met a **cruel** giant at the top of the beanstalk.
17. I'm **defenseless** in the rain with no umbrella.
18. **Sophomore** year in high school is also tenth grade.
19. Did you drain the **excess** water from the pasta?
20. Rama enjoys music, **especially** rock 'n' roll.

Spelling Strategy   *Page 69*
Discuss the spelling rule. Then, have students analyze each **list word**, identifying the "trick" in each one. Work with students to define each word, then ask volunteers to use the words in oral sentences.

Vocabulary Development Before the exercise, have students select a **list word** to match this clue: *beginning place; origin.* (*source*) Have volunteers consult dictionaries for other meanings for *source.*

Dictionary Skills If needed, use a dictionary to review guide words with students, pointing out examples and explaining their function.

Spelling Practice   *Pages 70–71*
Word Analysis Point out that this exercise will help students analyze the "tricks" in some of the **list words**. Urge them to check the **list words** on page 71 carefully to find the various letter components.

Analogies To review, have students name the **list word** that best completes this analogy: *Borrower is to library as _____ is to store.* (*customer*)

Word Application Before the exercise, write on the board: *manager, procedure, answer.* Then, write this phrase and have students select the word that best replaces the word in parentheses: *a standard (method).* (*procedure*)

50

TIP Some words are especially difficult to spell because they contain sounds that can be spelled by different letters. For example, the soft c sound in *fallacy* sounds very similar to the s sound in *defenseless.* In other challenging words, letters may stand for unusual sounds. For example, in *especially* the c stands for the sound of **sh.** Memorize the spellings of the **list words** so that you aren't fooled by their subtle "tricks."

Vocabulary Development
Write the list word that matches each synonym or definition.

1. costs — expenses
2. totally — entirely
3. client — customer
4. traditional — customary
5. lessen — diminish
6. unmerciful — cruel
7. polite behavior — courtesy
8. easily provoked — excitable
9. worry or fear — anxiety
10. particularly — especially

LIST WORDS
1. anxiety
2. customer
3. diminish
4. entirely
5. expenses
6. controversial
7. customary
8. eloquent
9. equally
10. fallacy
11. courtesy
12. decision
13. eminent
14. excitable
15. source
16. cruel
17. defenseless
18. sophomore
19. excess
20. especially

Dictionary Skills
Write the list word that comes between each pair of dictionary guide words.

1. entrance/equation — equally
2. sorrow/south — source
3. deal/defeat — decision
4. common/count — controversial
5. ember/empty — eminent
6. sole/soup — sophomore
7. examine/exchange — excess
8. decoy/dill — defenseless
9. either/emigrate — eloquent
10. fabulous/fame — fallacy
11. anvil/anything — anxiety
12. couple/cover — courtesy

69

DID YOU KNOW?
The study of knowledge and ideas is called *sophiology.* **Sophomore** comes from the Greek word *sophos*, for "wise," and *mros*, meaning "dull." Together, they mean "a wise fool." We use *sophomore* as a name for a person who is in the second year of high school or college. It is believed that the name came from the notion that sophomores are usually wiser than freshmen, but foolish enough to think that they "know it all."

Spelling Practice
Word Analysis
Write **list words** to answer the following questions. Some words will be used more than once.

Which words contain the double consonant ll?
1. equally   2. fallacy   3. especially

Which words contain the letter x?
4. anxiety   6. excitable   7. excess
5. expenses

Which words contain the letter q?
8. eloquent   9. equally

Which words contain no more than two syllables?
10. source   11. cruel   12. excess

Analogies
Write a **list word** to complete each analogy.
1. Fat is to thin as increase is to — diminish
2. Kind is to happiness as — cruel — is to sorrow.
3. Calm is to still as — excitable — is to active.
4. Two is to three as — sophomore — is to junior.
5. Disagree is to — controversial — as agree is to acceptable.
6. Profits are to in as — expenses — are to out.
7. Contentment is to happy as — anxiety — is to worried.

Word Application
Complete each of the following phrases by writing a **list word** to replace the word or words in parentheses.

1. the (famous) author — eminent
2. (origin) of the problem — source
3. common (polite behavior) — courtesy
4. (too much) baggage — excess
5. (completely) correct — entirely
6. a complete (falsehood) — fallacy
7. a (helpless) animal — defenseless
8. the (expressive) poet — eloquent
9. travel (costs) — expenses
10. a difficult (choice) — decision
11. (student class) dance — sophomore
12. his (usual) route — customary

LIST WORDS

anxiety	controversial	courtesy	equally
customer	customary	decision	fallacy
diminish	especially	eminent	source
entirely	defenseless	excitable	excess
expenses	sophomore	eloquent	cruel

Puzzle
Use the **list words** to complete the crossword puzzle.

ACROSS

2. easily provoked or excited
4. polite behavior
5. second year of high school or college
7. to lessen
9. helpless; unable to stand up for oneself
10. starting point; origin
12. totally
14. false or mistaken idea
15. mean; unmerciful
17. client or purchaser of goods or services
18. extreme concern, worry, or fear

DOWN

1. settlement, conclusion, or choice
2. costs; money spent
3. debatable; subject to divided opinions
6. distinguished; famous; above others in rank
8. following tradition, custom, or usual routine
11. in identical portions, sizes, or values
12. particularly
13. well-spoken; expressive; poetic
16. too much; more than enough

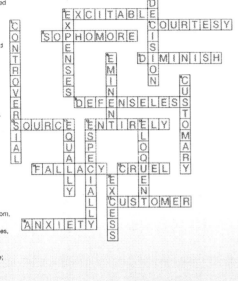

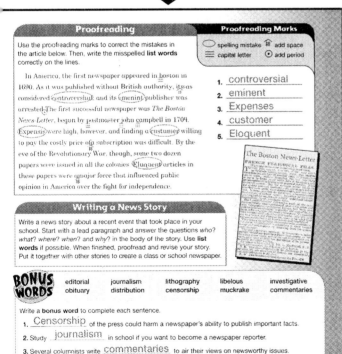

Proofreading

Use the proofreading marks to correct the mistakes in the article below. Then, write the misspelled **list words** correctly on the lines.

Proofreading Marks

- ◯ spelling mistake
- ≡ capital letter
- # add space
- ⊙ add period

In America, the first newspaper appeared in boston in 1690. As it was published without British authority, it was considered controvershil and its eminint publisher was arrested. The first successful newspaper was *The Boston News-Letter*, begun by postmaster john campbell in 1704. Expensis were high, however, and finding a custumer willing to pay the costly price of a subscription was difficult. By the eve of the Revolutionary War, though, some two dozen papers were issued in all the colonies. Eloquent articles in these papers were a major force that influenced public opinion in America over the fight for independence.

1. controversial
2. eminent
3. Expenses
4. customer
5. Eloquent

Writing a News Story

Write a news story about a recent event that took place in your school. Start with a lead paragraph and answer the questions *who? what? where? when?* and *why?* in the body of the story. Use **list words** if possible. When finished, proofread and revise your story. Put it together with other stories to create a class or school newspaper.

BONUS WORDS

editorial	journalism	lithography	libelous	investigative
obituary	distribution	censorship	muckrake	commentaries

Write a **bonus word** to complete each sentence.

1. Censorship of the press could harm a newspaper's ability to publish important facts.
2. Study journalism in school if you want to become a newspaper reporter.
3. Several columnists write commentaries to air their views on newsworthy issues.
4. On the editorial page, the newspaper presents its opinions on current issues.
5. Some newspapers published in the United States have worldwide distribution
6. Many newspapers are printed by using a process called lithography
7. Following a person's death, the obituary summarizes the events of his or her life.
8. Investigative reporters aim to find the facts behind a mystery or unsolved crime.
9. A story may be judged libelous if it unfairly injures or ridicules an individual.
10. To muckrake is to write a news story to expose corruption in business or politics.

Puzzle Urge students to use as clues not only the definitions, but also the number of spaces in each answer.

Spelling and Writing   *Page 72*

Proofreading Review with students the use of each of the proofreading marks shown in the box.

Writing a News Story Discuss examples of news articles. Show how the writers answered the questions *Who?, What?, Where?, When?,* and *Why?* Explain that the lead grabs the readers' attention and summarizes the story. Use a pyramid diagram to illustrate the lead and the layers of details supporting it. Then, discuss school-related topics, such as sporting events, debates, or other activities. Ask students to write the five "lead questions" in a vertical column on a sheet of paper. Have them take notes related to their topics to "answer" each question. When finished, urge students to submit their articles to the school paper or have them create a newsletter.

Bonus Words   *Page 72*

Newspapers With dictionaries and actual newspapers, define and discuss the **bonus words**. Relate them to the writing project and discussion.

Bonus Words Test

1. Teens are hired for **distribution** of the paper.
2. Ralph is an **investigative** reporter for *The Daily Sun*.
3. The term *muckrake* comes from a farming tool.
4. A **libelous** story is false and misleading.
5. The paper criticized the senator in an **editorial**.
6. Pete majored in **journalism** at the university.
7. Laurence Olivier's **obituary** was given a full page.
8. One method of printing is called **lithography**.
9. I always enjoy the **commentaries** of Art Buchwald.
10. **Censorship** of the press inhibits freedom of speech.

Final Test

1. Does the airline charge a fee for **excess** luggage?
2. She's a good **customer**; she buys food here often.
3. Set aside time each day **entirely** for relaxation.
4. The candidates debated many **controversial** issues.
5. Are your largest **expenses** rent and car payments?
6. The shelter **equally** distributes the food to people.
7. We were impressed by the waiter's **courtesy**.
8. Babe Ruth was an **eminent** baseball player.
9. The explorers discovered the **source** of the river.
10. Janell is a **sophomore** at Kenyon College.
11. Autumn is beautiful, **especially** in New England.
12. My **anxiety** disappeared when my lost cat returned.
13. The bright glow of the sunset will slowly **diminish**.
14. It is **customary** that our family gathers once a year.
15. Abraham Lincoln was an **eloquent** speaker.
16. Will scientists prove that theory to be a **fallacy**?
17. Check the facts before making your **decision**.
18. The **excitable** fans sat on the edge of their seats.
19. In the folk tale, the hero outwitted a **cruel** monster.
20. The goalie felt **defenseless** as the player scored.

Objectives
To review spelling words with Latin roots and unusual spellings

Spelling Strategy   *Page 73*

Tell students that in this lesson they will review the skills and spelling words studied in Lessons 13–17. You may wish to have students refer to previous spelling rules to review Latin roots and challenging words.

Spelling Practice   *Pages 73–75*

Lesson 13 To review the Latin roots *aqua, later, sim, liber, host/hosp, mort,* write on the board: *aquamarine, bilateral, similarity, liberty, hospice, mortician.* Then, have students identify the Latin roots in the **list words**. Point out the additional write-on lines to students and encourage them to add two words from Lesson 13 that they found especially difficult or assign certain words that seemed to be difficult for everyone. (Repeat this procedure for each lesson in the Review.)

Lesson 14 Have students identify the Latin roots in these words: *disrupt, perplexing, pendulum,* and *obstruct.* Then, discuss the Latin roots in the **list words**. Tell students to use context clues to determine the missing **list words**.

Lesson 15 Discuss the meanings of the Latin roots in these words: *revoke, invariable, vagabond, decentralize, termination,* and *terrestrial.* Then, have students identify the **list words'** Latin roots. To extend, have students write their own clues for the other **list words** in Lesson 15, and exchange them with classmates to solve.

Lesson 16 Have students identify the Latin roots in *spectacular, transpired, including,* and *matron.* Discuss how the Latin roots affect the meanings of the **list words**, and the subtle differences between *perspective, spectacle; conspiracy,* and *speculate.* Point out that all the puzzle clues are synonyms for **list words**.

Lesson 17 Ask students to spell: *entirely, sophomore, equally, excess,* and *diminish.* Tell students that these are examples of words with spellings that don't follow specific rules. Then, discuss the unusual spelling patterns in the **list words**. To review alphabetizing, have students put these words in order: *extinguish, expedition, delicious, expect,* and *disastrous.*

Show What You Know   *Page 76*

Point out that this review will help students know if they have mastered the words in Lessons 13–17. Have a volunteer restate the directions and tell which word in the first item should be marked as incorrect. *(acquarium)* When finished, have students write their misspelled words correctly.

TIPS

- Latin roots can help you determine the meanings of unfamiliar words. Knowing how a Latin root is spelled can help you figure out how to spell a difficult word. Here are some examples:

Latin Root (Meaning)	English Word	Latin Root (Meaning)	English Word
aqua ("water")	aquatic	**voc/vok** ("voice")	vocalize
later ("side")	unilateral	**var** ("different")	variety
sim ("like")	simulate	**vag** ("wander")	vagrant
liber ("free")	liberal	**centr** ("center")	centralize
host/hosp ("guest")	hostel	**term** ("end")	terminal
hostis ("warlike")	hostile	**terr** ("land")	terrace
mort ("death")	mortal	**spec** ("see")	inspection
plic/plex ("fold")	complex	**spir** ("breathe")	spiritual
rupt ("break")	abrupt	**clu/clud** ("shut")	preclude
pend ("hang")	pendant	**mater** ("mother")	maternity
struct ("build")	construct		

- Words that do not follow ordinary spelling rules present a challenge. Memorize and practice spelling tricky words such as these: <u>customer, eloquent,</u> and <u>eminent.</u>

Lesson 13

List Words

aquarium
lateral
hospice
dissimilar
hostage
mortgage
hospitalize
simultaneous
quadrilateral
liberate

Write **list words** to answer the questions.

Which list words have the Latin root **host** or **hosp** that means "guest"?
1. hospice   3. hospitalize
2. hostage

Which **list word** contains the Latin root **aqua** that means "water"?
4. aquarium

Which **list word** contains the Latin root **mort** that means "death"?
5. mortgage

Which **list words** contain the Latin root **sim** that means "like"?
6. simultaneous   7. dissimilar

Which **list words** contain the Latin root **later** that means "side"?
8. lateral   9. quadrilateral

Which **list word** contains the Latin root **liber** that means "free"?
10. liberate

73

Lesson 14

List Words

inexplicable
instruction
destruction
independently
suspended
duplicate
structural
suspense
interrupt
applicable

Write a **list word** to complete each sentence.

1. If you do a project without a partner, you work independently
2. If you see something you can't explain, it is inexplicable
3. If you read mystery stories, you enjoy suspense
4. If a tornado whips through town, it causes destruction
5. If a remark is off the subject, it is not applicable
6. When you duplicate something, you make an identical copy of it.
7. If a building collapses, it probably has structural deficiencies.
8. A balloon flying high is suspended in the air.
9. If you break into a conversation, you interrupt
10. To learn how to play the violin, you look for instruction

Lesson 15

List Words

advocate
terrain
concentric
exterminate
vague
various
determine
eccentric
territory
variation

Write a **list word** to match each clue.

1. circles   concentric
2. a change   variation
3. destroy   exterminate
4. unclear   vague
5. different   various
6. a region   territory
7. odd   eccentric
8. supporter   advocate
9. land   terrain
10. figure out   determine

Fill in the puzzle by writing a **list word** to match each synonym.

List Words

conspiracy
inspiration
matrimony
spectacle
disrespect
maternal
perspective
speculate
exclude
seclusion

ACROSS
2. keep out
7. privacy
8. view
9. display
10. marriage

DOWN
1. conjecture
3. plot
4. rudeness
5. encouragement
6. motherly

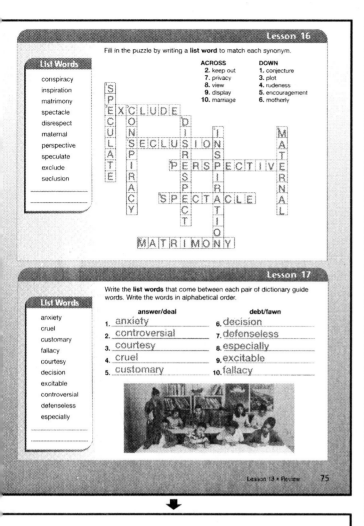

Write the **list words** that come between each pair of dictionary guide words. Write the words in alphabetical order.

List Words

anxiety
cruel
customary
fallacy
courtesy
decision
excitable
controversial
defenseless
especially

answer/deal
1. anxiety
2. controversial
3. courtesy
4. cruel
5. customary

debt/fawn
6. decision
7. defenseless
8. especially
9. excitable
10. fallacy

Show What You Know

One word is misspelled in each set of **list words**. Fill in the circle next to the **list word** that is spelled incorrectly.

#				
1.	○ exclude	● acquarium	○ provoke	○ applicable
2.	○ disrupt	○ territory	● hostal	○ inspection
3.	● maternel	○ lateral	○ vagrant	○ independently
4.	● pendalum	○ vocation	○ seclusion	○ mortuary
5.	○ transpired	● simultanious	○ eccentric	○ suspended
6.	○ revoke	○ controversial	○ bankrupt	● disimilar
7.	○ customer	○ duplicate	● hostege	○ terminal
8.	● aquadic	○ instruction	○ diminish	○ variation
9.	○ pendant	○ vocalize	○ entirely	● mortgadge
10.	○ expenses	● simmulate	○ suspense	○ conspiracy
11.	○ expire	○ complication	● angziety	○ hospitalize
12.	○ hostile	● customery	○ interrupt	○ impending
13.	● elloquent	○ destruction	○ liberal	○ inspiration
14.	● matrimoney	○ mortician	○ equally	○ perplexing
15.	○ spectacle	○ advocate	● falacy	○ unilateral
16.	○ courtesy	○ hospice	○ disrespect	● centralise
17.	○ mortal	● expectasion	○ terrain	○ decision
18.	○ vagabond	○ aquamarine	● eminnent	○ maternity
19.	○ excitable	● purspective	○ variety	○ quadrilateral
20.	○ source	○ concentric	○ liberate	● speckulate
21.	○ exclusive	● defensless	○ abrupt	○ exterminate
22.	○ complex	○ including	○ terrace	● sophemore
23.	● vage	○ implicate	○ cruel	○ matron
24.	○ preclude	○ various	● especialy	○ inexplicable
25.	○ excess	○ determine	○ structural	● spirtual

Final Test

1. What a perfect **aquarium** for your goldfish!
2. Her sudden, strange behavior was **inexplicable**.
3. Dad is an **advocate** for aiding the homeless.
4. A **conspiracy** was plotted against the captain.
5. May felt great **anxiety** when she lost her purse.
6. Lou made a perfect **lateral** pass to the right wing.
7. The house suffered **structural** damage in the fire.
8. How much of the Midwest has flat, fertile **terrain**?
9. What an **inspiration** to bring the video camera!
10. In debate class, we discuss **controversial** issues.
11. **Simultaneous** with your promotion is a raise.
12. That rule is **applicable** to many different situations.
13. Two circles sharing the same center are **concentric**.
14. Val is single and is not ready to consider **matrimony**.
15. It is **customary** to tip the food server in a restaurant.
16. A tall boy and a short girl are visibly **dissimilar**.
17. Jo works **independently** rather than with us.
18. Using insecticide is a way to **exterminate** ants.
19. Jake gets noticed by making a **spectacle** of himself.
20. His statement was a **fallacy**, based on incorrect facts.
21. The **hostage** was finally freed from his captors.
22. Privileges are **suspended** when you break the law.
23. Mel's **vague** response was confusing and unclear.
24. Rudeness and disobedience are forms of **disrespect**.
25. She held the door open out of **courtesy** toward me.
26. The City Bank holds the **mortgage** on our house.
27. That photo is a **duplicate** of the one that I have.
28. There are **various** ways to look at this problem.
29. Aunt Mary is very **maternal**, or motherly.
30. Was it a difficult **decision** to have the operation?
31. The doctor had to **hospitalize** Tara after she fell.
32. Ramón received **instruction** in woodworking.
33. A ruler helps **determine** the length of an object.
34. Ed stood back to get a full **perspective** of the view.
35. Hyperactive puppies are easily **excitable**.
36. With his **hostile** ways, he was considered a bully.
37. Mystery writers keep readers in **suspense**.
38. Our **eccentric** uncle had a strange sense of humor.
39. I can only **speculate** as to what might happen.
40. It is **cruel** to deprive an animal of food and water.
41. A **quadrilateral** figure has four sides and four angles.
42. If you **interrupt** the procedure, you must start over.
43. The **territory** west of the desert is still undeveloped.
44. The team did not **exclude** anyone from trying out.
45. The lame rabbit was **defenseless** against the fox.
46. Both nations decided to **liberate** their hostages.
47. The new model is a **variation** of the old one.
48. What terrible **destruction** after the storm!
49. Al enjoyed the quiet **seclusion** of his cabin retreat.
50. My mother loves fruit, **especially** peaches.

Prefixes Meaning "Together"

Objective
To spell words with prefixes that mean "together"

Pretest

1. Both doctors agreed to **coauthor** the book.
2. Can I use my car as **collateral** to get the loan?
3. The plane's pilot will be assisted by the **copilot**.
4. Fever is a **symptom** of many viral infections.
5. A **synagogue** is a place of worship.
6. The plants **coexist** in the same planter.
7. Haruko will **coordinate** everyone's schedules.
8. Stress the final **syllable** in the word *coincide*.
9. Both sides are alike, giving the vase **symmetry**.
10. **Synchronize** your watches so you'll meet on time.
11. Dr. Ball gave a simple, **coherent** talk about taxes.
12. Is this a **cooperative** task or an individual one?
13. I enjoyed the concert of **symphonic** music.
14. This product is the **synthesis** of six elements.
15. **Syncopate** the rhythm with a different beat.
16. How interesting that their birthdates **coincide**!
17. What does the figure of a heart usually **symbolize**?
18. My class will attend a poetry **symposium**.
19. **Syntax** refers to word order within a sentence.
20. A **syllabus** is an outline of a course of study.

Spelling Strategy   *Page 77*

Discuss the spelling rule and examples. Have students read the **list words** and identify their prefixes. If a word contains the prefix *syn* in any form, discuss any spelling changes and why they were made. Make sure students understand the words' meanings, having them refer to dictionaries if needed.

Vocabulary Development Explain to students that this exercise helps them learn the **list words'** meanings and spellings.

Dictionary Skills If needed, use a dictionary pronunciation key to review the letters and symbols used in sound-spellings. When students have finished, have them check their answers against a dictionary.

Spelling Practice   *Pages 78–79*

Word Analysis Write *synchronization* on the board and ask students which **list word** has the same root. (*synchronize*) Remind students that the words in the exercise may have different prefixes, suffixes, or both. If necessary, do the first item with students.

Word Application To extend the activity, have students create similar context clue sentences for the distractors, and then challenge their classmates to supply the correct answers.

54

Prefixes Meaning "Together"

TIP
The prefixes **co** and **syn** mean "together." However, the prefix **syn** changes the spelling to **syl** when it is used before words beginning with **l**; it changes to **sym** when it is used before words beginning with **b**, **m**, or **p**. Notice the spelling of these example words.

coauthor	syntheses	syllable
symbolize	symmetry	symptom

Vocabulary Development

Write the **list word** that matches each synonym or definition.

1. balance — symmetry
2. sentence structure — syntax
3. a temple — synagogue
4. to be identical or in accord — coincide
5. live together — coexist
6. understandable — coherent
7. musical — symphonic
8. a medical indicator — symptom
9. an outline of a course of study — syllabus
10. bring together — coordinate
11. word part — syllable
12. guaranteed by property — collateral

Dictionary Skills

Write the **list word** that matches each sound-spelling.

1. (kō′pī lət) copilot
2. (sim′b′l īz) symbolize
3. (kō′in sīd′) coincide
4. (simp′təm) symptom
5. (kō ô′thər) coauthor
6. (sin′taks) syntax
7. (sim pō′zē əm) symposium
8. (sin′thə sis) synthesis
9. (sig′krə nīz) synchronize
10. (sig′kə pāt) syncopate
11. (kō äp′ər ə tiv) cooperative
12. (kō hir′ənt) coherent

LIST WORDS
1. coauthor
2. collateral
3. copilot
4. symptom
5. synagogue
6. coexist
7. coordinate
8. syllable
9. symmetry
10. synchronize
11. coherent
12. cooperative
13. symphonic
14. synthesis
15. syncopate
16. coincide
17. symbolize
18. symposium
19. syntax
20. syllabus

77

DID YOU KNOW?
A **syncope** is a word that is made shorter by cutting out sounds in the middle. For example, writing *ne'er* in place of *never* would be a syncope. In music, to syncopate means "to make a rhythm feel shorter by cutting out beats in the middle."

Spelling Practice

Word Analysis

Write the **list word** that has the same root or base word as the word given.

1. syncopation — syncopate
2. synthetic — synthesis
3. authorize — coauthor
4. autopilot — copilot
5. cooperation — cooperative
6. coincidence — coincide
7. synchronicity — synchronize
8. symphony — symphonic
9. coexistence — coexist
10. symmetrical — symmetry
11. coordination — coordinate
12. symbolic — symbolize
13. symptomatic — symptom
14. coherence — coherent

Write the **list words** that contain double letters.

15. collateral
16. coordinate
17. syllable
18. symmetry
19. cooperative
20. syllabus

Word Application

Select a **list word** from the choices in parentheses to complete each sentence. Write the **list word** on the line.

1. A symposium on **symphonic** music will be held tomorrow night. (syntax, symphonic)
2. A **copilot** assists a pilot in flying a plane. (collateral, copilot)
3. The contestants had to **synchronize** their watches before the race. (synchronize, symbolize)
4. "What do the stripes on our flag **symbolize**?" asked a student. (coincide, symbolize)
5. We heard a **coherent** speech on the importance of computers. (syllable, coherent)
6. What beautiful symmetry of design on that **synagogue**! (synagogue, syntax)
7. Tomatoes and carrots are companion plants that **coexist** well in the garden. (coauthor, coexist)
8. Mr. Warren said, "Learn to spell each **syllable** in this word." (syllabus, syllable)
9. David and his coauthor attended the **symposium** introducing new science-fiction writers and the techniques that they use. (symposium, synthesis)
10. The sentence **syntax** can give you clues to a word's meaning. (syllable, syntax)
11. Sometimes **collateral** is needed in order to purchase expensive items. (coordinate, collateral)

78   Lesson 19 • Prefixes Meaning "Together"

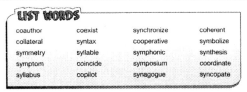

coauthor	coexist	synchronize	coherent
collateral	syntax	cooperative	symbolize
symmetry	syllable	symphonic	synthesis
symptom	coincide	symposium	coordinate
syllabus	copilot	synagogue	syncopate

Puzzle

Use the **list words** to complete the crossword puzzle.

ACROSS

1. having to do with the sounds a symphony makes
5. a writer who works with another writer
6. a meeting to discuss some particular subject
8. the assistant pilot of an airplane
9. a word or part of a word
12. the putting together of parts or elements to make a whole
16. speaking or thinking in a way that makes sense
17. the way words are put together in sentences; sentence structure
18. to be the symbol of something; represent

DOWN

2. to bring together in a proper relation
3. a sign that something else exists, especially in sickness
4. helpful; willing to cooperate
5. to happen at the same time
7. an outline or summary
9. a temple where Jewish people gather for worship
10. property given as a pledge to repay a loan
11. to make agree in time or rate of speed
13. to shift the musical accent of a beat
14. balance or harmony
15. living together in peace

Proofreading

Use the proofreading marks to correct the mistakes in the article below. Then, write the misspelled **list words** correctly on the lines.

Proofreading Marks

◯ spelling mistake   ⊓ add space
／ small letter
✓ᐢ add quotation marks

Through a cooperative effort with the Chicagoschool system, The Youth Education programs of the Chicago Symphony Orchestra provide in-depth classical music experiences to more than 100,000 area children each year. The school system works with the symphony to coordinate the program so that it will coinside with the school year calendar. Activities include an extensive series of Symphonic concerts for schools, a Sympozium for teachers, and opportunities for talented young musicians. "Our Concert was the best we have ever attended, wrote one teacher after this year's first show.

1. cooperative
2. coordinate
3. coincide
4. symphonic
5. symposium

Writing a Review

Write a review of a book you have read, a musical performance you have heard or a movie, TV show, or play you have seen recently. Give your opinion and explain why you liked or disliked it. Use as many **list words** as you can, then proofread and revise your review. Compile your work with that of other classmates in a book. Add new reviews to the book periodically.

 BONUS WORDS

amphitheater	coliseum	prologue	pageant	critique
melodrama	soliloquy	vaudeville	scenario	cinema

Write **bonus words** to answer the questions.

Which word relates to film or movies?

1. cinema

Which word might discuss a play or film in a critical way?

2. critique

Which words name buildings or structures?

3. coliseum   4. amphitheater

Which words describe or name kinds of performances?

5. pageant   6. vaudeville   7. melodrama

Which words name particular parts of plays?

8. soliloquy   9. prologue   10. scenario

Puzzle Briefly review crossword puzzle strategies with students, and remind them to print neatly.

Spelling and Writing   *Page 80*

Proofreading Use this sentence to review the proofreading marks: *Marsha said, Wat a wonderful day fora Picnic.*

Writing a Review Discuss with students where they have seen or heard reviews. Then, talk about why people like or dislike movies, shows, plays, books, or musical performances, and why two people might have different opinions about the same one. Explain that reviewers give facts and details to support their opinions, such as telling exactly how long a movie was.

Bonus Words   *Page 80*

Theater Explain that the **bonus words** are related to theater. Discuss words that students know, and help them define unfamiliar words through dictionary use. Point out unusual spellings in the words, such as the ending of *soliloquy* or the middle *e* in *vaudeville*.

Bonus Words Test

1. Hamlet's **soliloquy** begins, "To be or not to be . . ."
2. Plays are performed in the park's **amphitheater**.
3. In a **melodrama**, the hero and heroine are perfect.
4. In **cinema**, the camera's point of view is important.
5. *The Revels* is a **pageant** in medieval costume.
6. Read the **scenario** and tell me what you think.
7. A **prologue** is the opposite of an epilogue.
8. Each student wrote a **critique** of the performance.
9. Only a **coliseum** can hold such a big crowd.
10. Many **vaudeville** actors moved on to television.

Final Test

1. My cat and dog **coexist** without fighting.
2. Let's try to **coordinate** our chores for efficiency.
3. Which **syllable** is accented in the word *system*?
4. In nature, perfect **symmetry** is rarely seen.
5. Dancers must **synchronize** their steps to music!
6. The class's **syllabus** was handed out the first day.
7. To understand the **syntax**, diagram the sentence.
8. My mother attended a **symposium** on genetics.
9. A dove or an olive branch can **symbolize** peace.
10. If our schedules **coincide**, let's meet for lunch.
11. How many writers will **coauthor** the book?
12. Ken used his car as **collateral** for the loan.
13. What tasks do the pilot and the **copilot** share?
14. Fatigue is a **symptom** of many diseases.
15. In a **synagogue**, services are on Friday evenings.
16. The story was complex, but it was **coherent**.
17. Will you be **cooperative** and help with the project?
18. The poem has a **symphonic** quality to it.
19. A compound is the **synthesis** of elements.
20. As you play that song, **syncopate** the rhythm.

Prefixes Meaning "Not"

Objective
To spell words with prefixes that mean "not"

Pretest
1. **Anarchy** refers to the absence of government.
2. Sailing in such high winds would be **imprudent**.
3. That man can **impersonate** many people.
4. Many celebrities travel **incognito** to avoid fans.
5. My car's dent proves you've been **negligent**.
6. **Anesthesia** puts surgery patients to sleep.
7. Don't try to cut that board until you **immobilize** it.
8. The stranded traveler tapped her foot **impatiently**.
9. If you cannot make a decision, you are **indecisive**.
10. Which is healthier, a **negative** or a positive attitude?
11. **Anemia** is a blood condition that causes weakness.
12. His home is so clean, I'd call it **immaculate**!
13. If something is **inaccurate**, it is not correct.
14. Your permit is **invalid** because it has expired.
15. He acted very **nonchalant**, as if nothing happened.
16. To be **anonymous**, just don't give your name.
17. The **impromptu** party was not planned.
18. If I become more **inactive**, will I gain weight?
19. Do not **neglect** to dust underneath the couch.
20. These expenses make my savings **nonexistent**.

Spelling Strategy   *Page 81*
Discuss the spelling rule and examples. Have students read the **list words** and identify their prefixes and whether the prefixes changed spelling. Help students define unfamiliar words, showing that *invalid* has its stress on the second syllable and means "not logically correct." Students may confuse it with the identically spelled word, accented on the first syllable, meaning "a person in ill health."

Vocabulary Development This exercise helps students study the **list words'** meanings and spellings.

Dictionary Skills Briefly review the rules of syllabication, having students refer to Lesson 1 if necessary. When they have finished, have them check their answers against a dictionary.

Spelling Practice   *Pages 82–83*
Word Analysis Remind students to think about the first letters of words before adding prefixes.

Word Application Point out that the meaning and the part of speech of each underlined word or phrase are clues to the **list word** replacement. If necessary, do the first item with students.

TIP
Many different prefixes mean "not." Some of these prefixes change their spellings before certain letters. The prefix a, for example, becomes an before a vowel. The prefix in becomes im before m, b, and p. Look at how these words are spelled:

anarchy   incognito   immobilize   impromptu

Other prefixes meaning "not" include non and neg, as in nonexistent and negative.

Vocabulary Development
Write the **list word** that matches each definition or synonym.

1. unfavorable — negative
2. idle — inactive
3. in disguise — incognito
4. without advance planning — impromptu
5. unnamed — anonymous
6. null and void — invalid
7. cool and composed — nonchalant
8. prevent movement — immobilize
9. clean — immaculate
10. mimic or copy — impersonate
11. incorrect — inaccurate
12. hesitant — indecisive

Dictionary Skills
Rewrite each of the following **list words** to show how they are divided into syllables.

1. neglect — neg/lect
2. anemia — a/ne/mi/a
3. anarchy — an/arch/y
4. invalid — in/val/id
5. negligent — neg/li/gent
6. impatiently — im/pa/tient/ly
7. anesthesia — an/es/the/sia
8. immobilize — im/mo/bi/lize
9. nonexistent — non/ex/ist/ent
10. imprudent — im/pru/dent

LIST WORDS
1. anarchy
2. imprudent
3. impersonate
4. incognito
5. negligent
6. anesthesia
7. immobilize
8. impatiently
9. indecisive
10. negative
11. anemia
12. immaculate
13. inaccurate
14. invalid
15. nonchalant
16. anonymous
17. impromptu
18. inactive
19. neglect
20. nonexistent

81

DID YOU KNOW?
Nonchalant is a word borrowed from the French language and comes from two Latin words meaning "to be not warm." A person who is nonchalant does not get warm or passionate about things, but seems always to be cool or lukewarm.

Spelling Practice

Word Analysis
Write the **list word** formed by adding a prefix that means "not" to each base word given.

1. valid — invalid
2. decisive — indecisive
3. mobilize — immobilize
4. accurate — inaccurate
5. prudent — imprudent
6. active — inactive
7. patiently — impatiently
8. existent — nonexistent

Word Application
Replace the underlined word or words in each sentence with a **list word**. Write the **list word** on the line.

1. Make sure you do not abandon your duty. — neglect
2. These troops are not on active duty. — inactive
3. Ellen is so composed, and I am so nervous. — nonchalant
4. First, the doctor will have to prevent motion of that broken leg. — immobilize
5. We could not identify the voice of the nameless caller. — anonymous
6. The party was not planned; it was spur-of-the-moment. — impromptu
7. To avoid photographers, the celebrity traveled in disguise. — incognito
8. This surgery will require only local painkiller. — anesthesia
9. Make sure you do not make wrong claims about your product. — inaccurate
10. The Washington family keeps their home very clean. — immaculate
11. The nurse will test you for a blood disorder. — anemia
12. In the fog, my ocean view was not there. — nonexistent
13. People often try to pretend they are famous people. — impersonate
14. Spending all your money would be unwise. — imprudent
15. A leader is not allowed to be wavering. — indecisive
16. After the revolution, an absence of government ruled. — anarchy
17. The driver was careless in maintaining his car's brakes. — negligent
18. The critic gave the movie a bad review. — negative
19. My sister waited with annoyance for me to finish brushing my teeth. — impatiently

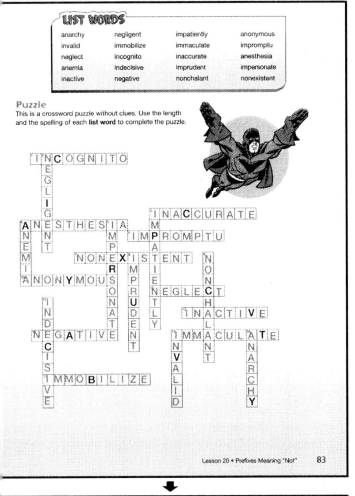

LIST WORDS

anarchy	negligent	impatiently	anonymous
invalid	immobilize	immaculate	impromptu
neglect	incognito	inaccurate	anesthesia
anemia	indecisive	imprudent	impersonate
inactive	negative	nonchalant	nonexistent

Puzzle
This is a crossword puzzle without clues. Use the length and the spelling of each **list word** to complete the puzzle.

Lesson 20 • Prefixes Meaning "Not"   83

Proofreading

Use the proofreading marks to correct the mistakes in the paragraphs below. Then, write the misspelled **list words** correctly on the lines.

The comic character Superman was created in the 1930s by Jerry Siegel and Joe Shuster Superman was first conceived as a negative character, a villain with superior strength, but Siegel became indicisive as the character developed. The idea to to make him a hero from another planet who fights against annarchy and and who can immobolise a villain with one blow, came to Jerry in the middle of the night. The next day, the first Superman story was written.

In 1938, Superman's alter ego, reporter Clark Kent, began working incognito at *The Daily Star*, which later became *The Daily Planet*. He has worked there now for for over 60 years!

Proofreading Marks
⬭ spelling mistake
! add exclamation mark
⊙ add period ⌒ delete word

1. negative
2. indecisive
3. anarchy
4. immobilize
5. incognito

Writing a Comic Strip

Create a superhero comic strip about a character whose incredible powers save an entire city from destruction. Write an introductory paragraph that tells the character's name and describes her or his super-human traits. Use as many **list words** as you can. After proofreading and revising your paragraph, illustrate and write the dialogue for the comic strip. Publish your comic strip in a class or school newspaper or newsletter.

BONUS WORDS

altruistic	articulate	arduous	unscathed	boisterous
laudable	winsome	staunch	vindictive	dynamic

Write the **bonus word** that matches each synonym.

1. vengeful — vindictive
2. difficult — arduous
3. intelligible — articulate
4. energetic — dynamic
5. cute — winsome

6. loud — boisterous
7. loyal — staunch
8. charitable — altruistic
9. uninjured — unscathed
10. praiseworthy — laudable

84   Lesson 20 • Prefixes Meaning "Not"

Puzzle Have volunteers describe how to solve crossword puzzles without clues. Remind students to print neatly and spell words carefully.

Spelling and Writing   *Page 84*

Proofreading Use this sentence to demonstrate the proofreading marks: *Wow That was a a fantastik game*

Writing a Comic Strip Discuss the different cartoon superheroes students have seen or read about. Make a list of the superheroes' special powers, and then add other traits they might have. As a group, make up names for new characters, encouraging students to be playful and inventive. Then, have students write their paragraphs and create their comic strips.

Bonus Words   *Page 84*

Descriptive Words Explain that the **bonus words** are descriptive words that would help writers create colorful descriptions. Through discussion and dictionary use, help students understand the words' meanings. Then, have students use the words in oral sentences.

Bonus Words Test
1. The children were polite, **winsome**, and attractive.
2. One hiker passed the brambles **unscathed**.
3. We were tired after such an **arduous** journey.
4. The waiter asked the **boisterous** family to be quiet.
5. Alan had **altruistic** motives for giving away money.
6. My mother is a **staunch** supporter of this candidate.
7. The first speaker was both **articulate** and funny.
8. You deserve a prize for such a **laudable** achievement.
9. Daryl is certainly a **dynamic** speaker and leader.
10. A **vindictive** person seeks revenge, not solutions.

Final Test
1. Local **anesthesia** is used for minor surgery.
2. Will the doctor **immobilize** that arm with a splint?
3. We waited **impatiently** while the bus was fixed.
4. If you are **indecisive**, someone will decide for you.
5. People with **negative** outlooks are not happy.
6. The entire project suffers if anyone is **negligent**.
7. She prefers to be **incognito** to avoid crowds of fans.
8. The way that you **impersonate** Mike is funny.
9. Driving in this storm would be **imprudent**.
10. When the government fell, **anarchy** reigned.
11. Do you worry about **nonexistent** problems?
12. I won't **neglect** your pets when you're gone.
13. Does the heat and humidity make you **inactive**?
14. The two pianists played an **impromptu** duet.
15. The tip came from an **anonymous** source.
16. A simple blood test can detect **anemia**.
17. The operating room must be **immaculate**.
18. The first estimates turned out to be **inaccurate**.
19. The check is **invalid** without a signature.
20. For being nervous, he sure looks **nonchalant**!

57

Words of Latin Origin

Objective
To spell words of Latin origin

Pretest

1. The **auditor** checked the tax return for errors.
2. What an **exorbitant** amount of money she spent!
3. The **molecular** formula of glucose is $C_6H_{12}O_6$.
4. An **ordinance** is a law made by a city government.
5. Is your senator a **Republican** or a Democrat?
6. She made a **documentary** film about the rain forest.
7. She uses **insecticide** to protect her garden.
8. Did you order your eyeglasses from the **optician**?
9. The **publicity** for the exhibit attracted large crowds.
10. **Suburban** areas are located outside the city limits.
11. Great Britain once had **dominion** over Canada.
12. The **juvenile** books are in the children's section.
13. You have the **option** of the matinee or the late show.
14. He is in **quarantine** until he is no longer contagious.
15. **Vermin** have gnawed holes in the attic floor.
16. I felt **exhilarated** after hiking up the mountain.
17. Is fifty the **maximum** or minimum amount?
18. The prince bought an **opulent** vacation home.
19. The **regime** of King Richard was brief.
20. What will the jury's **verdict** be—guilty or not guilty?

Spelling Strategy   *Page 85*

Discuss the spelling rule and examples. Then, discuss the **list words**, having students use dictionaries to find each one's Latin root. Ask volunteers to suggest other English words with the same Latin roots. Then, have students use the **list words** in oral sentences.

Vocabulary Development Before the exercise, have students select a **list word** to match this short definition: "lively or cheerful." (*exhilarated*)

Dictionary Skills If necessary, review etymologies by revisiting the spelling rule examples. Urge students to use both the structure and definitions of the Latin roots as clues.

Spelling Practice   *Pages 86–87*

Word Analysis As an example, ask students to name the **list word** that has the same Latin root or base word as the English word *ordinary*. (*ordinance*)

Analogies Have students select a **list word** to complete this analogy: *inexpensive is to low-cost as expensive is to _____*. (*exorbitant*)

Word Application Explain that students need to understand the **list words'** meanings to complete this exercise. To extend, have students create similar context-clue sentences for the distractors. Call on volunteers to challenge their classmates for the correct answers.

 TIP
You have already studied several words and prefixes that have Latin roots. Knowing the meanings of Latin roots that appear frequently in English words will help you to analyze unfamiliar words for correct meaning and spelling.

Latin Root	Meaning	English Words	Meaning
documentum	"lesson; example"	document / documentary	"paper relied on for proof" / "film that teaches"
optio	"wish; desire"	option / optional	"the power to choose" / "not mandatory; elective"
opticus	"eye"	optician	"one who makes eyeglasses"

Vocabulary Development

Write the **list word** that matches each definition clue.

1. law _ordinance_
2. excessive _exorbitant_
3. young _juvenile_
4. choice _option_
5. wealthy _opulent_
6. bug poison _insecticide_
7. promotion _publicity_
8. political party _Republican_
9. eye specialist _optician_
10. nonfiction film _documentary_

Dictionary Skills

Write the **list word** that matches each etymology.

1. Latin **sub** ("under; near") + **urbs** ("town") _suburban_
2. Latin **vermis** ("worm") _vermin_
3. Latin **vere** ("truly") + **dictum** ("said") _verdict_
4. Latin **dominus** ("master") _dominion_
5. Latin **regere** ("to rule") _regime_
6. Latin **ex** ("intensive") + **hilaris** ("glad") _exhilarated_
7. Italian **quaranta** ("forty") from Latin **quattuor** ("four") _quarantine_
8. Latin **audire** ("to hear") _auditor_
9. Latin **maximus** ("greatest") _maximum_
10. Latin **moles** ("mass") _molecular_

LIST WORDS
1. auditor
2. exorbitant
3. molecular
4. ordinance
5. Republican
6. documentary
7. insecticide
8. optician
9. publicity
10. suburban
11. dominion
12. juvenile
13. option
14. quarantine
15. vermin
16. exhilarated
17. maximum
18. opulent
19. regime
20. verdict

DID YOU KNOW?
Exorbitant is made by adding the prefix *ex*, which means "out," to the Latin root *orbita*, which means "path." It literally means "out of the path." So *exorbitant* means "too much" or "out of the normal amount."

Spelling Practice

Word Analysis

Write the **list word** with the same Latin root as the word given.

1. order _ordinance_   5. orbit _exorbitant_
2. maxim _maximum_   6. urban _suburban_
3. dominate _dominion_   7. adopt _option_
4. quarter _quarantine_   8. audition _auditor_

Analogies

Write a **list word** to complete each analogy.

1. Cell is to cellular as molecule is to _molecular_
2. Communist is to Socialist as Democrat is to _Republican_
3. Question is to answer as evidence is to _verdict_
4. Adult is to mature as adolescent is to _juvenile_
5. Rat is to _vermin_ as lion is to predators.
6. Tooth is to dentist as eye is to _optician_
7. Real is to _documentary_ as make-believe is to fiction.
8. Bed is to sleep as hospital is to _quarantine_
9. Least is to minimum as greatest is to _maximum_

Word Application

Select a **list word** from the choices in parentheses to complete each sentence. Write the **list word** on the line.

1. Ralph used _insecticide_ to rid his garden of aphids and beetles. (vermin, publicity, insecticide)
2. I was shaken but _exhilarated_ by the roller coaster ride. (exhilarated, exorbitant, opulent)
3. Your posters provided great _publicity_ for my campaign. (publicity, dominion, documentary)
4. The movie was set in the _opulent_ palace of Catherine the Great. (maximum, opulent, exhilarated)
5. The _regime_ of Queen Victoria lasted from 1837 to 1901. (opulent, regime, verdict)

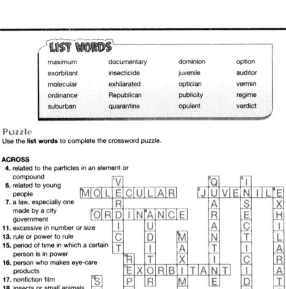

Puzzle
Use the **list words** to complete the crossword puzzle.

ACROSS
4. related to the particles in an element or compound
5. related to young people
7. a law, especially one made by a city government
11. excessive in number or size
13. rule or power to rule
15. period of time in which a certain person is in power
16. person who makes eye-care products
17. nonfiction film
18. insects or small animals, such as termites and rats
19. material geared to announce events or provide information to the public

DOWN
1. jury's decision
2. period in which a diseased person or animal is isolated
3. bug poison
6. feeling cheerful and lively
8. person who checks financial accounts and records
9. the greatest possible amount
10. a political party in the United States
12. related to areas situated near a city
14. power to choose; one particular choice
16. rich or luxurious

Proofreading

Use the proofreading marks to correct the mistakes in the article. Write the misspelled **list words** correctly on the lines.

The plague known as the Black Death erupted in the gobi Desert in mongolia in the late 1320s. No one knows why. Whatever the reason, Scientists know that the outbreak began there and spread outward, taking an exorbitent toll on the Earth's population. The bacteria that causes the Plague is carried by fleas that travel on virmin. In the middle ages, however, no one knew what caused the disease, and the only opshun people had when it appeared was to try and leave their town or city. Some city officials tried to qwarentine plague sufferers, and in Italy an ordinence was issued forbidding anyone who had come in contact with the plague to leave his or her home.

Proofreading Marks
- ◯ spelling mistake
- ⟍ᵥ add apostrophe
- ☰ capital letter
- / small letter

1. _exorbitant_
2. _vermin_
3. _option_
4. _quarantine_
5. _ordinance_

Writing a Report

Write a report about a modern-day plague that is occurring or could occur in the United States. Include facts about your topic, such as the personal, economic, and cultural impact of the disease, and use **list words** when possible. After proofreading and revising, share your report with the class.

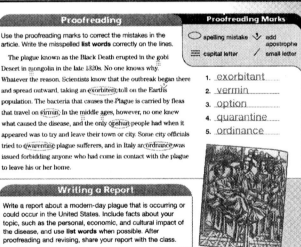

BONUS WORDS

topography	avalanche	erosion	mesa	crevasse
sedimentary	igneous	geyser	atoll	alluvial

Write the **bonus word** that matches each definition clue.

1. deep crack in land or ice _crevasse_
2. wearing away of soil _erosion_
3. ring-shaped island _atoll_
4. high, steep-sided plateau _mesa_
5. study of land surfaces _topography_
6. boiling spring _geyser_
7. containing matter deposited by water or wind, as sand or soil _sedimentary_
8. made up of sand or clay washed down by flowing water _alluvial_
9. matter produced by the action of volcanoes or other intense heat _igneous_
10. sudden, swift slide of a mass of loosened snow, earth, or rocks _avalanche_

Puzzle Urge students to use as clues not only the definitions, but the number of spaces in each answer.

Spelling and Writing   *Page 88*

Proofreading Use this sentence to demonstrate the proofreading marks: *Toms aunt is in midlands hospitel with Pneumonia.*

Writing a Report Relate the writing project to a cross-curriculum unit involving the history of diseases in areas of the world or current scientific disease research. Urge students to combine facts with imaginative descriptions. Allow time for students to share their completed work.

Bonus Words   *Page 88*

Earth Help students define the **bonus words**, then display pictures of a geyser, mesa, atoll, and avalanche. Discuss the differences between alluvial, sedimentary, and igneous rocks. Have students share their knowledge of the **bonus words**, and use each word in oral sentences.

Bonus Words Test
1. Molten lava cools to form **igneous** rocks.
2. **Topography** is the mapping of land features.
3. Fresh snow filled the glacier's deep **crevasse**.
4. **Sedimentary** rocks line the ocean's floor.
5. **Alluvial** clay deposits formed on the riverbank.
6. The **atoll** was formed by coral deposits.
7. Native Americans once lived on that **mesa**.
8. "Old Faithful" is a **geyser** in Yellowstone Park.
9. **Avalanche** warnings prevented us from skiing.
10. Trees on the riverbank may prevent **erosion**.

Final Test
1. Which **option** do you feel will be most beneficial?
2. The defense lawyer was anxious to hear the **verdict**.
3. Norma soon became the bank's head **auditor**.
4. What is the **molecular** structure of that chemical?
5. Harry is a **Republican**; his brother is a Democrat.
6. In London, I saw the **opulent** crown jewels.
7. We sprayed **insecticide** to kill the hornets.
8. The **optician** explained how to clean contact lenses.
9. The **documentary** about Spain won several awards.
10. The child was **exhilarated** after her day at the zoo.
11. They moved from the city to a **suburban** town.
12. The king claimed **dominion** over the colonies.
13. The bus can hold a **maximum** of 35 people.
14. The cartoon feature is meant for a **juvenile** audience.
15. **Vermin** have gnawed their way into the fire station.
16. What an **exorbitant** price for that tiny house!
17. World War II ended Hitler's **regime**.
18. To gain **publicity**, the store sponsored a contest.
19. Is there a city **ordinance** against double-parking?
20. The vet must **quarantine** the dog if it's sick.

Lesson 22

Words of Greek Origin

Objective
To spell words of Greek origin

Pretest

1. An **academy** is an educational institution.
2. All historic documents are filed in the **archive**.
3. A large city with diversity is a **cosmopolitan** city.
4. Is a compact car always **economical** and practical?
5. A **metropolis** is a large or important city.
6. Rocket scientists are experts in **aeronautics**.
7. The cave walls contained **archaic** hieroglyphics.
8. Did the reviewers **criticize** that film as being dull?
9. Jen secured her ponytail with an **elastic** band.
10. All citizens have equal rights in a **democracy**.
11. According to the **analysis**, the problem is resolvable.
12. Mrs. Wu hired an **architect** to design a new home.
13. What a **crisis** the drought created for local farmers!
14. There are many galaxies in the **cosmos**.
15. **Politics** is the science of government.
16. The word *dare* makes the **anagram** *read*.
17. This city is governed by a complex **bureaucracy**.
18. A total **eclipse** of the sun is a rare phenomenon.
19. Anything **magnetic** has the properties of a magnet.
20. **Theology** is the study of religious beliefs.

Spelling Strategy   *Page 89*

Discuss the spelling rule and examples. Using the Greek roots shown, have students speculate what *metromedia*, *psychology*, and *archduke* mean. Have them check their responses in a dictionary. Use these examples to stress that knowledge of the meanings of Greek roots will help them to figure out the meanings of unfamiliar words. Then, discuss the Greek roots in the **list words**, and work with students to define each word.

Vocabulary Development Before the exercise, have students select a **list word** to match this clue: "science of aircraft design." *(aeronautics)*

Dictionary Skills Urge students to use both the structure and definitions of the roots as clues.

Spelling Practice   *Pages 90–91*

Word Analysis As an example, ask students to name the **list word** that has the same Greek root as the English name *Theodore*. *(theology)*

Analogies To review analogies, have students select a **list word** to complete this example: *High is to low as expensive is to _____. (economical)*

Word Application To extend the activity, have students create riddles for the distractors, such as: *I am a large problem or an emergency. What am I? (crisis)* Call on volunteers to present their riddles to the class.

TIP
Many English words have Greek origins. Knowing the meanings of Greek roots and prefixes will help you spell and define unfamiliar words.

Prefix + Root	Meaning	English Word	Meaning
meter + polis	"mother" + "city"	metropolis	"major city"
theos + logos	"god" + "word"	theology	"religious studies"
archi + tekton	"chief" + "builder"	architect	"building designer"

Vocabulary Development

Write the **list word** that matches each synonym or definition clue.

1. school   academy
2. ancient   archaic
3. rubbery   elastic
4. urgent   crisis
5. find fault   criticize
6. universe   cosmos
7. government rules   bureaucracy
8. document library   archive
9. careful study   analysis
10. word puzzle   anagram
11. worldwide   cosmopolitan
12. attractive   magnetic

Dictionary Skills

Write a **list word** to match each Greek etymology.

1. aēr ("air") + naus ("ship")   aeronautics
2. theo ("god") + logos ("word")   theology
3. dēmos ("the people") + kratos ("strength")   democracy
4. Magnētis ("stone from Magnesia")   magnetic
5. politikos ("of a citizen")   politics
6. elatos ("to beat out")   elastic
7. Akadēmos ("figure in Greek myths")   academy
8. ana ("back") + gamma ("letter")   anagram
9. oikos ("house") + nomos ("one who manages")   economical
10. archi ("chief") + tekton ("builder")   architect
11. ana ("up") + lysis ("loosening")   analysis
12. ek ("out") + leipein ("to leave")   eclipse

LIST WORDS

1. academy
2. archive
3. cosmopolitan
4. economical
5. metropolis
6. aeronautics
7. archaic
8. criticize
9. elastic
10. democracy
11. analysis
12. architect
13. crisis
14. cosmos
15. politics
16. anagram
17. bureaucracy
18. eclipse
19. magnetic
20. theology

89

Spelling Practice

DID YOU KNOW?
Academy comes from the Greek word for "a grove of trees near Athens." Plato, an ancient Greek philosopher and teacher, taught his students in that grove. The Greeks thought that it had once belonged to a hero in a Greek legend named Akadēmos.

Word Analysis

Write the **list word** that has the same root as the word given.

1. polite   politics
2. magnesium   magnetic
3. economy   economical
4. Minneapolis   metropolis
5. analyze   analysis
6. airplane   aeronautics
7. academic   academy
8. telegram   anagram

Analogies

Write a **list word** to complete each analogy.

1. Difficult is to easy as archaic is to modern.
2. Communism is to Cuba as democracy is to the United States.
3. Portrait is to artist as building is to architect.
4. Brittle is to break as elastic is to stretch.
5. Archaeology is to early civilizations as theology is to religious doctrines.
6. Applaud is to "yes" as criticize is to "no."
7. Library is to book as archive is to document.
8. Island is to ocean as galaxy is to cosmos.

Word Application

Select a **list word** from the choices in parentheses to complete each sentence. Write the **list word** on the line.

1. Red tape is a slang term for the complexities of bureaucracy. (aeronautics, bureaucracy, crisis)
2. A cosmopolitan person travels all over the world with ease. (politics, cosmopolitan, democracy)
3. Scientists who design rockets are experts in aeronautics. (aeronautics, metropolis, crisis)
4. The moon may totally cover the sun in a solar eclipse. (bureaucracy, cosmos, eclipse)
5. The tornado created a crisis in the city. (metropolis, crisis, cosmos)
6. His lawyer's analysis of the problem was helpful. (anagram, criticize, analysis)

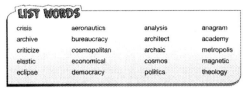

LIST WORDS

crisis	aeronautics	analysis	anagram
archive	bureaucracy	architect	academy
criticize	cosmopolitan	archaic	metropolis
elastic	economical	cosmos	magnetic
eclipse	democracy	politics	theology

Puzzle
Use the **list words** to complete the crossword puzzle.

ACROSS
1. universe
2. the science of aircraft
5. study of religion
9. able to fit into any culture
10. government by the people
11. hiding of the sun or moon
14. the most important city
15. person who designs buildings
16. rubbery
17. outdated or seldom used
18. to be critical of

DOWN
1. great danger
2. word made by changing the order of letters in another word
3. place of study
4. examination
6. where records are stored
7. saving money
8. attracting others
12. the science of government
13. government by officials who always obey all rules

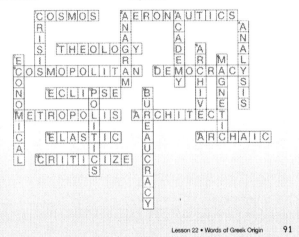

Lesson 22 • Words of Greek Origin   91

Proofreading

Use the proofreading marks to correct the mistakes in the article below. Then, write the misspelled **list words** correctly on the lines.

Proofreading Marks
○ spelling mistake   ? add question mark
¶ new paragraph   ⊙ add period

Did you know that cities exist for many reasons? In ancient times, cities could provide protection in times of crysis. During attacks, the population could flee behind the city walls. Today, with libraries and museums, many cities are an arkive for information, as well as centers for manufacturing. They also serve as hubs for state and federal burocracy. Washington, D.C., for example, displays the monumental buildings and large public spaces typical of a capital metropolis.

In ancient times and today, however, cities have always provided fertile ground for the development of human culture, with their cozmopolitan mixture of different people and ideas.

1. crisis
2. archive
3. bureaucracy
4. metropolis
5. cosmopolitan

Writing a Postcard

What cities have you visited? What cities around the world would you like to visit? Write a travel postcard in which you provide a friend with some details about your trip to the city of your choice. A travel postcard usually contains a brief greeting and a short summary of trip highlights. Try to use as many of the **list words** as you can in your message. When you have finished proofreading and revising, read your postcard aloud to your classmates.

BONUS WORDS

therapeutic	convalescent	surgery	gurney	dispensary
rehabilitate	intravenous	pediatrics	syringe	radiology

Write a **bonus word** to complete each sentence.

1. A __gurney__ is a stretcher or cot on wheels.
2. To __rehabilitate__ injured muscles, doctors often prescribe physical therapy.
3. Doctors sometimes perform __surgery__ to repair damaged organs.
4. Medicines are sometimes given by __intravenous__ injection.
5. A __syringe__ is a vial of medicine with a needle designed to penetrate a vein.
6. Drinking liquids and getting plenty of rest is __therapeutic__ for the common cold.
7. A patient's __convalescent__ period after surgery is sometimes spent in the hospital.
8. The hospital stores medicines in the __dispensary__.
9. __Radiology__ is a medical specialty involving X-rays.
10. __Pediatrics__ is a medical specialty involving the health of children.

92   Lesson 22 • Words of Greek Origin

Puzzle Urge students to use as clues not only the definitions, but the number of spaces in each answer.

Spelling and Writing   *Page 92*
Proofreading Ask students to give examples illustrating the use of each of the proofreading marks. Review the mark that shows that a new paragraph begins and should be indented.

Writing a Postcard If possible, read sample postcards to the class. Discuss the function of get-well, invitation, appointment, reminder, travel, and other messages that might be communicated in a postcard. Students may enjoy using card stock for their postcards and including colorful illustrations or photos. Provide time for them to share their postcards.

Bonus Words   *Page 92*
Medical Terms Have students use their own knowledge, as well as a dictionary, to define and discuss the **bonus words**. Point out the Greek roots in words such as *radiology* and *therapeutic*.

Bonus Words Test
1. The runner's knee **surgery** was successful.
2. Radiologists are doctors who specialize in **radiology**.
3. The patient was transported on a **gurney**.
4. The nurse took an **intravenous** blood sample.
5. Dr. Alvarez specializes in **pediatrics**.
6. A hot bath is often **therapeutic** for sore muscles.
7. Exercise can help **rehabilitate** injured muscles.
8. The antibiotic was administered with a **syringe**.
9. The clinic's **dispensary** provided the medicine.
10. Please stay in bed during the **convalescent** period.

Final Test
1. To save money, look for the most **economical** buys.
2. Do you believe there is other life in the **cosmos**?
3. Iron is attracted to **magnetic** substances.
4. The **elastic** rubber ball sprung back into shape.
5. I used the **archive** to research my geneaology.
6. A **bureaucracy** has several layers of management.
7. Pompeii, an **archaic** city, was destroyed in 79 A.D.
8. The **architect** drew the floorplans for the building.
9. Is every city considered a **metropolis**?
10. Many clergy members have degrees in **theology**.
11. Study law to prepare for a career in **politics**.
12. Ancient Greece was ruled by a **democracy**.
13. To design aircrafts, you must learn **aeronautics**.
14. The Air Force **Academy** is in Colorado Springs.
15. An **anagram** for *stop* is *pots*.
16. The chemist reported the results of his **analysis**.
17. The **eclipse** created a nighttime sky at high noon.
18. How dare you **criticize** her flawless performance!
19. Has world travel made you feel **cosmopolitan**?
20. An oil shortage can cause a temporary fuel **crisis**.

Words of Greek Origin

Objective
To spell words of Greek origin

Pretest

1. The novel is about a pauper turned **aristocrat**.
2. A **biography** is a book that tells someone's life story.
3. The **thermostat** keeps a stable temperature.
4. A stop sign is in the shape of an **octagon**.
5. A bug that lives on a plant is called a **parasite**.
6. A **barometer** measures atmospheric pressure.
7. A **chronic** illness lasts for a long time.
8. What are the **geographical** features of a desert?
9. Lined writing paper has several **parallel** lines.
10. I picked up my prescription at the **pharmacy**.
11. Digestion is a **biological** function of the body.
12. A **dialogue** is a conversation in a play or film.
13. We studied the **geological** properties of the fossil.
14. A **parable** is a simple story that illustrates a moral.
15. The network will **televise** the interview today.
16. Each fire **hydrant** in the city is painted yellow.
17. Come on, show your **enthusism** by cheering!
18. **Neon**, a gas, glows when charged with electricity.
19. **Paralysis** is the loss of power to feel or move.
20. How long will the **thermos** keep the soup hot?

Spelling Strategy　　　　　　　**Page 93**

Discuss the spelling rule and examples. Then, have students use dictionaries to find the Greek roots in *biography* and *geology*. Using the meanings of *bios*, *graphe*, *geo*, *logos*, *chronos*, *thermos*, and *metron*, have them define *geography*, *biology*, *geometry*, *thermography*, and *chronology*. Stress that knowing Greek roots will help students define and spell unfamiliar words. Then, discuss and define the **list words**.

Vocabulary Development To start, have students match a **list word** to this clue: "to broadcast by television." (*televise*)

Dictionary Skills Ask students which of these words would appear on a dictionary page with the guide words *transmission* and *transport*: *transportation*, *transparent*, *transpose*, *translucent*. (*transparent*)

Spelling Practice　　　　　　　**Pages 94–95**

Word Analysis If necessary, review the spelling rule discussion of Greek roots before students begin.

Analogies Have students complete this example with a **list word**: *occasional is to infrequent as unceasing is to* _____ . (*chronic*)

Word Application To extend, have students make up and present to the class similar context-clue sentences using other pairs of **list words**.

TIP

The **list words** contain Greek roots that appear frequently in English words. Many English words are a combination of two Greek roots.

Greek Root	Meaning	English Word	Meaning
chronos	"time"	chronic	"lasting a long time"
thermos	"hot; heat"	thermostat	"device for regulating a heating system"
metron	"measure"	thermometer	"device for measuring heat level"
		chronometer	"an extremely accurate clock"
baros	"weight"	barometer	"device for measuring atmospheric pressure"

Vocabulary Development

Write the **list word** that matches each synonym or definition clue.

1. drugstore __pharmacy__
2. eagerness __enthusiasm__
3. conversation __dialogue__
4. life story __biography__
5. short story __parable__
6. helpless inactivity __paralysis__
7. insulated bottle __thermos__
8. eight-sided figure __octagon__
9. recurring often __chronic__
10. colorless gas __neon__

Dictionary Skills

Write the **list word** that comes between each pair of dictionary guide words.

1. parade/parallelogram　__parallel__
2. biohazard/biometry　__biological__
3. geoid/geometry　__geological__
4. thermoscope/thesaurus　__thermostat__
5. humor/hydrogen　__hydrant__
6. telephone/thermodynamic　__televise__
7. geodesic/geologic　__geographical__
8. banner/beacon　__barometer__
9. aqua/aster　__aristocrat__
10. parameter/parboil　__parasite__

LIST WORDS

1. aristocrat
2. biography
3. thermostat
4. octagon
5. parasite
6. barometer
7. chronic
8. geographical
9. parallel
10. pharmacy
11. biological
12. dialogue
13. geological
14. televise
15. hydrant
16. enthusiasm
17. neon
18. paralysis
19. thermos

93

DID YOU KNOW?

Enthusiasm comes from the Greek words *en*, meaning "in or within" and *theos*, meaning "god." Poets and prophets long ago were thought to be inspired by a god. Today, *enthusiasm* usually means "a strong liking, excitement, or interest."

Spelling Practice

Word Analysis

Write the **list word** derived from the Greek roots given.

1. **para** ("beside") + **allelos** ("one another")　__parallel__
2. **bios** ("life") + **logos** ("word; thought")　__biological__
3. **geo** ("earth") + **logos** ("word; thought")　__geological__
4. **bios** ("life") + **graphe** ("writing")　__biography__
5. **para** ("beside") + **sitos** ("food")　__parasite__
6. **geo** ("earth") + **graphe** ("writing")　__geographical__
7. **para** ("beside") + **lusis** ("disable; loosen")　__paralysis__
8. **thermos** ("heat") + **statos** ("standing")　__thermostat__

Analogies

Write a **list word** to complete each analogy.

1. Radio is to broadcast as television is to __televise__
2. Food is to cooler as beverage is to __thermos__
3. Iron is to aluminum as helium is to __neon__
4. Influenza is to virus as barnacle is to __parasite__
5. Dread is to apprehension as eagerness is to __enthusiasm__
6. Fuel is to gas pump as water is to __hydrant__
7. *Yield* is to triangle as *Stop* is to __octagon__
8. Dancer is to waltz as reader is to __biography__

Word Application

Select a **list word** from the choices in parentheses to complete each sentence. Write the **list word** on the line.

1. The __biography__ of legendary cowboy Pecos Bill claims he rode a mountain lion and wielded a rattlesnake whip. (enthusiasm, biography)
2. The moral of the __parable__ is to treat others with kindness. (biography, parable)
3. The __aristocrat__ was last seen greeting the princess. (thermostat, aristocrat)
4. __Geological__ studies concern rocks and minerals. (geographical, geological)
5. A __barometer__ is a device that measures pressure in the atmosphere. (barometer, thermostat)

LIST WORDS

aristocrat	barometer	octagon	hydrant
biography	enthusiasm	dialogue	chronic
thermostat	geographical	parallel	neon
biological	geological	parasite	parable
paralysis	pharmacy	televise	thermos

Syllables

Write each **list word** under the correct category.

Words with Two Syllables	Words with Four Syllables	Words with Five Syllables
1. chronic	5. aristocrat	9. geographical
2. hydrant	6. biography	10. biological
3. neon	7. barometer	11. geological
4. thermos	8. paralysis	12. enthusiasm

Puzzle

Each clue is an example, or illustration, of a **list word**. Write the **list words** in the answer spaces. Then, transfer the numbered letters to the spaces below to answer the question.

1. She jumped for joy.   e n t h u s i(2) a(15) s m

2. *The Life of Helen Keller*   b(1) i o g r(6) a p h y(12)

3. a stop sign   o(5) c t a g o n(16)

4. a long illness   c h r o n i(11) c(8)

5. "Who's there?" "It's John."   d(13) i a l o g(3) u e

6. ▬▬▬▬▬   p a r a l l(10) e l(4)

7. Davidson's Drugstore   p h a(9) r m(14) a c y

8. to broadcast on a TV   t(17) e l e v i(7) s e

Question: What two **list words** could describe an elephant?

Answer: b(1) i(2) o(3) l(4) o(5) g(6) i(7) c(8) a(9) l(10)
h(11) y(12) d(13) r(14) a(15) n(16) t(17)

Proofreading

Use the proofreading marks to correct the mistakes in the paragraph below. Then, write the misspelled **list words** correctly on the lines.

Proofreading Marks
- ◯ spelling mistake
- ϑ add apostrophe
- ௸ delete word
- ∧ add comma

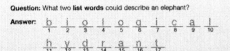 Have you heard of Pecos Bill? He was a a legendary cowboy hero who personified the frontier virtues of strength, courage, ingenuity, and enthuziasm. His biographey comprises a series of superhuman feats that illustrate these virtues. Pecos Bill is said to have been born in Texas in the 1830s. According to legend, after falling out of his parents wagon near the Pecos River, he became lost and was raised by coyotes. As an adult, Bill created many new geograficaland geoljical features throughout the West. During a cronic drought, he drained the Río Grande to water his ranch.

1. enthusiasm
2. biography
3. geographical
4. geological
5. chronic

Writing a Tall Tale

Have you ever felt as "hungry as a bear"? Such exaggerated expressions are called hyperboles. They are used in speech and literature to overstate reality, often for comic effect. Write a tall tale about a legendary character using an example of hyperbole to "stretch" the facts. Use as many **list words** as you can. After proofreading and revising, read your tall tale to the group.

BONUS WORDS

mimicry	synonymous	sarcasm	euphemism	memoir
rhetoric	anachronism	paradox	epigram	epithet

Write a **bonus word** to complete each sentence.

1. Words that are synonymous have similar meanings.
2. "He passed away" is a euphemism for he died.
3. "The child is father of the man" is an example of paradox.
4. "Early Romans driving fancy sports cars" is an example of anachronism.
5. The title *Richard the Lion-Hearted* is an example of epithet.
6. In a personal memoir, someone might recall important events in his or her life.
7. Edison's saying "Genius is 1% inspiration and 99% perspiration" is a famous epigram.
8. To say, "Thanks a lot!" to a person who has not been helpful is to use sarcasm.
9. To use eloquent "ten-dollar words" that do not communicate clearly is to use rhetoric.
10. Onomatopoetic words, such as *honk, sputter, clatter,* and *buzz,* are examples of mimicry.

Syllables To review, have students name the eight **list words** with three syllables.

Puzzle Point out to students that the number of spaces in each answer is also a clue.

Spelling and Writing   *Page 96*

Proofreading Demonstrate the proofreading marks.

Writing a Tall Tale Suggest further examples of hyperboles, such as "the smartest man in the whole world" and "Millions of people came to the game." Elicit hyperboles from students by suggesting such topics as big ("a dog as big as a horse"), funny, quiet, and noisy. Discuss how exaggeration can add drama to a humorous story.

Bonus Words   *Page 96*

Language Define and discuss the **bonus words**, giving examples similar to those in the exercise and Bonus Test sentences. Draw on students' knowledge of history for epithets and to create anachronisms. Many quotations by Ben Franklin, Mark Twain, and Dorothy Parker provide examples of witty epigrams.

Bonus Words Test

1. To practice **mimicry** is to imitate sounds.
2. "The last shall be first" is a **paradox**.
3. In a **memoir**, Thoreau explained his philosophy.
4. *Wristwatches in ancient Greece* is an **anachronism**.
5. Don't cloud your message with flowery **rhetoric**.
6. *Alexander the Great* is an example of an **epithet**.
7. The words *simple* and *easy* are **synonymous**.
8. **Sarcasm** is often a hurtful form of humor.
9. "Lost time is never found again" is an **epigram**.
10. *The remains* is a **euphemism** for *the dead body*.

Final Test

1. I recently read a **biography** of Dolly Madison.
2. Thanks to my **thermos**, my lemonade was icy cold.
3. Her **enthusiasm** for the play led me to see it.
4. A brain injury may cause **paralysis**.
5. The station chose to **televise** the soccer game.
6. The **neon** sign proclaimed, "Eat at Hal's Diner!"
7. The fire hose drew water from the **hydrant**.
8. Dr. Lee studied the cliffs' **geological** makeup.
9. What is the moral of the **parable** that she told?
10. I couldn't understand the French **dialogue**.
11. The **aristocrat** turned his old home into a museum.
12. Please set the **thermostat** at 68 degrees.
13. The leech is a wormlike **parasite** that lives in ponds.
14. It is possible to recover from a **chronic** illness.
15. Earl bought a jar of vitamins at the **pharmacy**.
16. Digestion is a **biological** process of all animals.
17. An **octagon** is a polygon with eight sides.
18. If the **barometer** falls, the weather may change.
19. Two **parallel** lines will never cross.
20. A **geographical** neighbor of Iowa is Kansas.

Lessons 19–23 · Review

Objectives
To review spelling words with prefixes and words of Greek and Latin origin

Spelling Strategy   *Page 97*

Discuss the spelling rules. For further examples of words with the prefixes *co, syn, syl, sym, non, neg, in, im,* and *a,* use: *copilot, syndicate, syllabus, symptom, nonfiction, negative, infirm, impure,* and *atypical.* To review the meanings of Greek and Latin prefixes and roots, discuss the etymologies of **list words** from Lessons 21–23.

Spelling Practice   *Pages 97–99*

Lesson 19 Review the meanings of *co* and *syn.* Have students paraphrase the rules about the different forms of *syn.* Then, have students use the **list words** in sentences. Point out the additional write-on lines and have them add two words from Lesson 19 that they found difficult, or assign words that were difficult for everyone. (Repeat this procedure for each lesson review that follows in this section.)

Lesson 20 Have students suggest other words with the prefixes *non, neg, im, in,* and *a,* and write them on the board. Discuss how prefixes change the meanings of roots or base words. Then, review the **list words**, having students use them in oral sentences. To extend, have students write similar "wrong word" sentences using their additional **list words**.

Lesson 21 Review the meanings of such Latin roots as *hilaris* and *orbitus.* Stress that knowing these roots will help students define many unfamiliar words. As examples, discuss *hilarious* and *orbit.* Then, review the **list words**.

Lesson 22 You may wish to review words of Greek origin by combining Lessons 22 and 23. Review the meanings of the roots *demos, graphe, bios, logos,* and *para.* Then, have students define *demography, paragraph,* and *graphologist.* Extend the exercise by having students create similar "definition" sentences for their additional words.

Lesson 23 Follow the procedure suggested in Lesson 22 to review Greek roots and prefixes.

Show What You Know   *Page 100*

Point out that this review will help students know if they have mastered the words in Lessons 19–23. Have a volunteer tell which word in the first item is incorrect. *(anesethesia)* When finished, have students write their misspelled words correctly.

- The prefixes **co** and **syn** mean "together." Examples include coauthor and synonym. When added to a root beginning with **l**, **syn** changes to **syl**, as in syllable. It changes to **sym** when it is added to roots beginning with **b**, **m**, or **p**. Examples include symbol, symmetry, and sympathy.
- The prefixes **non, neg, in, im,** and **a** mean "not." Examples include nonchalant, negligent, indecisive, impossible, and apolitical. The prefix **a** becomes **an** when it is added to a root beginning with a vowel. Examples include anarchy and anemia.
- Many English words have Greek or Latin origins. Knowing the meanings of Greek and Latin prefixes and roots will help you to define and spell many unfamiliar words.

Prefix/Root	Source	Meaning	English Word	Meaning
ex + orbita	Latin	"out of track"	exorbitant	"excessive"
optio	Latin	"wish; desire"	option	"power to choose"
sub + urbs	Latin	"near;" "town"	suburban	"just outside a city"
ex + hilaris	Latin	"very;" "glad"	exhilarated	"cheerful; lively"
aēr + naus	Greek	"air;" "ship"	aeronautics	"the science of aircraft"
theo + logos	Greek	"god;" "words"	theology	"the study of religion"
okto + gonia	Greek	"eight;" "angles"	octagon	"eight-sided figure"

Lesson 19

List Words

coherent
coordinate
synchronize
symphonic
synagogue
symmetry
symptom
syntax
coincide
symbolize

Select a **list word** from the choices in parentheses to complete each sentence. Write the **list word** on the line.

1. A rash of small red dots is a symptom of measles. (syntax, symptom)
2. Let's synchronize our watches. (synchronize, coincide)
3. In my poem, the sun will symbolize power. (synagogue, symbolize)
4. Hal has been chosen to coordinate the project. (coincide, coordinate)
5. He worships at a synagogue. (synagogue, symmetry)
6. This year, school vacation will coincide with my father's business trip to Argentina. (coincide, symbolize)
7. Mozart wrote many beautiful symphonic works. (symphonic, coordinate)
8. We study grammar and syntax. (syntax, coherent)
9. Maria got an A on her oral report because it was interesting and coherent. (symphonic, coherent)
10. Pieces of art that are balanced have symmetry. (symmetry, synchronize)

97

Lesson 20

List Words

anonymous
impersonate
inaccurate
negligent
nonexistent
immobilize
anemia
immaculate
incognito
anesthesia

Each of these sentences contains the wrong **list word**. Cross out the word and write the correct **list word** on the line.

1. No one knew who sent the ~~anesthesia~~ note. — anonymous
2. I'm afraid I was ~~nonexistent~~, and forgot to feed the cat last night. — negligent
3. Don't let shyness ~~immaculate~~ you when new friends invite you to join them in a game. — immobilize
4. To protect her privacy, the movie star decided to travel ~~negligent~~. — incognito
5. The comedian will ~~inaccurate~~ a gorilla. — impersonate
6. The doctor will administer ~~anemia~~ to the patient prior to surgery. — anesthesia
7. The city's plans to enlarge the library will be postponed because the funds are ~~anonymous~~. — nonexistent
8. Honest people tend to avoid ~~incognito~~ facts. — inaccurate
9. Eat foods that are rich in iron to protect yourself from ~~impersonate~~. — anemia
10. The players' ~~immobilize~~ uniforms became wet and grimy because the field was muddy. — immaculate

Lesson 21

List Words

auditor
exorbitant
exhilarated
juvenile
ordinance
quarantine
documentary
opulent
optician
molecular

Write a **list word** to answer each definition clue.

1. maker or seller of eyeglasses — optician
2. of or relating to molecules — molecular
3. luscious; prosperous — opulent
4. too much; excessive — exorbitant
5. an informative film based on facts — documentary
6. the act of isolating a diseased person or animal — quarantine
7. a child or young person — juvenile
8. very happy and excited — exhilarated
9. an examiner of financial accounts — auditor
10. a regulation or rule — ordinance

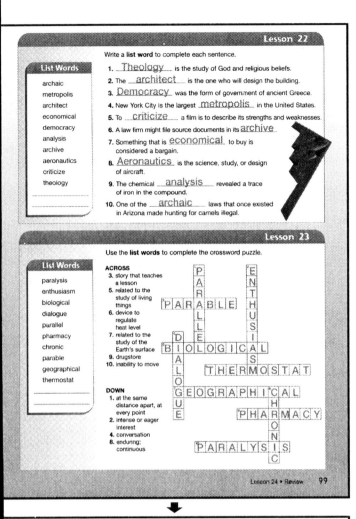

Write a **list word** to complete each sentence.

List Words

archaic
metropolis
architect
economical
democracy
analysis
archive
aeronautics
criticize
theology

1. __Theology__ is the study of God and religious beliefs.
2. The __architect__ is the one who will design the building.
3. __Democracy__ was the form of government of ancient Greece.
4. New York City is the largest __metropolis__ in the United States.
5. To __criticize__ a film is to describe its strengths and weaknesses.
6. A law firm might file source documents in its __archive__.
7. Something that is __economical__ to buy is considered a bargain.
8. __Aeronautics__ is the science, study, or design of aircraft.
9. The chemical __analysis__ revealed a trace of iron in the compound.
10. One of the __archaic__ laws that once existed in Arizona made hunting for camels illegal.

Use the **list words** to complete the crossword puzzle.

List Words

paralysis
enthusiasm
biological
dialogue
parallel
pharmacy
chronic
parable
geographical
thermostat

ACROSS
3. story that teaches a lesson
5. related to the study of living things
6. device to regulate heat level
7. related to the study of the Earth's surface
9. drugstore
10. inability to move

DOWN
1. at the same distance apart, at every point
2. intense or eager interest
4. conversation
8. enduring; continuous

Crossword answers: PARABLE, BIOLOGICAL, THERMOSTAT, GEOGRAPHICAL, PHARMACY, PARALYSIS, DIALOGUE (down), PARALLEL (down), ENTHUSIASM (down), CHRONIC (down)

Show What You Know

One word is misspelled in each set of **list words**. Fill in the circle next to the **list word** that is spelled incorrectly.

1. ○ coauthor ● anesethesia ○ bureaucracy ○ dominion
2. ● colateral ○ immobilize ○ juvenile ○ eclipse
3. ○ option ○ magnetic ● impatiantly ○ copilot
4. ○ theology ○ indecisive ● quaranteen ○ symptom
5. ○ negative ○ aristocrat ○ synagogue ● verman
6. ● exhilirated ○ immaculate ○ biography ○ anemia
7. ○ coexist ● maximmum ○ coordinate ○ thermostat
8. ○ syllable ○ inaccurate ○ nonchalant ● opulint
9. ○ regime ● symetry ○ cooperative ○ octagon
10. ○ verdict ○ barometer ○ synchronize ● parascite
11. ○ academy ● coherant ○ anonymous ○ chronic
12. ● archaive ○ invalid ○ geographical ○ impromptu
13. ○ inactive ○ symphonic ● cosmapolitan ○ parallel
14. ○ pharmacy ○ neglect ● economicle ○ synthesis
15. ○ syncopate ● metropolls ○ nonexistent ○ biological
16. ○ dialogue ○ coincide ● aironautics ○ auditor
17. ○ archaic ○ exorbitant ● symbolise ○ hydrant
18. ○ molecular ○ televise ○ symposium ● parabble
19. ● criticise ○ syntax ○ Republican ○ elastic
20. ○ syllabus ○ democracy ○ geological ● ordinence
21. ○ paralysis ● anarchey ○ documentary ○ analysis
22. ● insectiscide ○ architect ○ enthusiasm ○ imprudent
23. ○ crisis ○ optician ● impersonaite ○ neon
24. ○ politics ○ incognito ○ cosmos ● publcity
25. ● neglegent ○ thermos ○ suburban ○ anagram

Final Test

1. Gershwin wrote beautiful **symphonic** music.
2. Poets often use the word *dawn* to **symbolize** youth.
3. Architecture joins new ideas with classic **symmetry**.
4. Comics often **impersonate** politicians or celebrities.
5. A person with **anemia** may feel tired and weak.
6. A patient is put to sleep for surgery with **anesthesia**.
7. Will customs officials **quarantine** foreign pets?
8. The **molecular** formula for carbon dioxide is CO_2.
9. A new **ordinance** raised the fine for littering.
10. Is the steam engine considered an **archaic** device?
11. A reviewer may **criticize** the diner's poor service.
12. The priest teaches **theology** at a parochial school.
13. This particular disease may cause **paralysis**.
14. The actress studied the lines for the **dialogue**.
15. A **parable** often has a deep underlying message.
16. Mrs. Lee has a **chronic** allergy to pollen.
17. Madison Avenue runs **parallel** to Fifth Avenue.
18. The cheerleaders clapped with **enthusiasm**.
19. My mother, an **architect**, designed that building.
20. Free elections are a privilege of **democracy**.
21. The chemist did an **analysis** of the compound.
22. Laura Ingalls Wilder wrote **juvenile** fiction.
23. An **auditor** will examine the financial records.
24. Is Versailles the most **opulent** palace in France?
25. An **anonymous** tip helped solve the crime.
26. Highway construction may **immobilize** the traffic.
27. He was **negligent** with his wallet and lost it.
28. A persistent cough is a **symptom** of pneumonia.
29. Check your sentences for proper **syntax**.
30. If our vacations **coincide**, let's travel together.
31. Her rambling speech was not **coherent**.
32. We attend services at the **synagogue** on Saturdays.
33. He scrubbed the dirty floor until it was **immaculate**.
34. Robin Hood arrived at the tournament **incognito**.
35. That restaurant charges **exorbitant** prices for meals!
36. My **optician** has an office in a medical clinic.
37. Such a rare **archive** should be in a museum.
38. Benton's Market is an **economical** place to shop.
39. Isn't the Grand Canyon a **geographical** wonder?
40. A **thermostat** controls the furnace's heat.
41. **Biological** studies include botany and zoology.
42. We went to the **pharmacy** to buy hand lotion.
43. Denver is a leading **metropolis** in Colorado.
44. My aunt is an **aeronautics** engineer.
45. The **documentary** film describes the culture of Iran.
46. We were **exhilarated** by the exciting tennis match.
47. That figure is **inaccurate**; add the numbers again.
48. In today's world, live dinosaurs are **nonexistent**.
49. As a team leader, Ari will **coordinate** our efforts.
50. She will **synchronize** the dance to the music.

Words Ending in ize, ise, ent, ant

Objective
To spell words ending with *ize, ise, ent,* or *ant*

Pretest

1. We had such a relaxing, **pleasant** vacation.
2. Hire **competent** workers to do the best job.
3. Science can often **rationalize** unusual happenings.
4. The team that won the pennant was **jubilant**.
5. Wildflowers are **prevalent** in spring.
6. My first business **enterprise** was a lemonade stand.
7. We don't agree, but can we **compromise**?
8. Apply for a **franchise** to set up a television station.
9. Cut the fabric **lengthwise**, not across the pattern.
10. Is it **prudent** to borrow that much money?
11. Gee, Karen should **apologize** for being so late!
12. Children are **dependent** on their parents.
13. The four singers should **harmonize** on the chorus.
14. A good detective learns to be **observant**.
15. What you say is **relevant** and exactly to the point.
16. Turn the bolt to the right, or **clockwise**, to tighten it.
17. We can **economize** by spending less.
18. You can **itemize** all your expenses in a budget.
19. Did that stray cat find a **permanent** home?
20. Leah's speech had a **significant** effect on her grade.

Spelling Strategy   *Page 101*

After students have read the spelling rule, point out that they must memorize the spellings of these words, since no simple rule applies to them. Make sure students understand the meanings of the words, having them refer to dictionaries when necessary. Reinforce the meanings by having students use the words in oral sentences.

Vocabulary Development Remind students to pay attention to the spelling of each word as well as its meaning. To extend, have students write definition clues for additional **list words**.

Dictionary Skills Encourage students to first try completing this exercise without referring to a pronunciation key. When finished, have them check their answers against dictionaries.

Spelling Practice   *Pages 102–103*

Word Analysis The first part of this exercise will help students remember which ending each **list word** has. The second part will help them understand the words' derivations.

Word Application Point out that the meaning and the part of speech of each underlined word or phrase can be clues to help students know which **list word** to use. If needed, do the first item with students.

66

Words Ending in ize, ise, ent, ant

TIP Words ending in **ize, ise, ent** and **ant** are easy to confuse. Listen for the ending sounds of *enterprise* and *apologize*. They sound alike but are spelled differently. Other sounds are also easy to confuse. The ends of *prudent* and *relevant* sound alike but have different spellings. You must memorize which words end in **ise** or **ize** and which end in **ent** or **ant**.

Vocabulary Development
Write the **list word** that matches each definition clue.

1. eternal — permanent
2. a business — enterprise
3. joyful — jubilant
4. showing good judgment — prudent
5. express regrets — apologize
6. save money — economize
7. relying on another — dependent
8. agreeable or pleasing — pleasant
9. able — competent
10. watchful — observant
11. direction hands of clock move — clockwise
12. meaningful — significant
13. list — itemize
14. usual — prevalent

LIST WORDS
1. pleasant
2. competent
3. rationalize
4. jubilant
5. prevalent
6. enterprise
7. compromise
8. franchise
9. lengthwise
10. prudent
11. apologize
12. dependent
13. harmonize
14. observant
15. relevant
16. clockwise
17. economize
18. itemize
19. permanent
20. significant

Dictionary Skills
Write the **list word** that matches each sound-spelling.

1. (käm'prə mīz) compromise
2. (pur'mə nənt) permanent
3. (leŋkth'wīz) lengthwise
4. (əb zur'vənt) observant
5. (rash'ən ə līz') rationalize
6. (plez'n't) pleasant
7. (här'mə nīz) harmonize
8. (rel'ə vənt) relevant
9. (prev'ə lənt) prevalent
10. (fran'chīz) franchise

101

Spelling Practice

DID YOU KNOW?
Everyone knows that **clockwise** means "in the direction of the clock," but most people do not know where the word *clock* came from. The clock got its name from the bell that sounded its hours. It is derived from the Latin word, *clocca*, meaning "bell."

Word Analysis
Write each **list word** under its ending.

ise
1. enterprise
2. compromise
3. franchise
4. lengthwise
5. clockwise

ant
6. pleasant
7. jubilant
8. observant
9. relevant
10. significant

ize
11. rationalize
12. apologize
13. harmonize
14. economize
15. itemize

ent
16. competent
17. prevalent
18. prudent
19. dependent
20. permanent

Write the **list word** that has the same root as each word given.

1. economy — economize
2. please — pleasant
3. rational — rationalize
4. observe — observant
5. items — itemize
6. dependable — dependent
7. prevail — prevalent
8. unobserved — observant

Word Application
Replace the underlined word or words in each sentence with a **list word**. Write the **list word** on the line.

1. On the round edges, paint in the direction the clock hands turn, but on the floor, paint with the length. clockwise lengthwise
2. Mrs. Flores is supervising the entire job, and she seems delighted with the results. enterprise jubilant
3. It would be wise to try to save money on non-essential features. prudent economize
4. When their voices all sing in agreement, they make a pleasing sound. harmonize pleasant

102   Lesson 25 • Words Ending in ize, ise, ent, ant

LIST WORDS

pleasant	enterprise	apologize	compromise
prudent	clockwise	dependent	economize
itemize	franchise	harmonize	rationalize
jubilant	significant	observant	permanent
relevant	competent	prevalent	lengthwise

Puzzle
Use the **list words** to complete the crossword puzzle.

ACROSS
3. in the direction of the length
5. a right given to sell something
7. to make conform to reason
8. to sing in harmony
10. lasting forever
12. meaningful to a certain situation or thing
15. careful; cautious
16. having the ability to do what is needed
18. full of meaning
19. to list each item

DOWN
1. a settling of an argument by both sides giving in
2. in the direction of the clock
4. be thrifty
6. relying on another
9. a business or undertaking
10. happening over a wide area
11. to say that one is sorry
13. joyful and proud
14. paying careful attention
17. nice; agreeable

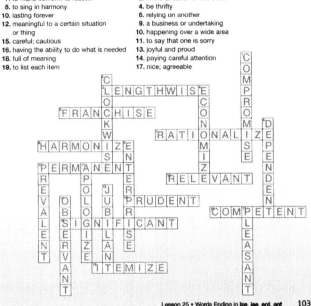

Lesson 25 • Words Ending in **ize, ise, ent, ant**   103

Proofreading

Use the proofreading marks to correct the mistakes in the article below. Then, write the misspelled **list words** correctly on the lines.

Proofreading Marks
○ spelling mistake   ╱ small letter
∧ add comma   # add space

A franchize is a legal agreement. It allows an Entirprise or organization with a product the right to grant another business owner the opportunity to sell that product. This kind of agreement first became popular in the 1950s. Since then it has had a significant and permenent effect on the rise of small business owners in the American Economy. Many fastfood businesses that are prevelent throughout the country are run this way.

1. franchise
2. enterprise
3. significant
4. permanent
5. prevalent

Writing an Ad

Think like a business person and write an advertisement using simile for a product of your choice. Here's an example of a simile: *These fans will sell like hot cakes!* Use as many of the **list words** as you can in your ad. When finished, proofread and revise your ad, and then share it with classmates.

BONUS WORDS

inflation	corporation	proprietary	mercantile	diversify
proxy	conglomerate	negotiation	securities	liquidate

Write the **bonus word** that matches each clue given.

1. discussion to reach agreement
   negotiation
2. authority to act for another
   proxy
3. more dollars buy less
   inflation
4. stocks and bonds, for example
   securities
5. commercial
   mercantile
6. give variety to
   diversify
7. a legal entity
   corporation
8. convert assets into cash
   liquidate
9. many companies in one big one
   conglomerate
10. held under patent or trademark
    proprietary

104   Lesson 25 • Words Ending in ize, ise, ent, ant

Puzzle Have volunteers tell what two strategies they can use to solve this puzzle. (*the definitions; the number of letters in each word*) Discuss why they should first fill in known answers. (*The letters can provide further clues.*)

Spelling and Writing   *Page 104*

Proofreading Ask students to provide an example to illustrate the use of each of the proofreading marks.

Writing an Ad Discuss similes with students, having them give several examples. If necessary, start them off with phrases, such as, "as red as . . . ," "like a house on fire . . . ," "as smart as. . . ." Then, discuss businesses and the types of products and services people buy and sell. Refer to a newspaper's classified section or telephone yellow pages for ideas. Finally, have students write their ads using similes.

Bonus Words   *Page 104*

Business Explain that all the **bonus words** are related to business. Through discussion and dictionary use, help students understand the words' meanings. To reinforce, have them use the words in oral sentences or phrases.

Bonus Words Test
1. Both parties called the **negotiation** a success.
2. Jack's small firm is part of a huge **conglomerate**.
3. Because of **inflation**, today's dollar is worth less.
4. My stockbroker showed me a list of my **securities**.
5. A shareholder can vote by **proxy** if needed.
6. The sale was designed to **liquidate** the firm's assets.
7. Don's specialty is **mercantile** finance, not personal.
8. Four of us have formed a legal **corporation**.
9. I'll **diversify** my investments with new stocks.
10. That beverage formula is **proprietary** information.

Final Test
1. Is your question **relevant** to this or another topic?
2. A good artist must be quite **observant**.
3. Your three voices **harmonize** beautifully!
4. Are you **dependent** on anyone for a ride to work?
5. I must **apologize** for leaving that book at home.
6. Do I turn the dial **clockwise** or counterclockwise?
7. To **economize**, we won't go out to eat so often.
8. Please **itemize** your expenses for each month.
9. The accident left an ugly, **permanent** scar.
10. The timeline shows the **significant** dates in the war.
11. That project is quite an **enterprise** for you!
12. To **compromise**, take turns at the computer.
13. Mr. Tien has bought a new restaurant **franchise**.
14. Sand the wood **lengthwise** with the grain.
15. My banker devised a **prudent** savings plan.
16. In this area, pick-up trucks are **prevalent**.
17. The doctors were **jubilant** when the child recovered.
18. I will **rationalize** my lateness by blaming traffic.
19. Sara, though not an expert, is **competent**.
20. July was stormy, but August was quite **pleasant**.

Noun-Forming Suffix ity

Objective
To spell words with the noun-forming suffix *ity*

Pretest

1. Due to our **punctuality**, the trip started on time.
2. People are drawn to her cheerful **personality**.
3. The owner has **liability** if the dog bites you.
4. There's a great deal of **practicality** in saving money.
5. The **formality** of the event required evening wear.
6. Does the way you dress express your **individuality**?
7. Due to a **technicality**, the first test was invalid.
8. Check the **availability** of water before you plant.
9. The **inferiority** of that brand of paper was obvious.
10. Pianists work to improve wrist and finger **mobility**.
11. What is the percentage of **visibility** in this fog?
12. Sasha thanked my parents for their **hospitality**.
13. Your **eligibility** will depend on your age and skill.
14. Our team has the **capability** of reaching the finals.
15. Such **generosity** deserves a gift in return.
16. The **eventuality** of a cancer cure is unknown.
17. This item's **superiority** is obvious by its quality.
18. The judge will decide on the **legality** of the issue.
19. I prefer the **flexibility** of plastic to stiff metal.
20. Despite our **similarity** in names, we're not sisters.

Spelling Strategy   *Page 105*

After students have read the spelling rule, discuss the spelling changes that were made to base words or roots when the suffix was added. To be sure students understand the words' meanings, have them use the words in oral sentences.

Vocabulary Development To extend the activity, you may wish to have students write the base word from which each **list word** is derived.

Dictionary Skills Encourage students to complete this exercise independently and then check their answers in dictionaries.

Spelling Practice   *Pages 106–107*

Word Analysis Remind students that the spelling of the adjectival form may change before the suffix is added. To reinforce this, have students write each word in its entirety, not just its suffix.

Word Application Point out to students that only one of the **list words** in parentheses makes sense in each sentence. To extend the activity, you may wish to have students write similar sentences, using some of the distractors.

Noun-Forming Suffix ity

TIP
The suffix **ity** can form a noun from an adjective. For example, legal becomes legality. When the suffix is added to words ending in **ble**, the ending of the base word changes, as in visible/visibility. A few other words, such as generous and hospitable, change in different ways to become generosity and hospitality.

Vocabulary Development

Write the **list word** that matches each definition clue.

1. ability to be on time	punctuality
2. ability to move	mobility
3. ability to be taken or purchased	availability
4. singularity	individuality
5. following prescribed customs	formality
6. abilities not yet developed	capability
7. ability to be seen	visibility
8. state of being lesser	inferiority
9. ability to bend	flexibility
10. temperament	personality
11. unselfish act	generosity
12. a possible event	eventuality

Dictionary Skills

Rewrite each of the following **list words** to show how they are divided into syllables.

1. legality	le/gal/i/ty	7. superiority	su/pe/ri/or/i/ty
2. similarity	sim/i/lar/i/ty	8. hospitality	hos/pi/tal/i/ty
3. eligibility	el/i/gi/bil/i/ty	9. practicality	prac/ti/cal/i/ty
4. liability	li/a/bil/i/ty	10. technicality	tech/ni/cal/i/ty
5. formality	for/mal/i/ty	11. capability	ca/pa/bil/i/ty
6. mobility	mo/bil/i/ty	12. generosity	gen/er/os/i/ty

LIST WORDS
1. punctuality
2. personality
3. liability
4. practicality
5. formality
6. individuality
7. technicality
8. availability
9. inferiority
10. mobility
11. visibility
12. hospitality
13. eligibility
14. capability
15. generosity
16. eventuality
17. superiority
18. legality
19. flexibility
20. similarity

DID YOU KNOW?
Technicality is formed from the word *technical* and the suffix *ity*. *Technical* comes from the Greek word *tekhnikos*, meaning "of art," which comes from the Greek word for "art," *tekhn*. It also shares the root *teks*, meaning "to weave" or "to fabricate," which is the basis for other English words such as *text*, *tissue*, *context*, *pretext*, *subtle*, *architect*, and *technology*.

Spelling Practice

Word Analysis

Form **list words** by adding the suffix *ity* to these adjectives to make nouns.

1. mobile	mobility	11. visible	visibility
2. inferior	inferiority	12. similar	similarity
3. practical	practicality	13. hospitable	hospitality
4. formal	formality	14. eventual	eventuality
5. liable	liability	15. superior	superiority
6. personal	personality	16. generous	generosity
7. punctual	punctuality	17. capable	capability
8. available	availability	18. legal	legality
9. individual	individuality	19. flexible	flexibility
10. technical	technicality	20. eligible	eligibility

Word Application

Select a **list word** from the choices in parentheses to complete each sentence. Write the **list word** on the line.

1. Due to his __punctuality__ Bill got to work on time. (punctuality, similarity)
2. This engine has the __capability__ to pull both boxcars. (formality, capability)
3. Bowing before the prince is merely a __formality__. (generosity, formality)
4. Tara called to let us know of her __availability__ for the job. (legality, availability)
5. Emily's clothing reflected her sense of __individuality__. (eventuality, individuality)
6. The glass door's breaking was an __eventuality__. (availability, eventuality)
7. Our insurance company has __liability__ for the accident. (flexibility, liability)
8. __Practicality__ was why Rick chose a small dog. (practicality, visibility)
9. Some exercises increase the body's __flexibility__. (visibility, flexibility)
10. Crossing guards wear orange vests for __visibility__. (punctuality, visibility)
11. Mark's and your voice have a great __similarity__. (similarity, practicality)
12. Jan's wheelchair has greatly increased her __mobility__. (mobility, liability)
13. The club thanked the donor for her __generosity__. (individuality, generosity)
14. A lawyer researched the __legality__ of the situation. (mobility, legality)

Puzzle

Unscramble the **list words** using the blank spaces to the right. Then, transfer the numbered letters to the spaces below to solve the riddle.

1. lenittchcaiy   t e c h n i c a l i t y
2. tivabyaililla   a v a i l a b i l i t y
3. cuttiypunal   p u n c t u a l i t y
4. pioyurerits   s u p e r i o r i t y
5. ernoitifiry   i n f e r i o r i t y
6. tyinegrose   g e n e r o s i t y
7. mitboily   m o b i l i t y
8. tiallibiy   l i a b i l i t y
9. undidailyivit   i n d i v i d u a l i t y
10. spoalyernit   p e r s o n a l i t y
11. sitopithaly   h o s p i t a l i t y
12. yuittneeval   e v e n t u a l i t y
13. mayrlfito   f o r m a l i t y

RIDDLE: Why isn't your nose twelve inches long?

ANSWER: t h e n   i t   w o u l d

b e   o n e   f o o t

Lesson 26 • Noun-Forming Suffix **ity**   107

Proofreading

Use the proofreading marks to correct the mistakes in the following article. Then, write the misspelled **list words** correctly on the lines.

Proofreading Marks
◯ spelling mistake   ⊙ add period
≡ capital letter   # add space

Good manners, such as punctuality when keeping an appointment, are always an admirable social asset. in the eventuality that you travel to another country, it is always a good idea to read upon what is considered polite and impolite in the country you will be visiting. After all, offending someone unknowingly can be a definite lyeability. In Japan, for example, it is impolite to eat something while walking down the street. Gift giving is very important in Japan, but extravagant gifts require an equally extravagant gift in return. It's best to avoid giving pricey gifts to repay a host's hospetality and genirosity.

1. punctuality
2. eventuality
3. liability
4. hospitality
5. generosity

Writing a Persuasive Paragraph

A metaphor compares two things without using the words like or as. For example, "Good manners are a paved road to success" is a metaphor. Write a short persuasive paragraph on why good manners are an asset, using one or two metaphors and as many **list words** as you can. Proofread and revise your paragraph, and then share it with the class.

BONUS WORDS

trigonometry	abacus	logarithm	correlation	statistical
geometric	finite	analytical	numerical	calculus

Write the **bonus word** that matches each clue.

1. not infinite   finite
2. having lines, circles, or other forms   geometric
3. early kind of calculator   abacus
4. kind of exponent   logarithm
5. a mutual relationship   correlation
6. able to analyze   analytical
7. based on numerical facts or data   statistical
8. math that deals with triangles   trigonometry
9. expressed by numbers   numerical
10. math dealing with changes   calculus

Puzzle Review that the number of letters in each scrambled word is a clue to its identity. Have students first unscramble all the words, and then transfer each letter to the appropriate blank. Ask a volunteer to read the riddle and its answer.

Spelling and Writing   *Page 108*

Proofreading Use this sentence to review the proofreading marks: *jean went to the libary afterschool*

Writing a Persuasive Paragraph Discuss metaphors with students, offering examples from poetry or songs, if possible. Then, have students give examples. It may help to start them with phrases, such as, "Life is a . . . ," "The full moon was a . . . ," "A smile is. . . ." You may wish to talk with students about why good manners can be an asset.

Bonus Words   *Page 108*

Mathematics Explain that all the **bonus words** are related to mathematics. Through discussion and dictionary use, help students understand the words' meanings. You may also wish to use definitions from math books or other sources.

Bonus Words Test

1. An **abacus** can be used to calculate sums quickly.
2. My brother is getting extra help in **trigonometry**.
3. Notice the **correlation** between size and cost.
4. In base 10, the **logarithm** of 1,000 is 3.
5. We have only a **finite** number of possible choices.
6. The board was covered with **geometric** figures.
7. My brother studied **calculus** in college.
8. Corporations use **statistical** charts to show profits.
9. An accountant needs an **analytical** mind.
10. This idea can be expressed by a **numerical** formula.

Final Test

1. **Visibility** was poor during the snowstorm.
2. Certain hotels are famous for their **hospitality**.
3. How is **eligibility** for a tax refund determined?
4. Does this machine have the **capability** to do that?
5. My dad's **generosity** helped me buy a bike.
6. My, what **similarity** there is among the siblings!
7. Bending and twisting exercises increase **flexibility**.
8. A citizen argued the **legality** of the new law.
9. Kim's **superiority** helped her win the game.
10. Hikers must be prepared for any **eventuality**.
11. Her **punctuality** is flawless; she is never late.
12. This funny-looking cat has a great **personality**.
13. A homeowner may have **liability** for accidents.
14. Abdul's **practicality** is useful on camping trips.
15. As a **formality**, I had to state my full legal name.
16. Will the tight garment limit your **mobility**?
17. Does low price always mean product **inferiority**?
18. The verdict was overturned on a legal **technicality**.
19. This artist expresses her **individuality** with color.
20. The **availability** of fresh fish may affect its price.

Lesson 27 — Words Ending in ary, ory

Objective
To spell words ending with *ary* or *ory*

Pretest
1. Did you hear the tornado **advisory** on the radio?
2. Mozart had **extraordinary** musical ability.
3. In some states, wearing seat belts is **mandatory**.
4. The **preliminary** step is to outline an idea.
5. Was his band performance **satisfactory**?
6. Is this a **compulsory** or optional class?
7. Does that nurse work in the **infirmary**?
8. This jewelry has sentimental, not **monetary**, value.
9. My **primary** goal is to just finish the marathon.
10. Eric made a **savory** sauce to pour over the pasta.
11. We won **complimentary** tickets to the concert.
12. Learn the basics with this **introductory** video.
13. We'll be inside, so a raincoat won't be **necessary**.
14. The **Revolutionary** War lasted from 1775 to 1783.
15. XYZ Co. is a **subsidiary** of a larger company.
16. Is that movie a **contemporary** film or a classic?
17. Pegasus was a **legendary** horse that flew.
18. The **observatory** has a show on comets.
19. Part of the bay is a **sanctuary** for marine wildlife.
20. Reading certainly improves a person's **vocabulary**.

Spelling Strategy **Page 109**
After students have read the spelling rule, discuss the sounds they hear at the ends of the **list words**. Help them understand the meanings and derivations of the words, using dictionaries when needed.

Vocabulary Development Remind students to pay attention to the meaning and the spelling of each **list word**. To extend the exercise, you may wish to have students provide definitions for additional **list words**.

Dictionary Skills If needed, review dictionary sound-spellings. After students have completed the exercise, have them check their answers in dictionaries.

Spelling Practice **Pages 110–111**
Word Analysis The first part of the exercise will familiarize students with the derivation of each word. The second part of the exercise focuses attention on the spelling of the words' endings.

Word Application When students have completed the exercise, you may wish to have them use each phrase in oral sentences, substituting the **list word** for the underlined word(s).

Words Ending in ary, ory — Lesson 27

TIP
Words ending in **ary** and **ory** sometimes sound alike. Listen for the ending sounds in compulsory and infirmary. They sound similar but are spelled differently. Study and memorize words that end with **ary** or **ory** carefully.

Vocabulary Development
Write the **list word** that matches each synonym or definition clue.

1. flattering — complimentary
2. mythical — legendary
3. words of a language — vocabulary
4. modern — contemporary
5. bringing radical change — revolutionary
6. meeting a need or wish — satisfactory
7. a safe place — sanctuary
8. a viewing place — observatory
9. first — primary
10. health clinic — infirmary
11. financial — monetary
12. tasty — savory
13. remarkable — extraordinary
14. needed — necessary
15. required — mandatory

LIST WORDS
1. advisory
2. extraordinary
3. mandatory
4. preliminary
5. satisfactory
6. compulsory
7. infirmary
8. monetary
9. primary
10. savory
11. complimentary
12. introductory
13. necessary
14. revolutionary
15. subsidiary
16. contemporary
17. legendary
18. observatory
19. sanctuary
20. vocabulary

Dictionary Skills
Write the **list word** that matches each sound-spelling.

1. (prī'mer'ē) primary
2. (səb sid'ē er'ē) subsidiary
3. (nes'ə ser'ē) necessary
4. (sā'vər ē) savory
5. (kəm pul'sər ē) compulsory
6. (man'də tôr'ē) mandatory
7. (sat'is fak'tər ē) satisfactory
8. (in'trə duk'tər ē) introductory
9. (ad vī'zər ē) advisory
10. (vō kab'yə ler'ē) vocabulary

109

Spelling Practice

DID YOU KNOW?
In colonial days, a child's first reading book was called a primer, and today, the first grades of school are called the primary grades. **Primary** is taken from the Latin word, *primus*, which meant "first." Today, we use this same word to describe the first or the best of something, like the prime rib of beef.

Word Analysis
Write **list words** to answer the following questions. Which **list word** contains the same root as the word given?

1. legend — legendary
2. infirm — infirmary
3. compliment — complimentary
4. observe — observatory
5. satisfy — satisfactory
6. prime — primary
7. savor — savory
8. advise — advisory
9. introduce — introductory
10. revolution — revolutionary
11. mandate — mandatory
12. compel — compulsory

Which **list words** end in **ory**?
13. advisory
14. mandatory
15. satisfactory
16. compulsory
17. savory
18. introductory
19. observatory

Word Application
Replace the underlined word or words in each phrase with a **list word**. Write the **list word** on the line.

1. a division of Worldwide Manufacturers — subsidiary
2. the opening round of competition — preliminary
3. an artist who is living and working today — contemporary
4. a free preliminary offer — introductory
5. a storm and hurricane warning bulletin — advisory
6. an out of the ordinary piece of music — extraordinary
7. a famous cartoon character — legendary
8. a national wildlife protected place for birds — sanctuary
9. many money considerations — monetary
10. the solar viewing place — observatory
11. medicines essential for the patient's recovery — necessary
12. the words on the English test — vocabulary
13. the health clinic where Dr. Jarvis works — infirmary

110   Lesson 27 • Words Ending in ary, ory

LIST WORDS

contemporary	infirmary	satisfactory	mandatory
extraordinary	advisory	introductory	legendary
compulsory	monetary	observatory	necessary
revolutionary	primary	preliminary	sanctuary
complimentary	savory	vocabulary	subsidiary

Puzzle

This is a crossword puzzle without clues. Use the length and the spelling of each **list word** to complete the puzzle.

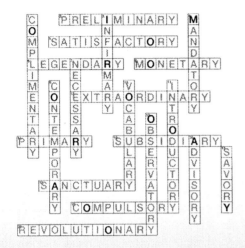

Proofreading

Use the proofreading marks to correct the mistakes in the article below. Then, write the misspelled **list words** correctly on the lines.

Did you know the invention of banking actually took place before the invention of monetory units such as as coins and paper money. Banking originated in in ancient mesopotamia where it was not only necessary but mandutory that the royal palaces and temples provide a sankchuary for the safe-keeping of grain. Receipts came to be used for transfers that the farmer who deposited the grain needed to give some of it to someone else. Over time, keeping track of grain and other goods in this fashion came to be a aprimary function of priests in mesopotamia. They became the world's first bankers.

Proofreading Marks

- ◯ spelling mistake
- ≡ capital letter
- ? add question mark
- ✗ delete word

1. monetary
2. necessary
3. mandatory
4. sanctuary
5. primary

Writing Sentences Using Alliteration

Alliteration is a literary device that employs two or more words with the same beginning sounds, such as "Sandy sang a simple song of sunny Sundays sailing." Write two sentences containing as much alliteration as possible on the topic of banking or U.S. or foreign currency, and try to use at least two **list words** in your sentences. After you proofread and revise your sentences, combine them with classmates' to create poems.

BONUS WORDS

franc	mark	rupee	yen	guilder
peso	ruble	pound	lira	shekel

Write the **bonus word** that is associated with each country given.

1. Netherlands guilder
2. Mexico peso
3. India rupee
4. Italy lira
5. Israel shekel

6. England pound
7. Russia ruble
8. France franc
9. Germany mark
10. Japan yen

Puzzle You may wish to ask a volunteer to remind the class how to solve a crossword puzzle without clues.

Spelling and Writing   *Page 112*

Proofreading Use this question to review the proofreading marks: *Do you you have any canadian curency.*

Writing Sentences Using Alliteration Discuss alliteration with students, pointing out that it is often used in tongue-twisters. If possible, show students examples from poems and songs. Have them make up their own examples, encouraging word play and humor.

Bonus Words   *Page 112*

Currencies Explain that the **bonus words** name some form of currency, or money. Use dictionaries, encyclopedias, and books about money to help students understand where each form is used. Point out that some forms of currency, such as the peso, are used in numerous countries. Encourage students to bring in currency collections and to research the topic further.

Bonus Words Test

1. The number of **yen** to the dollar keeps changing.
2. That bill looks like a **pound** note.
3. A **peso** is worth one hundred centavos in Cuba.
4. The **lira** is the basic monetary unit in Italy.
5. I have only one **ruble** in my money collection.
6. The word *shekel* is also a slang word for *money*.
7. The **franc** is used as money in many countries.
8. Dad brought me a **rupee** from India.
9. In Germany, this would cost a **mark**.
10. A **guilder** is worth more than a cent.

Final Test

1. Do you prefer **contemporary** or classical music?
2. Hank Aaron was a **legendary** baseball player.
3. We took a field trip to the **observatory**.
4. The **sanctuary** protects birds from hunters.
5. Each night, I learn ten more **vocabulary** words.
6. What a nice **complimentary** thing to say!
7. Try this free **introductory** offer for two weeks.
8. What is **necessary** for cooking a turkey?
9. Sliced bread was once a **revolutionary** idea.
10. I think that company is a **subsidiary** of a large one.
11. We will look to the **advisory** panel for suggestions.
12. That horse just made an **extraordinary** jump!
13. Wearing seat belts in the car is **mandatory**.
14. The **preliminary** match leads to the finals.
15. The service tonight was **satisfactory** but not great.
16. Our state has **compulsory** auto insurance laws.
17. The nurse sent my brother to the school **infirmary**.
18. The **monetary** unit of Mexico is the peso.
19. This position's **primary** task is data entry.
20. The **savory** salmon was made with dill sauce.

Lesson 28

Words of French Origin

Objective
To spell words of French origin

Pretest

1. Pat's hot beef **bouillon** warmed the tired campers.
2. Nam and his **fiancée** will be married next month.
3. The **opaque** window shade blocked the sun.
4. Sue bought a new tennis **racquet**.
5. Craig made a collage out of clam and **scallop** shells.
6. **Croquet** is an outdoor lawn game.
7. The gymnast's grace and **finesse** brought applause.
8. Did you choose a **corsage** at the new florist's?
9. A **résumé** lists your employment history.
10. The restaurant is famous for its cheese **soufflé**.
11. **Endive** is a green vegetable found in salad.
12. The puppeteer made the **marionette** dance.
13. Be careful! That teapot is antique **porcelain**!
14. How long do I **sauté** the vegetables in the wok?
15. Ravi bought a T-shirt as a **souvenir** of her trip.
16. **Etiquette** varies from country to country.
17. I've never seen such a varied **menu** at a restaurant!
18. The master carpenter trained his **protégé** well.
19. The hyena, a **scavenger**, eats rotting meat.
20. Is Dr. Nguyen a **surgeon** or a family doctor?

Spelling Strategy   **Page 113**

Discuss the spelling rule and examples of words that are derived or borrowed from the French language. Then, define the **list words** and discuss their French origins. Point out such spelling "tricks" as the different end sounds of *croquet* and *racquet*. Stress the accent marks in *fiancée, résumé, soufflé, sauté,* and *protégé,* pointing out that each represents the long *a* sound.

Vocabulary Development Before the exercise, have students select a **list word** to match this clue: "type of ceramic material." (*porcelain*)

Dictionary Skills Before the exercise, have volunteers look up the sound-spellings of *surgeon, bouillon,* and *etiquette* and write them on the board.

Spelling Practice   **Pages 114–115**

Word Analysis Explain that these exercises will help to unravel some of the spelling "tricks" of French words. Remind students to place the accent marks correctly.

Analogies If needed, review analogies using: *Beagle is to dog as _____ is to doll.* (*marionette*)

Word Application To extend the activity, have students make up context-clue sentences or "What am I?" riddles for the remaining **list words**. Call on volunteers to challenge their classmates for the correct answers.

Words of French Origin — Lesson 28

TIP
Several English words have French roots. For example, the English word porcelain comes from the French word *porcelaine.* The English word surgeon comes from the French word *cirurgien.*

Many other English words have been borrowed directly, in original form, from the French language. Examples include fiancée, bouillon, souvenir, and sauté. The spelling of such words can be tricky. Some, like sauté, contain accent marks. Others contain sounds spelled by letter combinations that are common to French words but rare in English words. For example, the letters et at the end of croquet and the ee at the end of fiancée stand for the long a sound.

Vocabulary Development

Write the **list word** that matches each synonym or definition.

1. manners — etiquette
2. puppet — marionette
3. keepsake — souvenir
4. shellfish — scallop
5. egg dish — soufflé
6. broth — bouillon
7. tennis equipment — racquet
8. to fry quickly — sauté
9. medical specialist — surgeon
10. dinner choices — menu
11. small bouquet — corsage
12. lawn game — croquet

Dictionary Skills

Write the **list word** that matches each sound-spelling.

1. (krō kā´) — croquet
2. (fē´an sā´) — fiancée
3. (en´dīv) — endive
4. (skav´in jər) — scavenger
5. (pôr´s'l in) — porcelain
6. (fi nes´) — finesse
7. (prōt´ə zhā) — protégé
8. (sōō flā´) — soufflé
9. (rez´oo mā) — résumé
10. (ō pāk´) — opaque
11. (sōō və nir´) — souvenir

LIST WORDS
1. bouillon
2. fiancée
3. opaque
4. racquet
5. scallop
6. croquet
7. finesse
8. corsage
9. résumé
10. soufflé
11. endive
12. marionette
13. porcelain
14. sauté
15. souvenir
16. etiquette
17. menu
18. protégé
19. scavenger
20. surgeon

113

Spelling Practice

DID YOU KNOW?
Etiquette is a French word that actually means "ticket," "label," or "list." It was first used on the lists of rules that were posted in a court or army camp. We might also say that etiquette can be a ticket that allows a person to enter polite society.

Word Analysis

Write **list words** to answer the following questions.

In which words does **et, é,** or **ée** spell the long a sound, as in day?

1. fiancée   3. résumé   5. sauté
2. croquet   4. soufflé   6. protégé

Which words contain the letter combination **que**?

7. opaque   9. croquet
8. racquet   10. etiquette

Which words contain these double consonants?

11. ss finesse   13. tt etiquette   15. ll bouillon
12. tt marionette   14. ff soufflé   16. ll scallop

Analogies

Write a **list word** to complete each analogy.

1. Bat is to baseball as racquet is to tennis.
2. Judge is to courtroom as surgeon is to operating room.
3. Gems are to bracelet as flowers are to corsage.
4. Fork is to silver as cup is to porcelain.
5. Flour is to bread as eggs are to soufflé.
6. Lion is to predator as buzzard is to scavenger.
7. Back is to forth as transparent is to opaque.
8. Apple is to lemon as cabbage is to endive.

Word Application

Write a **list word** to complete each sentence.

1. Ellen kept the ticket stub as a souvenir of her wonderful trip.
2. The waiter told us about the dinner specials that were not listed on the menu.
3. The magician fooled us with cleverness and finesse.
4. It is considered to be poor etiquette to talk with your mouth full of food.
5. Two weeks before the wedding, we had a party for Jeff and his fiancée, Josie.
6. Sara listed all of her summer jobs on her résumé.

LIST WORDS

bouillon	croquet	etiquette	endive
fiancée	finesse	marionette	menu
opaque	corsage	porcelain	scallop
racquet	résumé	scavenger	sauté
protégé	surgeon	souvenir	soufflé

Classification

Write a **list word** to complete each series.

1. chowder, soup, __bouillon__
2. glass, china, __porcelain__
3. ball, __racquet__, net
4. apprentice, student, __protégé__
5. bake, boil, __sauté__
6. style, cleverness, __finesse__

Puzzle
Use the **list words** to complete the crossword puzzle.

ACROSS
1. egg dish
3. not transparent
6. doctor who operates
9. animal that feeds on decaying organic matter
10. list of jobs and related experiences
17. list of dinner selections
18. sporting equipment
19. game with mallets, balls, and wickets
20. engaged female

DOWN
2. skill; artfulness; craft
4. leafy green plant
5. ceramic material used for dishes
7. bouquet that is worn
8. stringed puppet
11. scrapbook item
12. clear soup or broth
13. to fry briefly
14. shellfish
15. code of acceptable manners
16. person who receives help or guidance from another

Crossword answers:
SOUFFLE, OPAQUE, SURGEON, SCAVENGER, MARIONETTE, RESUME, CORSAGE, SAUTE, MENU, RACQUET, PORCELAIN, PROTEGE, CROQUET, FIANCEE, SCALLOP, ENDIVE, ETIQUETTE

Lesson 28 • Words of French Origin   115

Proofreading

Proofreading Marks

Use the proofreading marks to correct the mistakes in the article below. Then, write the misspelled **list words** correctly on the lines.

- ⊙ spelling mistake
- ⊕ add period
- ¶ new paragraph
- / small letter

Although, croquette and tennis do not look as if they would have anything in common, they have many striking similarities⊙ Both are thought to have originated in France—tennis, around the twelfth century, and croquet, perhaps around the thirteenth century. While one game is played with a mallet and the other is played with a racket, both require a great deal of finese⊙ During the Nineteenth century, guidebooks of rules and playing etiquitte appeared.

Today, Tennis has become so popular that a souvenir from a tennis match such as Wimbledon can cost a great deal of money⊙

1. __croquet__
2. __racquet__
3. __finesse__
4. __etiquette__
5. __souvenir__

Writing a Comparison

Choose two sports you have played or enjoy watching. Make a list in which you compare and contrast the two sports, and then use this information to write a comparison of them. Try to use as many **list words** as you can. Proofread and revise your writing, then share it with your classmates.

BONUS WORDS

impurity	refraction	crystallize	turquoise	obsidian
facets	dispersion	amethyst	sapphire	diamond

Write a **bonus word** to complete each sentence.

1. The __obsidian__ is a hard, black stone that is formed by the intense heat of volcanoes.
2. A tiny crack or __impurity__, even if invisible to the eye, can make a gem's value plunge.
3. The polished surfaces of a cut gem are called __facets__
4. The __dispersion__ of light reflecting off a cut gem can create a rainbow effect.
5. Due to __refraction__ of light, you'll see a distorted image by looking through a cut gem.
6. The __diamond__ is a colorless stone that is the hardest natural substance known.
7. The __sapphire__, which is named after the planet Saturn, is usually deep blue.
8. Most gems are formed when minerals __crystallize__
9. The __turquoise__ is greenish-blue and contains aluminum, copper, and phosphorus.
10. The __amethyst__, which is purple or violet, is a variety of quartz or corundum.

116   Lesson 28 • Words of French Origin

Classification If needed, use the following series to review classification skills: *clam, oyster, _____.* (scallop)

Puzzle Urge students to use as clues not only the definitions, but the number of spaces in each answer.

Spelling and Writing   *Page 116*
Proofreading Ask students to provide examples illustrating the use of each of the proofreading marks.

Writing a Comparison Invite students to name two similar games they enjoy, and then describe them. Have students research the games, taking careful notes and citing their sources in brief bibliographies to include with their comparisons. Then, provide time for students to present their comparisons to the class.

Bonus Words   *Page 116*
Gemstones Define the **bonus words**, then invite students to research gemstones. Have students write reports that use the **bonus words** to share what they have learned. To extend, discuss the differences between the refraction and dispersion of light.

Bonus Words Test
1. A prism causes **dispersion** of light.
2. Light **refraction** creates illusions underwater.
3. An **impurity** made the gem inexpensive.
4. Diamonds form as pieces of carbon **crystallize**.
5. An **obsidian** is a crystallized volcanic rock.
6. A **diamond** can be used as a cutting tool.
7. Gems sparkle when light reflects off their **facets**.
8. The queen wore a priceless **amethyst** necklace.
9. My uncle sent me a **turquoise** pin from Arizona.
10. The **sapphire** is a beautiful, rich shade of blue.

Final Test
1. The violinist took pride in introducing his **protégé**.
2. Keep unexposed film in an **opaque** container.
3. Don't miss the **croquet** tournament this Saturday!
4. Badminton requires a lighter **racquet** than tennis.
5. Each job applicant should submit a **résumé**.
6. Does the recipe for the **soufflé** call for a dozen eggs?
7. His fingers move the strings of a **marionette**.
8. In our garden, we grow tomatoes and **endive**.
9. Can **bouillon** be served either hot or chilled?
10. Danielle found a **scallop** shell on the beach.
11. Tyrell has great **finesse** with difficult customers.
12. The operation requires more than one **surgeon**.
13. The vulture is a **scavenger**.
14. The florist made her a wrist **corsage**.
15. Ed met his **fiancée** while attending graduate school.
16. The **porcelain** tea set was in a London antique shop.
17. Is licking your plate proper **etiquette**?
18. **Sauté** the onions until they are golden brown.
19. I bought a **souvenir** cowboy hat in Texas.
20. Jaime asked the waiter for the dessert **menu**.

Challenging Words

Objective
To spell difficult words with unusual spelling patterns

Pretest
1. Use this scarf as an **accessory** for your dress.
2. I **emphatically** deny any involvement in the plot!
3. The station **attendant** checked the car's oil.
4. What activities are on the weekly **schedules**?
5. The village was **vulnerable** to enemy attack.
6. Each member was **allotted** only two tickets.
7. This cute program will **fascinate** the children.
8. Notary publics certify, or **notarize**, documents.
9. The poet led a quiet, **tranquil** life in the country.
10. Joe got a job unloading freighters at the **wharf**.
11. The empty, **dilapidated** shed was condemned.
12. Her wish to see Ireland again was finally **fulfilled**.
13. The central police **precinct** is the busiest.
14. The colonists revolted against the king's **tyranny**.
15. How high will the **yeast** make the dough rise?
16. A **disastrous** earthquake devastated the town.
17. Firefighters put their life in **jeopardy** every day.
18. A **scarcity** of lumber caused housing prices to rise.
19. The huge **umbrella** protected us from the rain.
20. The florist added an orange **zinnia** to the bouquet.

Spelling Strategy *Page 117*

Discuss with students how there are some English words to which no usual spelling rules apply. Stress that the pronunciation of these words provides little help in spelling them. Instead, they must study and practice them. Then, discuss the **list words**, helping students see each word's special spelling challenge.

Vocabulary Development When finished, you may wish to have students find synonyms for additional **list words**.

Dictionary Skills If needed, use a dictionary to review the function of guide words with students.

Spelling Practice *Pages 118–119*
Word Analysis Remind students that repeating the word to themselves may not help them recall the letters that are missing. Have them refer to the **list words** on page 119 if needed.

Classification To review classification, have students complete this series using a **list word**, then explain their answer: *police, patrol, _____. (precinct)*

Word Application Discuss the directions with the class. As an example, read the first sentence together. Ask students to find the **list words** that fit the meaning of the sentence.

74

Challenging Words

TIP
Many English words do not follow ordinary spelling rules. The best way to become familiar with these challenging words is to study, memorize, and practice using them.

Challenging Word	"Trick"
schedules	d = sound of j
emphatically	ph = sound of f
jeopardy	eo = sound of short e
accessory	cc, ss double consonants

Vocabulary Development
Write the **list word** that matches each synonym.

1. servant attendant
2. pier wharf
3. shabby dilapidated
4. allowed allotted
5. peaceful tranquil
6. danger jeopardy
7. dictatorship tyranny
8. timetables schedules
9. completed fulfilled
10. intrigue fascinate
11. sensitive vulnerable
12. terrible disastrous

LIST WORDS
1.
2.
3.
4.
5.
6.
7.
8.
9.
10.
11.
12.
13.
14.
15.
16.
17.
18.
19.
20.

Dictionary Skills
Write the **list word** that comes between each pair of dictionary guide words.

1. scan/scene scarcity
2. wheat/zinc yeast
3. instant/key jeopardy
4. display/far emphatically
5. tyrant/vulgar umbrella
6. yellow/zoom zinnia
7. mystery/odd notarize
8. over/python precinct
9. dimple/embrace disastrous
10. able/alive accessory

117

DID YOU KNOW?
In England during the sixteenth century, when a chess player was forced to make a move with which he could lose the game, his position was called *iuparti*. This term came from the French *jeu parti*, which meant "divided game." Today, we know the word as **jeopardy**, which can describe any situation in which winning or losing hangs in a delicate balance.

Spelling Practice
Word Analysis
Fill in the missing letters to form **list words**. Then, write the completed list words on the lines.

1. vuln**e r a**ble vulnerable
2. not**a r**i**z**e notarize
3. di**s**as**t r o**us disastrous
4. a**c c e s s o**ry accessory
5. **e m p h**atica**l l**y emphatically
6. fa**s c**inate fascinate
7. t**y r a n n**ny tyranny
8. w**h a r f** wharf
9. tra**n q u i l** tranquil

Classification
Write a **list word** to complete each series.

1. waiter, valet, attendant
2. charm, enchant, fascinate
3. calm, restful, tranquil
4. raincoat, boots, umbrella
5. trouble, danger, jeopardy
6. scarf, pin, accessory
7. witness, sign, notarize
8. freighter, harbor, wharf
9. marigold, petunia, zinnia
10. dough, bread, yeast

Word Application
Replace each underlined word or words in the sentences with a **list word**. Write the list word on the line.

1. He strongly denied that he was responsible for the ruinous accident.
   emphatically disastrous

2. The landlord satisfied his promise to repair the run-down apartment building.
   fulfilled dilapidated

3. Due to the shortage of seats, each graduate was given only four tickets.
   scarcity allotted

4. The sergeant posted lists of times for officers assigned to his division.
   schedules precinct

LIST WORDS

accessory	allotted	zinnia	disastrous
emphatically	scarcity	wharf	jeopardy
dilapidated	notarize	precinct	fascinate
schedules	tranquil	tyranny	umbrella
vulnerable	fulfilled	yeast	attendant

Puzzle
Use the **list words** to complete the crossword puzzle.

ACROSS
3. great danger or peril
6. something extra
7. free from disturbance
9. to witness a legal signing
11. a wooden structure in a harbor where ships load and unload goods
12. substance used in baking to make dough rise
13. a person who helps or serves someone
15. to have made happen; completed
17. having great destruction or misfortune
18. lists of arriving and departing trains and buses
19. very cruel and unjust use of power

DOWN
1. a portable covering to protect from rain
2. a showy garden flower
4. the district or area patrolled by police
5. open to harm or danger
8. distributed little by little
10. run down; in ruin
14. with force of expression
15. to delight or charm
16. a lacking or shortage of something

Lesson 29 • Challenging Words   119

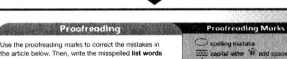

Use the proofreading marks to correct the mistakes in the article below. Then, write the misspelled **list words** correctly on the lines.

Proofreading Marks
◯ spelling mistake
≡ capital letter # add space
⁙ add exclamation mark

If you are lucky enough to live where wolves are common, you may sometimes hear them howl. The howl is one important method wolves use to communicate with each other. It certainly is an eerie sound. Unfortunately, although wolves have always tended to fascinate people, they have also been a source of fear. As a result, there is a scarsity of wolves in the lower 48 states. For many years, wolves were vulnerable to hunters and ranchers who wanted to remove them from wilderness areas. Once in jeopardy, wolves are now making a comeback in states like minnesota and maine, with attendant laws to protect them.

1. fascinate
2. scarcity
3. vulnerable
4. jeopardy
5. attendant

Writing Sentences Using Onomatopoeia

Onomatopoeia is a word in which the sound gives the word meaning. "Plink, plink went the raindrops as they fell into the puddle" is an example. Write several sentences with onomatopoeia, using as many **list words** as you can. Proofread and revise your onomatopoeic sentences, then compare them with those of your classmates and discuss which ones work best.

BONUS WORDS

vociferous	enunciate	strident	amplification	taciturn
reverberate	inaudible	timbre	intonation	reticent

Write the **bonus word** that matches each clue given.

1. cause a sound to echo   reverberate
2. cannot be heard   inaudible
3. loud; noisy; vehement   vociferous
4. say clearly and distinctly   enunciate
5. making sound louder   amplification
6. harsh-sounding; shrill   strident

Write the **bonus words** that are synonyms or near-synonyms for the phrases given.

distinguishing quality of a voice		almost always silent
7. timbre	9.	taciturn
8. intonation	10.	reticent

120   Lesson 29 • Challenging Words

Puzzle Remind students to use capital letters and to print clearly and neatly as they fill in the puzzle.

Spelling and Writing   *Page 120*
Proofreading Use the following to demonstrate the proofreading marks: *Look. Their's meg's babysister*

Writing Sentences Using Onomatopoeia Discuss the unusual spelling patterns in *onomatopoeia*. Then, have students identify the example of onomatopoeia in the sentence. (*Plink, plink*) Before writing, urge students to brainstorm two or three sounds for each item they wish to describe, or for **list words** such as *tranquil, vulnerable, wharf, tyranny, disastrous*, and *umbrella*. Encourage them to use these words as they write.

Bonus Words   *Page 120*
Sound Discuss the **bonus words**. Have students give examples of when each word might apply to a certain sound. For example, an angry person might speak in a *strident* voice; a crowd's cheers might *reverberate* in a gymnasium. Elicit from students the **bonus words** that are near-synonyms. (*taciturn, reticent*) Discuss the shades of difference in their meanings.

Bonus Words Test
1. The **timbre** of the tenor's voice vibrated in the hall.
2. The angry crowd responded with a **vociferous** cry.
3. The song needs more **amplification** to hear it.
4. The newborn baby's cry was practically **inaudible**.
5. Try to **enunciate** each word clearly as you speak.
6. Her voice was **strident** as she lost her temper.
7. The excited cheers **reverberate** off the gym walls.
8. The **reticent** child spoke in a shy, quiet whisper.
9. Her voice's **intonation** showed her impatience.
10. The **taciturn** man spoke only when necessary.

Final Test
1. The mayor campaigned heavily in our **precinct**.
2. A **disastrous** fire destroyed the factory.
3. A **zinnia** is a brightly colored, showy garden flower.
4. Was his job in **jeopardy** because of the economy?
5. Towns near rivers are **vulnerable** to flooding.
6. Complicated software programs **fascinate** Dora.
7. The zoo **attendant** was feeding the tiger.
8. The governor spoke longer than her **allotted** time.
9. The cruel dictator ruled with **tyranny** and deceit.
10. Our busy **schedules** kept us from getting together.
11. The bread recipe calls for two packets of **yeast**.
12. Do you always carry an **umbrella** on cloudy days?
13. Ken nodded his head **emphatically** in approval.
14. What is the attorney's fee to **notarize** our will?
15. That old car is run down and **dilapidated**.
16. The **scarcity** of rain caused an awful drought!
17. From the **wharf**, Kate watched the ship dock.
18. Leon **fulfilled** his promise to pick me up.
19. Do you prefer a **tranquil** or a fast-paced life?
20. A bright **accessory** will improve this dull outfit.

Lessons 25–29 · Review

Objectives
To review spelling patterns of words with different suffixes, of French origin, and with no usual spelling patterns

Spelling Strategy   *Page 121*

This lesson will help students review the spelling patterns of words they studied in Lessons 25–29. Read and discuss the spelling rules with students, having them identify root words or base words and suffixes or endings, where appropriate. Then, have students give other examples of challenging words, telling what trick makes each word hard to spell.

Spelling Practice   *Pages 121–123*

Lesson 25 Use the words *lengthwise, rationalize, prudent,* and *significant* as examples of words with confusing suffixes. Then, have students identify the root or base word of each **list word** and tell how its suffix was added. Explain that the words given may have prefixes or suffixes or both. Point out the additional write-on lines and have students add two words from Lesson 25 that they found difficult, or assign words that were hard for everyone. (Repeat this procedure for each lesson review in this section.)

Lesson 26 Use *civility, ability,* and *possibility* to review the *ity* suffix. Then, have students identify the root or base word of each **list word** and tell them how its suffix was added.

Lesson 27 Write *contemporary, observatory, savory,* and *vocabulary* on the board. Use the words to review the *ory* and *ary* endings. Help students hear the difference in sound between the words, when applicable. Then, have students say each **list word**, emphasizing the ending sound.

Lesson 28 Use *fiancée, corsage,* and *sauté* to review words that come from the French language. Discuss such letter combinations as *ette* and *illon* and the use of the accent mark and how it changes a letter's sound.

Lesson 29 Write *emphatically, fascinate, notarize,* and *zinnia* on the board. Use the words to discuss how some words can be hard to spell. Have students suggest other words that are not spelled the way they sound, and then discuss ways to remember their spellings.

Show What You Know   *Page 124*

Point out to students that this review will help them know if they have mastered the words in Lessons 25–29. Have a volunteer restate the directions and tell which word in the first item should be marked as incorrect. *(pleasent)* When finished, have students write their misspelled words correctly.

TIPS
- Understanding word endings can help you spell many words correctly. Some are easy to confuse, such as **ise** and **ize**, **ent** and **ant**, and **ary** and **ory**. Pay close attention to the spelling of words with similar endings. Here are several examples:

  prevalent, relevant, franchise, harmonize, advisory, preliminary
- The suffix **ity** forms a noun from an adjective, as when formal becomes formality. When this suffix is added to words ending in **ble**, an **i** is inserted before the **l**, so that words like liable become liability. In some words, the base word changes in different ways. For example, hospitable becomes hospitality.
- Many English words come from French and may contain letter combinations that are common in French words but unusual in English words, such as the ending of finesse. Other words from the French may contain accent marks, as in sauté.
- Our language also has words that do not follow the usual spelling rules. These may contain unusual spellings for certain sounds or unexpected double consonants. In the word jeopardy, for example, the vowel sound for short **e** is spelled **eo**. The word allotted has two pairs of double consonants.
- The best way to learn words with unusual spellings is to study them and use them.

Lesson 25

List Words

pleasant
apologize
compromise
dependent
observant
competent
economize
jubilant
enterprise
itemize

Replace the underlined word or words in each sentence with a **list word**. Write the **list word** on the line.

1. The swimmer was very happy when she won. ___jubilant___
2. Make sure you go to a skilled mechanic. __competent__
3. An aware neighbor called the fire dept. __observant__
4. The breeze makes this room quite nice. __pleasant__
5. If you can reach an agreement through negotiation, you can both get what you want. __compromise__
6. This business will not be sold! __enterprise__
7. We can save money by buying generic brands. __economize__
8. When we go camping, we are no longer relying on city facilities for entertainment. __dependent__
9. I want to say I'm sorry for arriving late. __apologize__
10. Make a list of the ingredients you need. __itemize__

121

Lesson 26

List Words

hospitality
availability
individuality
eligibility
similarity
flexibility
generosity
personality
capability
visibility

Write the **list word** with the same base word or root as the word given.

1. dissimilar — __similarity__		6. invisibly — __visibility__
2. individualized — __individuality__		7. generously — __generosity__
3. inhospitable — __hospitality__		8. unavailable — __availability__
4. inflexible — __flexibility__		9. ineligible — __eligibility__
5. incapable — __capability__		10. impersonate — __personality__

Lesson 27

List Words

infirmary
legendary
mandatory
necessary
satisfactory
monetary
primary
sanctuary
extraordinary
complimentary

Write a **list word** to complete each sentence.

1. If people or animals are safe in a place, the place may be a __sanctuary__.
2. Financial plans affect a nation's __monetary__ system.
3. If something is essential, it is __necessary__.
4. If someone says that Seth looked wonderful, that person is making a __complimentary__ statement.
5. The __legendary__ pitcher was inducted into the Baseball Hall of Fame.
6. If you feel sick, go to the __infirmary__.
7. Health is the __primary__ reason for exercising.
8. If you and your family are generally pleased, the carpenter did a __satisfactory__ job.
9. If a dancer's performance is truly outstanding, you might also call it an __extraordinary__ performance.
10. If seatbelts are required, they are __mandatory__.

122   Lesson 30 • Review

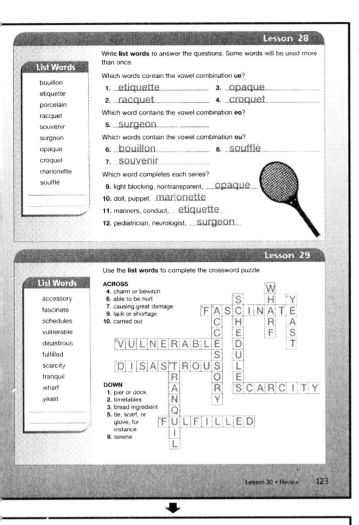

Lesson 28

List Words

bouillon
etiquette
porcelain
racquet
souvenir
surgeon
opaque
croquet
marionette
soufflé

Write **list words** to answer the questions. Some words will be used more than once.

Which words contain the vowel combination **ue**?

1. etiquette   3. opaque
2. racquet   4. croquet

Which word contains the vowel combination **eo**?

5. surgeon

Which words contain the vowel combination **ou**?

6. bouillon   8. soufflé
7. souvenir

Which word completes each series?

9. light blocking, nontransparent, opaque
10. doll, puppet, marionette
11. manners, conduct, etiquette
12. pediatrician, neurologist, surgeon

Lesson 29

List Words

accessory
fascinate
schedules
vulnerable
disastrous
fulfilled
scarcity
tranquil
wharf
yeast

Use the **list words** to complete the crossword puzzle.

ACROSS
4. charm or bewitch
6. able to be hurt
7. causing great damage
9. lack or shortage
10. carried out

DOWN
1. pier or dock
2. timetables
3. bread ingredient
5. tie, scarf, or glove, for instance
8. serene

Crossword answers:
W H Y
FASCINATE
WHARF
YEAST
VULNERABLE
DISASTROUS
SCHEDULES
TRANQUIL
SCARCITY
FULFILLED

Show What You Know

Lessons 25–29 • Review

One word is misspelled in each set of **list words**. Fill in the circle next to the **list word** that is spelled incorrectly.

#				
1.	○ individuality	● pleasent	○ introductory	○ etiquette
2.	○ technicality	○ necessary	● compitent	○ menu
3.	○ revolutionary	○ availability	● rationalise	○ protégé
4.	○ inferiority	● subcidiary	○ contemporary	○ jubilant
5.	○ scavenger	○ prevalent	○ observatory	● surgeaon
6.	○ enterprise	● legendery	○ accessory	○ visibility
7.	● compromize	○ hospitality	○ emphatically	○ mobility
8.	○ eligibility	○ franchise	○ sanctuary	● attendent
9.	● vocabulery	○ schedules	○ lengthwise	○ capability
10.	○ vulnerable	○ generosity	● bouillion	○ prudent
11.	○ eventuality	○ fiancée	● alloted	○ apologize
12.	○ dependent	● opacque	○ superiority	○ fascinate
13.	○ notarize	● flexability	○ harmonize	○ legality
14.	● observent	○ tranquil	○ similarity	○ racquet
15.	○ scallop	○ relevant	● dilapidatted	○ advisory
16.	○ clockwise	○ croquet	● extrordinary	○ wharf
17.	● economise	○ fulfiled	○ mandatory	○ finesse
18.	○ preliminary	○ corsage	○ precinct	● itemise
19.	○ permanent	○ savory	○ résumé	● tyranney
20.	● compulsery	○ yeast	○ significant	○ souffle
21.	○ disastrous	○ endive	○ punctuality	● infirmery
22.	○ personality	○ monetary	○ marionette	● jeopurdy
23.	● porcelin	○ liability	○ scarcity	○ primary
24.	● satisfactory	○ sauté	○ practicality	○ umbrella
25.	○ souvenir	● zinia	○ complimentary	○ formality

Final Test

1. Please **itemize** the office supplies that you need.
2. The school nurse is not in the **infirmary** right now.
3. The peseta is the **monetary** unit of Spain.
4. Our school can **economize** by using recycled paper.
5. This entire meadow is a **sanctuary** for waterfowl.
6. Notice the **similarity** between these two leaves.
7. We can't forecast the **availability** of fuel next year.
8. Many twins try to maintain their **individuality**.
9. A perfect mission made the astronauts **jubilant**.
10. Her kind **hospitality** to guests is legendary.
11. What is the proper **etiquette** for formal dinners?
12. Her **primary** goal is to make good grades.
13. Try a lighter **racquet** and see if your swing improves.
14. What an **extraordinary** view of the lunar eclipse!
15. This new **enterprise** will boost the town's economy.
16. A hot cup of **bouillon** will warm you up quickly.
17. What are the **eligibility** requirements for the loan?
18. This cup is made from **porcelain**, not earthenware.
19. Maria is a responsible, **competent** employee.
20. This poster is a **souvenir** of my trip to California.
21. Mike **fulfilled** his dream to become a doctor.
22. Both sides negotiated to reach a **compromise**.
23. We camped in a **tranquil** spot by the lake.
24. The flight is delayed due to poor **visibility**.
25. Matzoh is a kind of bread made without **yeast**.
26. I am grateful for your kind **generosity**.
27. This laser light show will **fascinate** most children.
28. A bicycle helmet is **necessary** for your safety.
29. A wooden house is **vulnerable** to termite damage.
30. Her admirer gave her **complimentary** remarks.
31. The **surgeon** performed a heart transplant.
32. The window is **opaque**, and we can't see through it.
33. At a garage sale, Steve bought a used **croquet** set.
34. Each **marionette** had a carved face and lifelike hair.
35. For dessert, I ordered the lemon **soufflé**.
36. Thank goodness the accident was not **disastrous**!
37. Among fans, Elvis Presley has a **legendary** status.
38. Wearing proper footwear is **mandatory** in the gym.
39. Check the bus **schedules** for the departure times.
40. Your work performance has been **satisfactory**.
41. Imagine the **flexibility** it takes to be a gymnast!
42. You need a bright **accessory**, such as a scarf or belt.
43. The cheery house reflected her **personality**.
44. With her medical **capability**, she'll be a fine doctor.
45. The boats will unload the fish onto the **wharf**.
46. The weather is warm and **pleasant** this week.
47. My sister wanted to **apologize** for interrupting me.
48. The **scarcity** of water can be a problem in summer.
49. Koalas are **dependent** upon leaves for food.
50. She's **observant** and described the scene in detail.

Words from Science

Objective
To spell words from science

Pretest
1. His **allergy** to grass made him sneeze constantly.
2. Eating too quickly may cause **indigestion**.
3. **Physics** is the study of matter and motion.
4. A **neutron** is a particle of the nucleus of an atom.
5. Will the nurse **vaccinate** children against smallpox?
6. Mildew is just one type of **fungus**.
7. Kayla lost her voice due to an inflamed **larynx**.
8. **Psychology** is the study of human behavior.
9. Was the television **transmitter** struck by lightning?
10. **Voltage** is the measure of electrical current.
11. Specific symptoms help to **diagnose** an illness.
12. Bacteria is a kind of **microorganism**.
13. The moon is a **satellite** that orbits the Earth.
14. Did the accident victim need a blood **transfusion**?
15. Rubbing surfaces together creates **friction**.
16. **Iodine** is used to cleanse wounds.
17. A **perennial** plant blooms from year to year.
18. **Respiration** will cease if the airways are blocked.
19. A water wheel is a type of **turbine**.
20. She studied **zoology** because of her love for animals.

Spelling Strategy   *Page 125*
Discuss the spelling rule. Encourage students to name other words they know that come specifically from science. Then, have volunteers define the **list words**. Have students consult a dictionary or science book for any words that are unfamiliar. Emphasize that because scientific words are often a challenge to pronounce and spell, it is necessary to study and practice these words.

Classification Encourage students to use dictionaries for **list words** whose meanings they are unsure of. When finished, you may wish to challenge students to work in pairs to find another science word related to each category.

Dictionary Skills Remind students to check their dictionaries if they are unsure of the diacritical marks used in this exercise.

Spelling Practice   *Pages 126–127*
Word Analysis Students may wish to review the **list words** on page 127 before completing this activity.

Word Application Remind students that in this exercise the meanings of the **list words** are as important as the spellings.

Words from Science

Lesson 31

TIP

The study of science involves the recognition and comprehension of many unfamiliar words. Words such as indigestion, microorganism, and respiration may seem complicated and difficult to spell. With practice, you can master these challenging words.

All the **list words** are from science. Memorize and practice spelling these words.

Classification
Write a **list word** to complete each series.
1. current, wattage, **voltage**
2. air, lungs, **respiration**
3. space, orbit, **satellite**
4. esophagus, trachea, **larynx**
5. inoculate, serum, **vaccinate**
6. electron, proton, **neutron**
7. mold, parasite, **fungus**
8. annual, biennial, **perennial**
9. mammals, birds, **zoology**
10. microscope, bacteria, **microorganism**
11. pollen, sneezing, **allergy**
12. mind, thought, **psychology**

LIST WORDS
1. allergy
2. indigestion
3. physics
4. neutron
5. vaccinate
6. fungus
7. larynx
8. psychology
9. transmitter
10. voltage
11. diagnose
12. microorganism
13. satellite
14. transfusion
15. friction
16. iodine
17. perennial
18. respiration
19. turbine
20. zoology

Dictionary Skills
Write the **list word** that matches each sound-spelling.
1. (tur′bin) **turbine**   6. (trans mit′ər) **transmitter**
2. (ī′ə dīn) **iodine**   7. (in′di jes′chən) **indigestion**
3. (fiz′iks) **physics**   8. (trans fyo͞o′zhən) **transfusion**
4. (frik′shən) **friction**   9. (sī käl′ə jē) **psychology**
5. (al′ər jē) **allergy**   10. (dī′əg nōs′) **diagnose**

125

DID YOU KNOW?
A **turbine** is a rotary engine that generates power. It may have gotten its name from the Latin word *turb* meaning "spinning top," or from the Greek word *.urb*, meaning "turmoil." Either is quite reasonable since a turbine must be turning in order to work. Indeed, if you were spinning about in a turbine, you would certainly be in a great deal of turmoil.

Spelling Practice
Word Analysis
Write each **list word** under the correct category.

Words with Two Syllables
1. physics
2. neutron
3. fungus
4. larynx
5. voltage
6. friction
7. turbine

Words with Three Syllables
8. allergy
9. vaccinate
10. transmitter
11. diagnose
12. satellite
13. transfusion
14. iodine

Words with Four Syllables
15. indigestion   18. respiration
16. psychology   19. zoology
17. perennial

Word with Six Syllables
20. microorganism

Word Application
Underline the **list word** in each sentence that is used incorrectly. Write the correct **list word** on the line.
1. That voltage plant comes up year after year despite the cold weather. **perennial**
2. The pneumonia in Kim's lungs had a severe effect on her vaccinate. **respiration**
3. A bacteria is an example of a neutron. **microorganism**
4. High-respiration towers carry a tremendous amount of electrical power. **voltage**
5. Sandy suffered from perennial after she ate some bad food. **indigestion**
6. Atoms have particles that include the electron, the proton, and the iodine. **neutron**
7. Be sure to larynx your pet so that it won't get the rabies virus. **vaccinate**
8. My brother sneezes all the time due to his microorganism to dust. **allergy**
9. The thyroid gland uses indigestion to help the body function properly. **iodine**
10. Tom injured his allergy and couldn't talk for weeks. **larynx**

Puzzle
Use the **list words** to complete the crossword puzzle.

ACROSS

1. mold; mildew; mushroom
4. something that sends signals
6. the study of human behavior
9. discomfort caused by inability to digest foods properly
11. a sensitivity to a substance such as food or plants
13. science dealing with energy, matter, and movement
14. detect an illness
17. inject a serum to protect against a disease
18. upper part of the throat
19. returning or becoming active again and again

DOWN

2. uncharged particle of an atom
3. an object in orbit around the Earth
5. bacteria not visible to the human eye
7. the act of moving blood from one person to another
8. the study of animals and their behavior
10. reddish-colored disinfectant
12. breathing
15. the resistance to motion of two objects that touch
16. a steam engine
17. measurement of electrical current

Proofreading   Proofreading Marks

Use the proofreading marks to correct the mistakes in the article. Then, write the misspelled **list words** correctly on the lines.

Proofreading Marks:
- ◯ spelling mistake   ↑ add comma
- ¶ new paragraph   ⌿ delete word

The best way to prevent an allergy is to recognize that you have one. Many people diagnoze it as a cold or flu. Colds are short-lived and are passed from person to to person. Allergies are an immune-system reaction to a normally harmless substance, like pollen or fungis. Sneezing, watery eyes, or resperation trouble that lasts for more than 10 days without a a fever may actually be allergic symptoms.

Food allergies have different symptoms. They may cause indigestion. Whatever the cause however there are many treatments available for allergies today.

1. allergy
2. diagnose
3. fungus
4. respiration
5. indigestion

Writing a Persuasive Speech

Which field of science interests you — zoology, biology, microbiology, or physics? Write a persuasive speech that tells why the field you're interested in should receive more grants for research than any other field. Use **list words** when possible. After proofreading and revising your speech, get together with others that wrote about the same field. Hold a class debate to decide which field of science merits more funding.

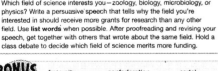

BONUS WORDS

fraternity	confederation	cartel	sorority	clique
syndicate	affiliation	guild	faction	troupe

Write the **bonus word** that matches each definition clue.

1. a small exclusive circle of people — clique
2. a small group within an organization working against goals of the main body — faction
3. a group of women or girls with similar interests — sorority
4. an alliance; a political union of states — confederation
5. an association that fixes prices and monopolizes an industry — cartel
6. connected with a particular group — affiliation
7. a group of actors, singers, performers — troupe
8. a group of men or boys with similar interests — fraternity
9. an association formed to transact a planned financial project — syndicate
10. a trade union — guild

Puzzle You may wish to remind students to print neatly and clearly as they write the letters in the boxes.

Spelling and Writing   *Page 128*

Proofreading Ask students to give examples of when to use the proofreading marks. Then, review the use of the comma with the word *however*.

Writing a Persuasive Speech Ask students if they have ever heard or seen a political or activist speech or ad. Elicit elements of these types of speeches, such as the use of strong persuasive language, emotional appeal, and so on. If desired, encourage students to incorporate these elements in their persuasive speeches.

Bonus Words   *Page 128*

Organizations Ask students to name the different groups or organizations that they belong to. Then, discuss the **bonus words**, having students consult a dictionary to define the words. Help students contrast the different kinds of organizations. Students may wish to prepare a report on medieval guilds, the effect of cartels, or the history of fraternities and sororities.

Bonus Words Test

1. Ruby felt isolated from her new neighbors' **clique**.
2. His column is published by a nationwide **syndicate**.
3. The provinces united to form a **confederation**.
4. Amy joined a **sorority** while in college.
5. That **faction** of the union will not support the strike.
6. The oil **cartel** controls oil prices around the world.
7. George joined a **troupe** of Shakespearean actors.
8. Mrs. Franklin is a member of the Fine Jeweler's **Guild**.
9. Don's **fraternity** sponsored a campus fund-raiser.
10. His store has an **affiliation** with a major corporation.

Final Test

1. Akule's rate of **respiration** rose when he ran.
2. The astronauts repaired the **satellite**.
3. We are studying mammals in **zoology** class.
4. Hydrogen is the only element without a **neutron**.
5. My, that machine requires a lot of **voltage**!
6. Aida has a dog because she has an **allergy** to cats.
7. The vocal chords are found in the **larynx**.
8. Water moving a **turbine** produces electricity.
9. Was it difficult for doctors to **diagnose** her disease?
10. **Iodine** is often used as an antiseptic.
11. There is less **friction** between smooth surfaces.
12. A **transfusion** of nutrients will keep up his strength.
13. Is antacid an effective remedy for her **indigestion**?
14. A radio signal is sent through a **transmitter**.
15. Years ago, doctors didn't **vaccinate** against tetanus.
16. We learned about energy in **physics** class.
17. Athlete's foot is caused by a **fungus**.
18. The human eye can't see a **microorganism**.
19. Is a hosta a **perennial** or an annual plant?
20. Maya will study child **psychology** in college this fall.

Words from Occupations

Objective
To spell words from occupations

Pretest

1. Miss Romero is an excellent school **administrator**.
2. The **librarian** helped Kim find the reference book.
3. Juan's physical **therapist** helped him exercise his legs.
4. Ken Yee is the **proprietor** of Ken Yee's Shoe Store.
5. The **electrician** installed new fuses.
6. The strikers met with a neutral **arbitrator**.
7. Carol bought a scarf from the street **vendor**.
8. The **paramedic** treated the accident victim.
9. Did the **veterinarian** cure your sick rabbit?
10. The **chemist** told why certain chemicals are toxic.
11. What funny jokes the **comedian** told!
12. The X-ray **technician** saw the fractured bone.
13. Who is your **representative** in the state legislature?
14. The **announcer** mispronounced the pitcher's name.
15. The **pharmacist** filled Mr. Chan's prescription.
16. The **hygienist** showed me how to floss my teeth.
17. The **analyst** may help you manage your finances.
18. The **manicurist** filed and polished Rosie's fingernails.
19. The woman with the toolbelt is a **carpenter**.
20. Will that **researcher** find a cure for cancer?

Spelling Strategy   Page 129

Review the spelling rules for adding *or, er, an, ist,* and *ive.* Write on the board: *publisher, dentist, aviator,* and *musician.* Have students identify the meaning and then the derivation of each word. (*publish, dental, aviation, music*) Then, ask volunteers to define the **list words** and name their derivations.

Classification You may wish to have students write additional series of words using other **list words**.

Dictionary Skills Remind students that breaking words into syllables can help them spell multisyllabic words such as *administrator, proprietor,* and *representative.*

Spelling Practice   Pages 130–131

Word Analysis Write the example *ch__mi__ __* on the board. Ask students to fill in the missing letters to make a **list word**. (*chemist*) Provide other examples as needed.

Vocabulary Development Write the word pairs *announce/announcer* and *manicure/manicurist* on the board. Build meanings for each word. Point out that each word in this activity will require a spelling change to become a **list word**.

Word Application Stress that students should use the context clues to select a **list word** that makes sense in each sentence.

Words from Occupations

TIP
Words that name occupations are usually another form of a word related to that occupation. The suffixes *or, er, an, ist,* or *ive* are added to make the word mean "one who does something." For example, a *librarian* is one who works in a library. Here are some other examples.
manicure – manicurist   announce – announcer
arbitrate – arbitrator   represent – representative
The **list words** name occupations. Notice the special spelling patterns of each word. Memorize and practice spelling them.

Classification

Write a **list word** to complete each series.

1. hammer, nails, __carpenter__
2. jokes, laughter, __comedian__
3. prescription, drugstore, __pharmacist__
4. books, catalogue cards, __librarian__
5. animals, medicine, __veterinarian__
6. microphone, radio, __announcer__
7. dentist, teeth, __hygienist__
8. nail file, polish, __manicurist__
9. wiring, outlets, __electrician__
10. laboratory, chemicals, __chemist__
11. owner, manager, __proprietor__

Dictionary Skills

Rewrite each of the following **list words** to show how they are divided into syllables.

1. proprietor __pro/pri/e/tor__
2. researcher __re/search/er__
3. arbitrator __ar/bi/tra/tor__
4. therapist __ther/a/pist__
5. representative __rep/re/sent/a/tive__
6. administrator __ad/min/is/tra/tor__
7. analyst __an/a/lyst__
8. vendor __ven/dor__
9. paramedic __par/a/med/ic__
10. technician __tech/ni/cian__

LIST WORDS
1. administrator
2. librarian
3. therapist
4. proprietor
5. electrician
6. arbitrator
7. vendor
8. paramedic
9. veterinarian
10. chemist
11. comedian
12. technician
13. representative
14. announcer
15. pharmacist
16. hygienist
17. analyst
18. manicurist
19. carpenter
20. researcher

129

DID YOU KNOW?
The word **comedian** once referred to a person who wrote comedies, or humorous works. William Shakespeare was the first to use it to mean "a humorous actor" in his play *Twelfth Night,* and it has carried that meaning to this day.

Spelling Practice

Word Analysis

Fill in the missing letters to form **list words**. Then, write the completed **list words** on the lines.

1. ph__a__r__m__a__c__l__st   __pharmacist__
2. res__e__a__rch__e__r   __researcher__
3. lib__r__a__r__i__an   __librarian__
4. p__a__r__a__med__i__c   __paramedic__
5. rep__resen__t__a__t__ive   __representative__
6. ven__d__o__r   __vendor__
7. pr__o__p__r__i__e__or__r   __proprietor__
8. arb__i__t__r__a__t__o__r   __arbitrator__
9. a__n__n__ounce__r   __announcer__
10. man__i__c__u__r__i__st   __manicurist__

Vocabulary Development

Write the **list word** that matches each derivative given.

1. chemistry __chemist__   6. analyze __analyst__
2. electricity __electrician__   7. comedy __comedian__
3. therapy __therapist__   8. administrate __administrator__
4. technical __technician__   9. hygiene __hygienist__
5. carpentry __carpenter__   10. veterinary __veterinarian__

Word Application

Write a **list word** to complete each sentence.

1. The __pharmacist__ filled Grandpa's medicine prescription.
2. The __proprietor__ of the store listened to the customer's complaint.
3. Mr. Ortega is an __arbitrator__ who settles disputes between labor and management.
4. Fatimah is a __researcher__ trying to find new ways to recycle trash.
5. The __paramedic__ treated the injured people at the scene of the accident.
6. Kitty, our pet cat, was examined by Dr. Schwartz, the __veterinarian__
7. The __carpenter__ built new bookcases for the library.

130   Lesson 32 • Words from Occupations

LIST WORDS

vendor	arbitrator	administrator	paramedic
librarian	comedian	veterinarian	technician
therapist	hygienist	representative	manicurist
analyst	proprietor	announcer	carpenter
chemist	electrician	pharmacist	researcher

Puzzle
Use the **list words** to complete the crossword puzzle.

ACROSS
1. one who fixes fingernails
3. a specialist in physical or mental disorders
7. a doctor for animals
9. a person who installs electrical wiring
10. an expert in chemistry
12. a person who examines the details of something
13. one who assists a trained medical professional
14. a person who tells jokes and amusing stories
17. one who sells; a peddler
19. one who investigates in order to establish facts
20. one who manages or directs

DOWN
2. one who builds and repairs wooden things
4. one who dispenses medicines
5. a person skilled in the technicalities of a subject
6. one who speaks or acts for someone or something
8. one who introduces radio or television programs
11. a person who assists a dentist
15. one who settles disputes
16. one who owns and operates a business
18. a person who manages a library

Crossword answers:
MANICURIST, THERAPIST, VETERINARIAN, ELECTRICIAN, ANALYST, CHEMIST, PARAMEDIC, COMEDIAN, VENDOR, RESEARCHER, ADMINISTRATOR, TECHNICIAN, CARPENTER, PROPRIETOR, REPRESENTATIVE, ANNOUNCER, HYGIENIST, LIBRARIAN, ARBITRATOR, VENDOR

Lesson 32 • Words from Occupations   131

Proofreading
Use the proofreading marks to correct the mistakes in the article. Write the misspelled **list words** correctly on the lines.

A representative at a job-counseling center can give you a variety of helpful tips when you're looking for that first career job. For example, it doesn't matter whether you are looking for a position that requires a great deal of specialized training—such as a veterinarian or a chemist—or a job that requires less training, such as a manicurist or an announcer. Most Job Counselors will tell you to avoid ruling out excellent jobs on the basis of geographic preferences. You probably won't be at your first job forever and may need to apply for lots of jobs before getting one you really like.

Proofreading Marks
⟲ spelling mistake   / small letter
∨ add apostrophe   ⊙ add period

1. representative
2. veterinarian
3. chemist
4. manicurist
5. announcer

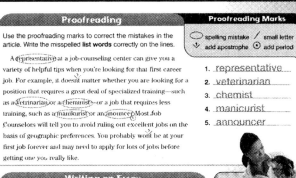

Writing an Essay
Imagine that you have graduated from school and are looking for your first position. What would you pursue? Choose an occupation from one of the **list words** and write a short informative essay on why this kind of job would interest you. Use as many of the other **list words** in your essay as you can. When finished, proofread and revise your essay, and then share it with the class.

BONUS WORDS

cholesterol	plaque	arthritis	stimulant	addiction
hypertension	enzyme	nicotine	depressant	tolerance

Write the **bonus word** that matches each definition clue.

1. a complete dependence on a substance — addiction
2. poisonous substance found in tobacco leaves — nicotine
3. organic compound that aids in digestion — enzyme
4. high blood pressure — hypertension
5. a waxy substance found in animal fats — cholesterol
6. the ability to resist the effects of stimuli — tolerance
7. lowers the rate of nervous or muscular activity — depressant
8. increases the rate of brain-cell activity — stimulant
9. inflammation of the joints — arthritis
10. sticky film on teeth — plaque

132   Lesson 32 • Words from Occupations

Puzzle Encourage students to print neatly and clearly as they write the letters in the puzzle boxes.

Spelling and Writing   *Page 132*
Proofreading Write the proofreading marks in this lesson on the board and ask volunteers to write a sentence illustrating the use of each one.

Writing an Essay Discuss what the jobs of administrators, therapists, arbitrators, paramedics, technicians, hygienists, analysts, and other occupations involve. Encourage students to research their chosen occupations further before writing their essays.

Bonus Words   *Page 132*
Health Discuss the **bonus words**, having students consult a dictionary or science book to define the words. This may be a good opportunity to invite a health-care professional to speak to the class about the realities and dangers of drug addictions.

Bonus Words Test
1. Susan has a high **tolerance** to pain.
2. Her **cholesterol** level was dangerously high.
3. The dentist scraped the **plaque** from Mandy's teeth.
4. **Arthritis** is a painful and crippling disease.
5. She was given a **depressant** before the operation.
6. High blood pressure may indicate **hypertension**.
7. **Nicotine** is used in some medicines.
8. Amylase is an **enzyme** that aids digestion.
9. Heavy dependence on any substance is an **addiction**.
10. A **stimulant** increases the activity of brain cells.

Final Test
1. My **manicurist** said that gelatin makes nails strong.
2. Nam asked the **pharmacist** for a flu remedy.
3. The audio **technician** repaired the sound system.
4. The **arbitrator** used finesse to end the strike.
5. The **chemist** studied the results of the experiment.
6. The speech **therapist** helped Cal overcome a lisp.
7. Lynn is the chief **administrator** of a large company.
8. We need an **analyst** to examine the problem.
9. My funny brother wants to be a **comedian**.
10. A **researcher** will investigate many different ideas.
11. A **representative** of the court explained the law.
12. Did the **carpenter** build an addition on your house?
13. The **paramedic** administered CPR to the victim.
14. The **librarian** oversees the collection and the staff.
15. The **hygienist** specializes in oral hygiene.
16. The **electrician** installed a new outlet.
17. The **vendor** sells his wares at flea markets.
18. Is Laura the owner and **proprietor** of a small cafe?
19. A retired athlete can become a sports **announcer**.
20. Dr. Lee, the **veterinarian**, operated on Liza's horse.

Words from Literature

Objective
To spell words related to literature

Pretest

1. Repetition of sounds in a phrase is **alliteration**.
2. Cartoonists often **caricature** politicians.
3. Music, art, and **literature** are bases of culture.
4. **Parody** aims to inject humor into serious issues.
5. "Every cloud has a silver lining" is a **proverb**.
6. In an **allegory**, a villain might be named Pride.
7. A **couplet** is two lines of rhymed poetry.
8. *Moby Dick* was written as a first-person **narrative**.
9. Using **personification** gives objects life.
10. Is that the author's **pseudonym** or her real name?
11. Her **analogy** helped me grasp the concept.
12. His **exposition** of the novel was informative.
13. Do you enjoy reading both **fiction** and nonfiction?
14. We studied the **poetic** works of Robert Frost.
15. The phrase *as hard as steel* is a **simile**.
16. List all your sources in your **bibliography**.
17. "It's on me" is an **idiom** meaning "I'll pay for it."
18. Is Alice Walker known for poetry as well as **prose**?
19. Please read the second **stanza** of the poem silently.
20. On what rhyme pattern is this **sonnet** based?

Spelling Strategy   *Page 133*

Discuss the spelling rule. Then, discuss and define the **list words**, relating each one to the field of literature. Have students give examples of similes, analogies, proverbs, and idioms. Point out that in addition to the form familiar to students, analogies may appear in less formal structures, such as "To save money in a bank is to have an umbrella for a rainy day."

Vocabulary Development Before the exercise, have students select a **list word** to match this definition: "figure of speech that endows nonhuman objects with human qualities." (*personification*)

Dictionary Skills To extend the activity, have students divide the words into syllables, checking their work in dictionaries.

Spelling Practice   *Pages 134–135*

Word Analysis To extend the activity, have students look up the etymologies of the **list words** or use what they have learned about Greek and Latin prefixes and roots to explain the meanings of such words as *parody* (Greek *para* [*beside*] + *oide* [*song, ode*]).

Word Application You may wish to have students make up and present to the class similar context-clue sentences for other pairs of **list words**.

TIP Like science and math, the field of literature and composition has a specific vocabulary of technical terms. Words like *fiction*, *sonnet*, and *prose* describe types of literature. Other words, including *simile*, *metaphor*, and *personification*, describe types of figurative language.

All of the **list words** are related to literature and composition. Knowing how to define and spell them will be of great benefit to you throughout your studies.

Vocabulary Development

Write the **list word** that matches each definition.

1. list of source materials for a nonfiction work — bibliography
2. art or writing that exaggerates someone's features — caricature
3. false "pen" name used by a writer — pseudonym
4. poem of fourteen lines with one central theme — sonnet
5. old, familiar saying that states a simple truth — proverb
6. repetition of the same beginning sound — alliteration
7. symbolic story that teaches or explains — allegory
8. all literature that is not poetry — prose
9. literature that explains true facts or events — exposition
10. two lines of poetry — couplet

Dictionary Skills

Write the **list words** in alphabetical order.

1. allegory
2. alliteration
3. analogy
4. bibliography
5. caricature
6. couplet
7. exposition
8. fiction
9. idiom
10. literature
11. narrative
12. parody
13. personification
14. poetic
15. prose
16. proverb
17. pseudonym
18. simile
19. sonnet
20. stanza

LIST WORDS

1. alliteration
2. caricature
3. literature
4. parody
5. proverb
6. allegory
7. couplet
8. narrative
9. personification
10. pseudonym
11. analogy
12. exposition
13. fiction
14. poetic
15. simile
16. bibliography
17. idiom
18. prose
19. stanza
20. sonnet

133

Spelling Practice

DID YOU KNOW? The word **allegory** comes from two words in Greek, one meaning "different" or "other" and the second meaning "to speak openly" or "to speak publicly." Allegories are stories with hidden meanings, or meanings different from the ones at the surface of the story.

Word Analysis

Write the **list word** that has the same base word or root as the word given.

1. verb — proverb
2. personally — personification
3. sonic — sonnet
4. narrate — narrative
5. analogous — analogy
6. stand — stanza
7. ode — parody
8. couple — couplet
9. similar — simile
10. expose — exposition

Word Application

Select a **list word** from the choices in parentheses to complete each sentence. Write the **list word** on the line.

1. _Poetic_ lines contain rhythm, meter, and often rhyme. (poetic, simile)
2. _Fiction_, a general class of literature, includes novels and plays. (exposition, fiction)
3. Through _analogy_, the relationships between words are analyzed. (allegory, analogy)
4. "The shifting sands of summer" is an example of _alliteration_. (simile, alliteration)
5. A section of a poem, usually four or more lines in length, is a _stanza_. (stanza, couplet)
6. An example of _personification_ is "My dog voted to sample my lunch." (personification, allegory)
7. Stories, nonfiction articles, and plays are _literature_. (exposition, literature)
8. The movie was a _parody_ of old science-fiction films. (bibliography, parody)
9. The _idiom_ "I heard it through the grapevine" means "I heard it through gossip." (idiom, proverb)
10. The cartoonist drew a _caricature_ of the president. (narrative, caricature)
11. Entries are alphabetized, by author's last name, in the _bibliography_. (exposition, bibliography)
12. All literature that is not poetry is called _prose_. (narrative, prose)
13. A story about a character overcoming a dragon named "Greed" is an _allegory_. (allegory, analogy)
14. John was thinking of writing a _narrative_ history of skateboarding. (pseudonym, narrative)

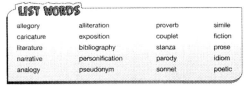

LIST WORDS

allegory	alliteration	proverb	simile
caricature	exposition	couplet	fiction
literature	bibliography	stanza	prose
narrative	personification	parody	idiom
analogy	pseudonym	sonnet	poetic

Puzzle

Each of the clues below is an example of a literary term defined by a **list word**. Write your answers in the spaces. Then, transfer the numbered letters to the spaces below to answer the question.

1. "A stitch in time saves nine."
   — Ben Franklin
   P R O V E R B
   1   15   11

2. "I shall be as secret as the grave."
   — Miguel de Cervantes
   S I M I L E
   10   9   12

3. "A little Madness in the Spring
   is wholesome even for the King."
   — Emily Dickinson
   C O U P L E T
   4   18

4. "Go put your creed into your deed,
   Nor speak with double tongue."
   — Ralph Waldo Emerson
   I D I O M
        5

5. "Hail, Columbia! happy land! Hail,
   ye heroes! heaven-born band!"
   — Joseph Hopkinson
   A L L I T E R A T I O N
            19   16   7

6. "Thy head is as full of quarrels as an
   egg is full of meat."
   — William Shakespeare
   A N A L O G Y
   20   6

7. "Hunger is the handmaid of genius."
   — Mark Twain
   P E R S O N I F I C A T I O N
   2   14   17

8. "A young man named Ernest Hemingway
   lives in Paris, writes for the *Transatlantic
   Review*, and has a brilliant future."
   — F. Scott Fitzgerald
   E X P O S I T I O N
   3   8   6   13

Question: Who was Mrs. Silence Dogwood?

Answer: one of many P S E U D O N Y M S used by
1 2 3 4 5 6 7 8 9 10

B E N   F R A N K L I N
11 12 13   14 15 16 17   18 19 20

↓

Proofreading

Use the proofreading marks to correct the mistakes in the article below. Then, write the misspelled **list words** correctly on the lines.

Like jazz, science fictoin is a a native 20th-century art form, and it boasts an impressive track record. Did you know that atom bombs, spaceships, cloning—even credit cards—all appeared in works of this genre before they became reality. Still, for many years, it was not considered "real literachure. Some authors in in the field even took to writing under a psudonym beçause there was such a lack of respect for the genre. Today, however, writers who use their imaginations to conceive what the future might be like, or to picture other worlds, are as respected as a poet who labors over his couplt or sonet.

Proofreading Marks
⌒ spelling mistake   ᵔ delete word
ᴠ⁄ᴠ add quotation mark
? add question mark

1. _____
2. _____
3. _____
4. _____
5. _____

Writing a Science-Fiction Story

Most science fiction is set in the future. It builds on today's established facts, stretching them to imagine new technologies or areas of exploration. Write a science-fiction story that includes a new invention, alien creature, and/or bold exploration. Use as many **list words** as you can. Proofread and revise your story, then share it with others.

BONUS WORDS

nebula	module	luminosity	planetarium	centrifugal force
inertia	relativity	celestial	momentum	encapsulate

Write a **bonus word** to complete each sentence.

1. You can view stars and constellations at a _____.
2. The planet Saturn is a _____ body surrounded by rings.
3. A _____ is a cloud of interstellar gas or dust.
4. According to Einstein's theory of _____, no energy can travel faster than light.
5. The tendency for a being at rest to stay at rest is called _____.
6. When something orbits around a central core, _____ pulls it outward.
7. To calculate the _____ of a moving object, physicists multiply mass times speed.
8. The moon's _____ is created by reflected light from the sun.
9. Astronauts _____ themselves in suits equipped with oxygen supplies.
10. In 1969, the first lunar _____ to be piloted by humans landed on the moon.

Puzzle You may wish to review the differences between *exposition/narrative* and *simile/analogy*.

Spelling and Writing   Page 136

Proofreading Use this sentence to review the proofreading marks: *Do you think its a a "fool's erand.*

Writing a Science-Fiction Story Discuss features of the science-fiction genre, inviting students to share their own knowledge. Talk about possible topics and characters. Urge students to prewrite, using note-taking, outlining, or story-mapping. When finished, have students read their stories aloud as part of a simulated radio broadcast entitled "Science-Fiction Theater."

Bonus Words   Page 136

Space Using science texts and encyclopedias, define and discuss the **bonus words**. Draw on students' own knowledge as well, and use athletic contexts for examples of *inertia* and *momentum*. As an example of *centrifugal force*, discuss how the body leans in the direction of the curve when taking a sharp turn on a bicycle. Amusement park rides provide other examples.

Bonus Words Test

1. The astronauts prepared to land the **module**.
2. **Centrifugal force** is at play on a roller coaster.
3. The **nebula** created a haze around the star cluster.
4. The moon's **luminosity** creates a soft, white light.
5. A **planetarium** was established on Nantucket.
6. We'll **encapsulate** our stories and bury them.
7. **Inertia** causes moving trains to jolt to a stop.
8. A brick has more **momentum** than a feather.
9. Einstein developed the theory of **relativity**.
10. Planets and stars are **celestial** bodies.

Final Test

1. *As silent as a faraway star* is a **simile**.
2. This **sonnet** was written by William Shakespeare.
3. Isak Dinesen is the **pseudonym** of Karen Blixen.
4. Is "All's well that ends well" a **proverb**?
5. A sonnet ends in a rhymed **couplet**.
6. A **caricature** contains humorous exaggeration.
7. The phrase *in the meantime* is an **idiom**.
8. Her **exposition** of the evidence convinced the jury.
9. How many sources are listed in your **bibliography**?
10. *Cold is to hot as up is to down* is an **analogy**.
11. In Dante's **allegory**, the fire was named Avarice.
12. *George the gentle giant* has **alliteration**.
13. "The Iliad" is a **narrative** poem about the Trojan War.
14. Elizabeth Barrett Browning wrote poetry and **prose**.
15. The **literature** of Mark Twain is highly respected.
16. The **fiction** of Charlotte Brontë includes *Jane Eyre*.
17. The revue was a **parody** of musical comedies.
18. T.S. Eliot's "The Wasteland" is a **poetic** masterpiece.
19. *The sun kissed the rose* shows **personification**.
20. Will you read the fourth **stanza** of the poem?

Words from Language Arts

Objective
To spell words related to language arts

Pretest

1. UFO is an **acronym** for *unidentified flying object*.
2. A **conjunction** is a word that joins words or phrases.
3. A **gerund** is a verb ending with *ing* used as a noun.
4. Which of these adjectives is **modifying** the noun?
5. That curved line is a **parenthesis**.
6. Karen forgot to put an **apostrophe** in *we'll*.
7. An **exclamation** that Joy uses often is *Wow!*
8. There are so many **grammar** rules to learn!
9. Did you look up the word in the **glossary**?
10. A **preposition** shows a word relationship.
11. The verb is found in the **predicate** of the sentence.
12. The **definition** of a word shows its meaning.
13. *Cent*, a penny, is a **homonym** for *scent*, the odor.
14. I will try to **paraphrase** what he said in a few words.
15. Does a **transitive** verb take a direct object?
16. What are the **capitalization** rules for proper nouns?
17. A sentence **fragment** is missing a subject or a verb.
18. *To run* is an **infinitive**.
19. The past **participle** form of *see* is *have seen*.
20. An **interrogative** sentence asks a question.

Spelling Strategy   *Page 137*

Discuss the spelling rule with the class. Then, elicit the definitions of the **list words** from students and have them provide examples of as many language arts terms as possible. If necessary, provide examples for unfamiliar terms. Discuss the spelling patterns in frequently misspelled words such as *grammar*, *parenthesis*, and *apostrophe*, and any other words that you think pose a particular spelling challenge.

Vocabulary Development You may wish to have students review the definitions of the **list words** before completing the activity.

Dictionary Skills Point out to students that when they alphabetize, they are forced to focus on the spelling pattern of each word.

Spelling Practice   *Pages 138–139*

Word Analysis You may wish to have students make up questions for additional **list words** to exchange with partners.

Word Application Encourage students to use context clues to help them determine the **list word**.

Word Application Have students use actual examples of each language arts term to determine the correct **list word**.

Words from Language Arts

You are probably familiar with many words that refer to English usage and language arts. Many of these common words, such as grammar, preposition, capitalization, and homonym are often misspelled.

All the **list words** name words from language arts. Study the spelling patterns of each word. Memorize and practice spelling them.

Vocabulary Development

Write the **list word** that matches each definition clue.

1. shows surprise — exclamation
2. an incomplete sentence — fragment
3. the mark used in a contraction — apostrophe
4. a word's meaning — definition
5. a joining word — conjunction
6. the use of upper-case letters — capitalization
7. changing the meaning of — modifying
8. word formed from beginnings of other words — acronym
9. verb used as a noun, ending in ing — gerund
10. verb that takes a direct object — transitive
11. curved line used for explanations — parenthesis

LIST WORDS

1. acronym
2. conjunction
3. gerund
4. modifying
5. parenthesis
6. apostrophe
7. exclamation
8. grammar
9. glossary
10. preposition
11. predicate
12. definition
13. homonym
14. paraphrase
15. transitive
16. capitalization
17. fragment
18. infinitive
19. participle
20. interrogative

Dictionary Skills

Write the **list words** that come between each pair of dictionary guide words. Write the words in alphabetical order.

gesture/interrupt
1. glossary
2. grammar
3. homonym
4. infinitive
5. interrogative

parade/press
6. paraphrase
7. parenthesis
8. participle
9. predicate
10. preposition

137

DID YOU KNOW?
The word **acronym** means "tip of the name," and is a word made up of the beginnings of other words. Although acronyms have been in use for a long time, the word *acronym* was made up in 1943, when many acronyms were created by the military during World War II.

Spelling Practice

Word Analysis

Write the **list words** to answer the following questions.

Which words contain the letter combination **nym**?
1. acronym   2. homonym

Which words contain the following double consonants?
3. rr interrogative   5. mm grammar
4. ss glossary

Word Application

Write a **list word** to complete each sentence.

1. A word's first definition listed in the dictionary is its most common meaning.
2. Adjectives are usually found modifying a noun or another adjective.
3. *Soar* is a homonym for the word *sore*.
4. A sentence fragment is a part of a sentence missing a subject or a predicate.
5. A comma and a conjunction can join two complete sentences.
6. A verb that ends with *ing* and is used as a noun is called a gerund.
7. The complete predicate includes the verb and all its modifiers in a sentence.
8. Look up the word in the glossary at the end of your reading textbook.
9. When you repeat something in different words, you paraphrase it.
10. *Radar* is an acronym for "radio detecting and ranging."
11. In the phrase "to the store," *store* is the object of the preposition.
12. Grammar is the study of English usage.
13. A transitive verb shows action and takes a direct object.

Word Application

Write the **list word** that matches each clue.

1. (— parenthesis
2. Wow! — exclamation
3. Mary's — apostrophe
4. to go — infinitive
5. Why? — interrogative
6. Washington — capitalization
7. in, for, at — preposition
8. The boy to the store — fragment

138   Lesson 34 • Words from Language Arts

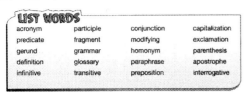

LIST WORDS

acronym	participle	conjunction	capitalization
predicate	fragment	modifying	exclamation
gerund	grammar	homonym	parenthesis
definition	glossary	paraphrase	apostrophe
infinitive	transitive	preposition	interrogative

Puzzle

Unscramble the **list words** to complete the crossword puzzle.

ACROSS
2. CMINELAOTAX
4. PPRAEAHASR
5. REPPIOISNTO
8. OAYLSGSSR
9. NERIOITEARGTV
12. MOMOYHN
14. EUDRGN
15. TAEFGRMN
16. PAIACIANTILZTO
17. FNEINIIITV

DOWN
1. FNDIINIETO
3. IAIERNSTTV
4. EIEPADRCT
5. RPETEASNHSI
6. DIYMOGFIN
7. RCNOMAY
8. RMRMAGA
10. POTESPAROH
11. ONCCJINUNTO
13. ACIERPTIPL

Lesson 34 • Words from Language Arts   139

Proofreading

Use the proofreading marks to correct mistakes in the article. Write the misspelled **list words** correctly on the lines.

The most beautiful thoughts in the world will move no one unless the writer who expresses them uses proper grammer.For example, an infinetive and a participe are both capable of conveying the idea of action in time,so it is important to observe the appropriate tense sequence when using them. Pay close attention to the rules of capitalisation and to the proper use of an apostrofe to indicate a contraction.

Also, providing a transition between ideas is something many writers neglect. You may be able to go from one idea to another, but your readers may need stepping stones—a conjunction such as and, but, or nevertheless.

Proofreading Marks

- ◯ spelling mistake
- ¶ new paragraph
- ⌃ add comma
- ⊙ add period

1. _grammar_
2. _infinitive_
3. _participle_
4. _capitalization_
5. _apostrophe_
6. _conjunction_

Writing Survey Questions and a Summary

How do students feel about the importance of using proper grammar? Write a questionnaire to conduct a survey to find out. Include at least six questions. Try to use **list words** in your questions. After proofreading and revising, conduct the survey in your classroom or among your friends. Tally and write a summary of the results, then present your findings.

Here's Bert. He's a gud Dog.

BONUS WORDS

intramural	participation	tournament	facility	skiing
volleyball	interscholastic	racquetball	lacrosse	rugby

Write the **bonus word** that matches each definition clue.

1. sport similar to handball played with a small racquet _racquetball_
2. among or between schools _interscholastic_
3. a form of football _rugby_
4. a series of games played to determine a championship _tournament_
5. a winter snow sport _skiing_
6. between teams of the same school _intramural_
7. a place or building where sporting events are held _facility_
8. playing an active role _participation_
9. sport in which two teams are separated by a net _volleyball_
10. team sport played with long-handled, pouched sticks _lacrosse_

140   Lesson 34 • Words from Language Arts

Puzzle Elicit from students that the exercise requires them to (1) unscramble each group of letters to make **list words** and (2) use the **list words** to solve the puzzle.

Spelling and Writing   *Page 140*

Proofreading Write the proofreading marks in this lesson on the board and ask volunteers to write a sentence illustrating the use of each one.

Writing Survey Questions and a Summary

Ask students what they think the important issues are in using good grammar. Write their ideas on the board. Encourage students to use these ideas as they prepare their questionnaires. Students may enjoy conducting an actual survey by distributing their questionnaires and tallying the responses.

Bonus Words   *Page 140*

Sports Discuss the sports-related **bonus words**, having students define each word. Encourage groups of students to select a sport and prepare a visual demonstration of how the sport is played.

Bonus Words Test

1. Tanya's soccer team won the **tournament**.
2. Jon went downhill **skiing** on Mount Monadnock.
3. **Lacrosse** is played with long, pouched rackets.
4. **Rugby** was the forerunner of American football.
5. The school encourages **participation** in team sports.
6. Rob served the **volleyball** over the net.
7. **Racquetball**, played with a racquet, is like handball.
8. I am on the school's **intramural** soccer team.
9. The **interscholastic** contest was held at DeKalb High.
10. The state college built a beautiful new sports **facility**.

Final Test

1. The present **participle** of *stay* is *staying*.
2. This sentence **fragment** needs a subject.
3. Always use **capitalization** to begin a sentence.
4. *Laughing*, used as a noun, is a **gerund**.
5. Set off the **parenthesis** with curved lines.
6. What does the **acronym** SCUBA stand for?
7. An **exclamation** shows strong feelings.
8. Always use proper **grammar** when you write.
9. Begin a prepositional phrase with a **preposition**.
10. An **apostrophe** is used to show possession.
11. A **glossary** is a list of special words and definitions.
12. Underline the simple **predicate** in that sentence.
13. Marcus found the **definition** in the dictionary.
14. It's absolutely impossible to **paraphrase** his words!
15. *Dye*, a tint, is a **homonym** for *die*, to expire.
16. The object of the **transitive** verb *draw* is *picture*.
17. Is the word *and* a **conjunction**?
18. *Happy* is the adjective **modifying** the word *girl*.
19. An **infinitive** may be preceded by an auxiliary verb.
20. *Who*, *what*, and *where* are **interrogative** pronouns.

Challenging Words

Objective
To spell difficult words with unusual spelling patterns

Pretest
1. Gina bought a **device** to improve her hearing.
2. The chemist gave us a tour of the **laboratory**.
3. The fallen tree was an **obstacle** for traffic.
4. The tools used by cavemen were quite **primitive**.
5. An emergency **situation** requires a quick response.
6. The loss of their passports created a **dilemma**.
7. Two years after their **marriage**, they had a son.
8. My job offers **opportunities** for travel.
9. The assembly **procedure** is done by steps.
10. We have found a **solution** to the problem.
11. Is this car's price **equivalent** to the other one's?
12. The commuter was used to **metropolitan** traffic.
13. Paul's father did not **oppose** his career plans.
14. What **scheme** lured Carol to the surprise party?
15. The kangaroo is **peculiar** to Australia.
16. Kathy helped to organize the photography **exhibit**.
17. I need a **miniature** frame for my class picture.
18. Alex always tries to have an **optimistic** attitude.
19. Did you read a few or **several** books last summer?
20. **Zinc** is a metal that is a chemical element.

Spelling Strategy   *Page 141*
Discuss the spelling rules about silent letters and the different spellings of the schwa sound. Stress the identical sounds of /ə/ in the examples given. Then, discuss and define the **list words**, having students analyze the spelling "trick" in each one. Have students use the **list words** in oral sentences.

Vocabulary Development Before starting this exercise, have students select a **list word** that matches this clue: "method." *(procedure)*

Dictionary Skills Have students tell which of the following words would not appear on a dictionary page containing the guide words *opposable* and *optometer*: *opportunities, oppose, optimistic.* (opportunities)

Spelling Practice   *Pages 142–143*
Word Analysis To review, have students determine the **list word** with the same root as *prohibit.* (exhibit)

Analogies Have students select a **list word** to complete this analogy: *Negative is to positive as discouraged is to _____.* (optimistic)

Word Application To extend the activity, have students make up similar context-clue sentences for the distractors and other **list words.** Call on volunteers to challenge their classmates for the correct answers.

86

Challenging Words

TIP Some words are especially difficult to spell because they contain silent letters, such as the h in scheme and the i in marriage. Other challenging words contain the schwa sound in unstressed syllables. Although /ə/ sounds like short u, or the sound of uh, it may be spelled with any of the vowels. Examples include the first o in oppose, the a and final e in equivalent, and the o and io in solution.

Vocabulary Development
Write the **list word** that matches each synonym or definition.

1. many — several
2. hopeful — optimistic
3. problem — dilemma
4. wedding — marriage
5. equal — equivalent
6. answer — solution
7. tiny — miniature
8. show — exhibit
9. contraption — device
10. strange or odd — peculiar
11. disagree with — oppose
12. urban — metropolitan
13. chances — opportunities
14. circumstances — situation
15. testing room — laboratory
16. simple; rough — primitive

LIST WORDS
1. device
2. laboratory
3. obstacle
4. primitive
5. situation
6. dilemma
7. marriage
8. opportunities
9. procedure
10. solution
11. equivalent
12. metropolitan
13. oppose
14. scheme
15. peculiar
16. exhibit
17. miniature
18. optimistic
19. several
20. zinc

Dictionary Skills
Write the **list word** that comes between each pair of dictionary guide words.

1. oat/open — obstacle
2. pebble/pray — peculiar
3. zebra/zoo — zinc
4. say/scratch — scheme
5. private/prune — procedure
6. mauve/mince — metropolitan
7. prime/probe — primitive
8. mace/meter — marriage
9. eon/ether — equivalent
10. opposite/option — optimistic

141

DID YOU KNOW?
One of the meanings of **miniature** is "a small painting." from the Latin root *miniare,* meaning "to paint with red lead." In the Middle Ages, manuscripts were created by hand, and paintings called miniatures were placed on the pages. Because of their small size, the word *miniature* now also means "a copy of reduced size."

Spelling Practice
Word Analysis
Write the **list word** containing the same root as the word given.

1. primates — primitive
2. dissolve — solution
3. unequal — equivalent
4. unopposed — oppose
5. obstruction — obstacle
6. inopportune — opportunities
7. pessimistic — optimistic
8. politician — metropolitan

Analogies
Write a **list word** to complete each analogy.

1. Kitchen is to chef as laboratory is to scientist
2. Gate is to go as obstacle is to stop.
3. Performance is to drama as exhibit is to photograph.
4. Gigantic is to redwood as miniature is to bonzai.
5. Wood is to oak as metal is to zinc
6. Memories are to past as opportunities are to future.
7. "Yes" is to agree as "no" is to oppose
8. Three is to few as eight is to several

Word Application
Select a **list word** from the choices in parentheses to complete each sentence. Write the **list word** on the line.

1. John was hopeful that his scheme would work. (optimistic, scheme)
2. The situation became chaotic during the reconstruction. (solution, situation)
3. The paint roller is a clever, time-saving device. (device, dilemma)
4. Many friendships have led to marriage. (dilemma, marriage)
5. Will you accept the terms or will you oppose them? (scheme, oppose)
6. His quirky sense of humor is very peculiar. (peculiar, procedure)
7. We used to have just one bunny, but now we have several. (situation, several)
8. The stone tools are very primitive, but they work. (primitive, metropolitan)
9. Many of metropolitan New York's buildings are giant, steel skyscrapers. (metropolitan, laboratory)
10. An optimistic person looks at the bright side of life. (obstacle, optimistic)

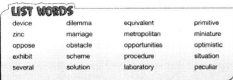

LIST WORDS

device	dilemma	equivalent	primitive
zinc	marriage	metropolitan	miniature
oppose	obstacle	opportunities	optimistic
exhibit	scheme	procedure	situation
several	solution	laboratory	peculiar

Classification

Write a **list word** to complete each series.

1. invention, machine, _device_
2. chances, occasions, _opportunities_
3. _miniature_, average, enormous
4. ancient, simple, _primitive_
5. hurdle, sand trap, _obstacle_
6. gallery, museum, _exhibit_
7. many, a lot, _several_
8. plot, plan, _scheme_
9. copper, aluminum, _zinc_
10. sum, remainder, _solution_

Puzzle
Use the **list words** to complete the crossword puzzle.

ACROSS
2. a place for experiments
7. chances
8. a metallic element
9. something that gets in the way
11. pertaining to a large city
13. position or circumstances
15. ancient; simple; rough
17. the answer to a problem
18. many; more than a few
19. a difficult problem

DOWN
1. union; wedding
3. to disagree or work against
4. a tool or machine
5. a method of doing something
6. strange; unusual; rare
10. tiny
12. equal
14. hopeful
16. a public show
18. a plan or system

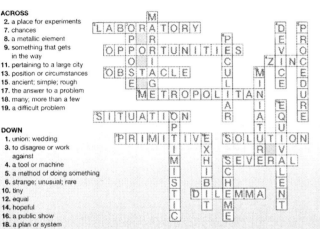

Lesson 35 • Challenging Words   143

Proofreading

Use the proofreading marks to correct the mistakes in the article. Write the misspelled **list words** correctly on the lines.

The first primitive computer, a calculating device called the Difference Engine, was designed in 1822 by the English mathematician, Charles babbage. In 1833, he started designing the Analytical Engine, a more sophisticated machine. The programming procedure for this invention was developed by Ada byron Lovelace. Opportunities for women were few in the early nineteenth century, but lovelace became an expert in several subjects, including math and foreign languages. She translated and added extensive notes to a paper on Babbage's Engines written in French by an Italian engineer. Her document was the best contemporary description of the engines.

Proofreading Marks
- ◯ spelling mistake
- ≡ capital letter
- ⟋ add space
- ⟋ delete word

1. _primitive_
2. _device_
3. _procedure_
4. _Opportunities_
5. _several_

Writing a Description

Thomas Edison changed the world when he invented the electric light bulb. Now it's your turn. Invent a machine. Draw a diagram of it, labeling its parts. Then, write a description of what it does, how it works, and why it will "change the world," using as many **list words** as you can. Proofread and revise your work, then display it. Discuss which inventions might really work.

 BONUS WORDS

hydraulic	implement	electromagnetic	combustion	conduit
fabricate	ventilator	mechanical	incinerator	lathe

Write a **bonus word** to complete each sentence.

1. Rubbish can be burned in the _incinerator_.
2. A _ventilator_ allows for the passage and circulation of fresh air.
3. _Implement_ is synonymous with *tool*.
4. A stapler is a _mechanical_ device for attaching sheets of paper together.
5. _Hydraulic_ brakes are operated by the movement and force of brake fluid.
6. A _lathe_ is a carpentry device that can turn square timbers into cylindrical poles.
7. In a _combustion_ engine, fuel mixes with oxygen and is then ignited to create energy.
8. Workers on that assembly line manufacture, or _fabricate_, automobiles.
9. Current passes through wire, creating _electromagnetic_ energy to run the motor.
10. The electric wires are encased in a protective _conduit_ to avoid fires and shocks.

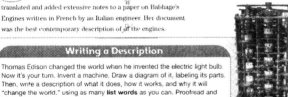

144   Lesson 35 • Challenging Words

Classification Review classification skills by having students select a **list word** to complete this series: *birthday, graduation, _____. (marriage)*

Puzzle Urge students to use as clues not only the definitions, but the number of spaces in each answer.

Spelling and Writing   *Page 144*

Proofreading To review the proofreading marks, use this sentence: *jackand jill eight lunch at at noon.*

Writing a Description You may wish to display examples of the cartoons of Rube Goldberg, who created fantastic, often hilarious "contraptions" to accomplish simple tasks. Then, urge students to think creatively about their own inventions. Provide time for students to present their drawings and descriptions.

Bonus Words   *Page 144*

Machines Define and discuss the **bonus words**, displaying diagrams of an electromagnet, a hydraulic device, and a combustion engine. Have students share their own knowledge of the **bonus words** and use them in oral sentences.

Bonus Words Test
1. Workers **fabricate** machines by assembling parts.
2. The plow is a farming **implement**.
3. The carpenter used a **lathe** to make the spindles.
4. The truck was equipped with a **hydraulic** lift.
5. Do not put aerosol cans in the **incinerator**.
6. A dishwasher is a **mechanical** aid that saves time.
7. The **conduit** insulates the wires to prevent accidents.
8. Your car is powered by a **combustion** engine.
9. The sewing machine has an **electromagnetic** motor.
10. The chemistry lab needs a good **ventilator**.

Final Test
1. **Zinc** becomes extremely malleable when heated.
2. Brianna had to maneuver past the **obstacle**.
3. A smoke alarm is an essential **device** at home.
4. I faced a **dilemma** as to which job to accept.
5. Do you prefer **primitive** art to modern art?
6. The detective knew who plotted the **scheme**.
7. We saw an **exhibit** of paintings by Picasso.
8. Will you lend me **several** of your carpentry tools?
9. The surgeon explained the operating **procedure**.
10. I was an usher at my cousin's **marriage** ceremony.
11. **Metropolitan** Detroit has many car factories.
12. Are they still **optimistic** that the dog will be found?
13. The ostrich is a **peculiar** bird in that it can't fly.
14. The new chemistry **laboratory** is ready to use.
15. How at ease she seems in every **situation**!
16. You'll have many **opportunities** after graduation.
17. She has a **miniature** of the Statue of Liberty.
18. A cup is **equivalent** to a half pint.
19. Kareem will **oppose** Earl in today's debate.
20. The principal offered a **solution** to the problem.

Lessons 31–35 · Review

Objective
To review spelling patterns of words from science, occupations, literature, and language arts; and challenging words

Spelling Strategy   *Page 145*
Tell students that in this lesson they will review the spelling words studied in Lessons 31–35. If needed, have students refer to the lessons' spelling rules to review the information on words from science, occupations, literature, and language arts; and challenging words.

Spelling Practice   *Pages 145–147*
Lesson 31 Have students identify what the following words have in common: *indigestion, fungus, friction, perennial,* and *turbine.* (*They are all words related to the study of science.*) Then, discuss the **list words.** Point out the additional write-on lines and encourage students to add two words from Lesson 31 that they found difficult, or assign words that were difficult for everyone. (Repeat this procedure for each lesson review that follows.)

Lesson 32 Have students tell what people with the following occupations do: *arbitrator, therapist, comedian, announcer,* and *representative.* Discuss the sufixes *er, or, ist, ian,* and *ive* that are added to make jwords mean "one who does something." Then, discuss the **list words.** To extend, have students make up riddle-type sentences for additional **list words.**

Lesson 33 Write on the board *metaphor, sonnet, prose, onomatopoeia,* and *fiction.* Have students tell which words refer to types of literature and which refer to figures of speech. Then, discuss the **list words.** Students should look closely at the spelling patterns of each word as they answer questions.

Lesson 34 Ask students to identify and define the grammar terms in this list: *gerund, exposition, modifying, predicate, transitive,* and *infinitive.* Discuss the meanings of the **list words** before students complete the activity.

Lesson 35 Have students spell these words: *situation, opportunities, procedure,* and *zinc.* Discuss the unexpected spellings of these challenging words, then apply the discussion to the **list words.** To extend, have students create crossword puzzle clues and grid spaces for the words they added to their lists.

Show What You Know   *Page 148*
Point out to students that this review will help them know if they have mastered the words in Lessons 31–35. Have a volunteer tell which word in the first item should be marked as incorrect. (*arbitrater*) When finished, have students write their misspelled words correctly.

Lessons 31–35 · Review

TIPS
- Knowing how to define and spell words from various fields of study is an advantage to any student. In this unit, you learned many words related to specific subjects. Practice using and spelling these words.
- Here are examples of words from science.
  physics,   psychology,   zoology
- Pay special attention to the endings of words that name occupations.
  librarian,   paramedic,   chemist
- The field of literature has its technical terms.
  caricature,   parody,   exposition
- Words from language arts are familiar but often difficult to spell.
  exclamation,   transitive,   capitalization
- Some words have unexpected spellings, with irregular spelling patterns. These words are especially difficult to spell because they do not follow normal spelling rules. Memorize and practice spelling these challenging words.
  device,   dilemma,   metropolitan,   several

Lesson 31

Write the **list word** that matches each definition.

List Words
allergy
neutron
vaccinate
larynx
voltage
diagnose
microorganism
satellite
iodine
respiration

1. the measure of electrical force ..... voltage
2. inhaling and exhaling air ..... respiration
3. a hypersensitivity to a specific substance ..... allergy
4. muscle and cartilage in the throat ..... larynx
5. to inject a serum in an attempt to ward off a disease ..... vaccinate
6. to decide the nature of a disease after careful examination ..... diagnose
7. a man-made object rocketed into orbit around the Earth ..... satellite
8. an uncharged elementary particle of an atom with the same mass as a proton ..... neutron
9. a chemical element used as an antiseptic ..... iodine
10. any microscopic animal or vegetable organism ..... microorganism

145

Lesson 32

Write a **list word** to complete each sentence.

List Words
hygienist
proprietor
vendor
analyst
comedian
technician
representative
pharmacist
administrator
veterinarian

1. If you are fascinated by radios, televisions, and computers, be an electronics ..... technician
2. If people talk to you about money problems, you are a financial ..... analyst
3. If you purchase a store, you are the ..... proprietor
4. If you clean people's teeth, you are a dental ..... hygienist
5. If you practice medicine dealing with diseases in animals, you are a ..... veterinarian
6. If you stand on a corner selling trinkets, you are a street ..... vendor
7. To speak for the voters, be a state ..... representative
8. If you can make people laugh, be a ..... comedian
9. To share medical expertise about prescriptions, be a ..... pharmacist
10. To manage or direct a business or office, be an ..... administrator

Lesson 33

Write **list words** to answer the questions.

List Words
alliteration
allegory
couplet
narrative
bibliography
pseudonym
poetic
simile
personification
idiom

Which words contain the vowel combination **io**?
1. alliteration   3. bibliography
2. personification   4. idiom

Which words contain the following vowel combinations?
5. oe poetic   7. eu pseudonym
6. ou couplet

Which word contains the double consonant **rr**?
8. narrative

Which word begins with the Latin root **sim** meaning "alike"?
9. simile

Which word contains letters in the same order as these four words: all, leg, ego, gory?
10. allegory

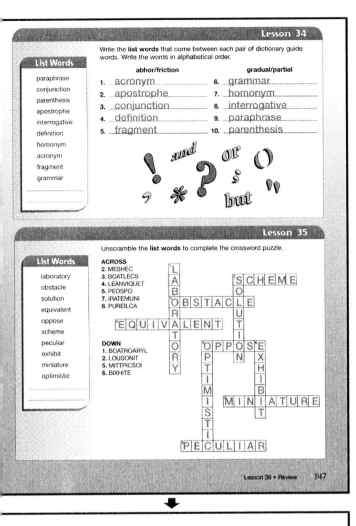

Lesson 34

List Words

paraphrase
conjunction
parenthesis
apostrophe
interrogative
definition
homonym
acronym
fragment
grammar

Write the **list words** that come between each pair of dictionary guide words. Write the words in alphabetical order.

abhor/friction
1. acronym
2. apostrophe
3. conjunction
4. definition
5. fragment

gradual/partial
6. grammar
7. homonym
8. interrogative
9. paraphrase
10. parenthesis

Lesson 35

List Words

laboratory
obstacle
solution
equivalent
oppose
scheme
peculiar
exhibit
miniature
optimistic

Unscramble the **list words** to complete the crossword puzzle.

ACROSS
2. MESHEC
3. BOATLECS
4. LEANVIQUET
5. PEOSPO
7. IRATEMUNI
8. PUREILCA

DOWN
1. BOATROARYL
2. LOUSONIT
5. MITTPICSOI
6. BIXHITE

Crossword answers: SCHEME, OBSTACLE, EQUIVALENT, OPPOSE, MINIATURE, PECULIAR, LABORATORY, OPTIMISTIC

Lesson 36 • Review   147

Show What You Know

Lessons 31—35 • Review

One word is misspelled in each set of **list words**. Fill in the circle next to the **list word** that is spelled incorrectly.

#				
1.	○ pseudonym	○ apostrophe	● arbitrater	○ allergy
2.	● exclamaition	○ vendor	○ indigestion	○ analogy
3.	○ paramedic	● grammer	○ exposition	○ physics
4.	● nutron	○ fiction	○ veterinarian	○ glossary
5.	○ predicate	● vacinate	○ preposition	○ chemist
6.	○ homonym	○ comedian	○ metropolitan	● fungas
7.	● tecknician	○ larynx	○ paraphrase	○ transitive
8.	● pyschology	○ fragment	○ representative	○ zinc
9.	○ several	○ announcer	● transmittor	○ optimistic
10.	○ pharmacist	● infinnitive	○ capitalization	○ voltage
11.	● participal	○ diagnose	○ hygienist	○ miniature
12.	○ peculiar	○ exhibit	● microrganism	○ analyst
13.	○ satellite	○ manicurist	● interogative	○ scheme
14.	○ poetic	○ definition	○ transfusion	● carpentor
15.	○ oppose	○ friction	○ researcher	● similie
16.	○ situation	● equivlent	○ alliteration	○ iodine
17.	○ perennial	○ caricature	● opportunitites	○ idiom
18.	○ literature	● proze	○ respiration	○ marriage
19.	○ stanza	○ turbine	● bibiliography	○ parody
20.	● sonet	○ proverb	○ procedure	○ zoology
21.	○ solution	○ acronym	● administrater	○ allegory
22.	○ primitive	● librarien	○ conjunction	○ obstacle
23.	○ therapist	○ couplet	● labrotory	○ gerund
24.	○ dilemma	● proprieter	○ modifying	○ narrative
25.	○ parenthesis	○ electrician	● personifcation	○ device

148   Lesson 36 • Review

Final Test

1. Do you have an **allergy** to any type of medication?
2. Mr. Wan is a high school **administrator**.
3. Point out examples of **alliteration** in that poem.
4. NASA is an example of an **acronym**.
5. The chemistry students had class in the **laboratory**.
6. A **neutron** is a fundamental particle of matter.
7. José is the **proprietor** of a clothing store.
8. An **allegory** is a story that teaches a lesson.
9. A **conjunction**, like *but*, joins other words.
10. Consider the setback an **obstacle** you can overcome.
11. The doctor will **vaccinate** the baby against the mumps.
12. Which **vendor** is selling popcorn?
13. The last **couplet** of your sonnet should rhyme.
14. Use a **parenthesis** instead of a bracket.
15. There is more than one **solution** to his problem.
16. She lost her voice because of an infected **larynx**.
17. The **veterinarian** examined the sick calf.
18. Bo's **narrative** about the trip was informative.
19. Add an **apostrophe** and an *s* to the noun to show possession.
20. Twelve inches is the **equivalent** of one foot.
21. High **voltage** is needed to transmit electrical power.
22. That **comedian** will star in a funny new movie.
23. **Personification** brings inanimate objects to life.
24. English **grammar** has many rules to study.
25. The people will **oppose** the law to raise taxes.
26. Dr. Kent could not **diagnose** the illness.
27. The lab **technician** prepared slides for the biologist.
28. Mark Twain is Samuel Clemens' **pseudonym**.
29. Lydia looked up the **definition** of the word *enigma*.
30. That's a get-rich **scheme** if I ever heard one!
31. A spore is a microscopic **microorganism**.
32. An ambassador is a nation's **representative**.
33. **Poetic** language is rich in imagery.
34. *Deer* is a **homonym** for *dear*.
35. Ruth liked the **peculiar** hat with the big bow.
36. A **satellite** has been launched to photograph Mars.
37. The **pharmacist** suggested a cold remedy.
38. A comparison using *like* or *as* is a **simile**.
39. **Paraphrase** these thoughts in brief sentences.
40. We saw the toy train **exhibit** at the museum.
41. The nurse applied **iodine** to my scrapes and cuts.
42. Did the **hygienist** insist that you floss every day?
43. List your reference sources in the **bibliography**.
44. A **fragment** doesn't express a complete thought.
45. The **miniature** barn is next to the model train.
46. Bronchitis or pneumonia can hinder **respiration**.
47. What training is required to be a computer **analyst**?
48. *Take a test* is an example of a common **idiom**.
49. An **interrogative** sentence asks a question.
50. Leroy said it would rain but I was **optimistic**.

Review Word List

Lesson 6

Lesson 1
affidavit
appetite
commemorate
dominate
guardian
installation
resurrect
saturate
tendency
voluntary

Lesson 2
accidental
artificial
colossal
criminal
experimental
hysterical
logical
perpetual
revival
tropical

Lesson 3
acceptance
assistance
cancellation
depression
immense
immigration
necessity
possession
successive
summon

Lesson 4
ancestors
angular
conqueror
glacier
investor
murmur
particular
perpendicular
reflector
vinegar

Lesson 5
admitting
conferred
deferred
handicapped
incurred
occasionally
occurring
omitted
preferred
unforgettable

Lesson 12

Lesson 7
centimeter
decade
deciliter
duplex
kilowatt
milligram
monologue
myriad
semiannual
semiprecious

Lesson 8
antecedent
anterior
epidermis
epilogue
epistle
epitaph
preamble
prejudice
premier
procession

Lesson 9
abhor
absurd
affiliate
affirmative
aggravate
aggressive
annihilate
announcement
antihistamine
antisocial

Lesson 10
benefactor
benign
collaborate
colleague
collision
commencement
contradict
contrary
contrast
eulogy

Lesson 11
deception
decompose
deplete
descendant
dissolve
distort
malevolent
malice
metamorphosis
metaphor

Review Word List

Lesson 18

Lesson 13
aquarium
dissimilar
hospitalize
hostage
hospice
lateral
liberate
mortgage
quadrilateral
simultaneous

Lesson 16
conspiracy
disrespect
exclude
inspiration
maternal
matrimony
perspective
seclusion
spectacle
speculate

Lesson 14
applicable
destruction
duplicate
independently
inexplicable
instruction
interrupt
structural
suspended
suspense

Lesson 17
anxiety
controversial
courtesy
cruel
customary
decision
defenseless
especially
excitable
fallacy

Lesson 15
advocate
concentric
determine
eccentric
exterminate
terrain
territory
vague
variation
various

Lesson 24

Lesson 19
coherent
coincide
coordinate
symbolize
symmetry
symphonic
symptom
synagogue
synchronize
syntax

Lesson 22
aeronautics
analysis
archaic
architect
archive
criticize
democracy
economical
metropolis
theology

Lesson 20
anemia
anesthesia
anonymous
immaculate
immobilize
impersonate
inaccurate
incognito
negligent
nonexistent

Lesson 23
biological
chronic
dialogue
enthusiasm
geographical
parable
parallel
paralysis
pharmacy
thermostat

Lesson 21
auditor
documentary
exhilarated
exorbitant
juvenile
molecular
optician
opulent
ordinance
quarantine

Review Word List

Lesson 30

Lesson 25
apologize
competent
compromise
dependent
economize
enterprise
itemize
jubilant
observant
pleasant

Lesson 28
bouillon
croquet
etiquette
marionette
opaque
porcelain
racquet
soufflé
souvenir
surgeon

Lesson 26
availability
capability
eligibility
flexibility
generosity
hospitality
individuality
personality
similarity
visibility

Lesson 29
accessory
disastrous
fascinate
fulfilled
scarcity
schedules
tranquil
vulnerable
wharf
yeast

Lesson 27
complimentary
extraordinary
infirmary
legendary
mandatory
monetary
necessary
primary
sanctuary
satisfactory

Lesson 36

Lesson 31
allergy
diagnose
iodine
larynx
microorganism
neutron
respiration
satellite
vaccinate
voltage

Lesson 34
acronym
apostrophe
conjunction
definition
fragment
grammar
homonym
interrogative
paraphrase
parenthesis

Lesson 32
administrator
analyst
comedian
hygienist
pharmacist
proprietor
representative
technician
vendor
veterinarian

Lesson 35
equivalent
exhibit
laboratory
miniature
obstacle
oppose
optimistic
peculiar
scheme
solution

Lesson 33
allegory
alliteration
bibliography
couplet
idiom
narrative
personification
poetic
pseudonym
simile

Name _____

Read each set of words. Fill in the circle next to the word that is spelled correctly.

1. ⓐ saturrate ⓒ satureate
   ⓑ saturate ⓓ satturate

2. ⓐ colosal ⓒ collosal
   ⓑ callosal ⓓ colossal

3. ⓐ summen ⓒ sumen
   ⓑ sommon ⓓ summon

4. ⓐ handicapped ⓒ handycapped
   ⓑ handycaped ⓓ handicaped

5. ⓐ vinerger ⓒ vinager
   ⓑ vinargar ⓓ vinegar

6. ⓐ cansellation ⓒ cancelation
   ⓑ canselation ⓓ cancellation

7. ⓐ lodgicle ⓒ logical
   ⓑ logicle ⓓ lodgical

8. ⓐ murmur ⓒ murmar
   ⓑ murmor ⓓ murmer

9. ⓐ gaurdian ⓒ gardian
   ⓑ guardian ⓓ gaurdean

10. ⓐ ocurring ⓒ occurring
    ⓑ ocuring ⓓ occuring

11. ⓐ resurect ⓒ ressurect
    ⓑ resurrect ⓓ ressurrect

12. ⓐ reflecter ⓒ riflector
    ⓑ riflecter ⓓ reflector

13. ⓐ revival ⓒ rivivle
    ⓑ rivival ⓓ revivle

Name _____

Read each set of words. Fill in the circle next to the word that is spelled correctly.

14. (a) ocassionally   (c) occasionaly
    (b) occasionally   (d) ocassionaly

15. (a) voluntary   (c) volluntary
    (b) voluntery   (d) volluntery

16. (a) successive   (c) sucesive
    (b) sucessive   (d) succesive

17. (a) ancesters   (c) ansesters
    (b) ansestors   (d) ancestors

18. (a) hystarical   (c) histerical
    (b) hysterical   (d) histarical

19. (a) preferred   (c) prefered
    (b) perferred   (d) perfered

20. (a) unforgettible   (c) unforgetible
    (b) unforgetable   (d) unforgettable

21. (a) apetite   (c) appitite
    (b) apitite   (d) appetite

22. (a) acceptence   (c) acceptance
    (b) aceptance   (d) aceptence

23. (a) particular   (c) particulor
    (b) particuler   (d) perticuler

24. (a) necessity   (c) neccessity
    (b) neccesity   (d) necesity

25. (a) traupical   (c) tropical
    (b) traupicle   (d) tropicle

Name _____

Read each set of phrases. Fill in the circle next to the phrase with an underlined word that is spelled correctly.

1. (a) the unexpected <u>announcement</u>   (c) a formal <u>announcment</u>
   (b) his wedding <u>anouncement</u>   (d) an official <u>anowncement</u>

2. (a) <u>decilliter</u> of acid   (c) <u>decileter</u> of fluid
   (b) <u>deciliter</u> of water   (d) <u>decilitter</u> of gasoline

3. (a) <u>disolve</u> in water   (c) will easily <u>dissolve</u>
   (b) add fluid to <u>dessolve</u>   (d) will quickly <u>desolve</u>

4. (a) <u>dipleet</u> the rations   (c) <u>deplete</u> the stock
   (b) <u>diplete</u> the supplies   (d) <u>depleet</u> the reserves

5. (a) your <u>absurde</u> assumption   (c) totally <u>abserd</u>
   (b) an <u>abserde</u> suggestion   (d) an <u>absurd</u> accusation

6. (a) the <u>anterior</u> claws   (c) an <u>anteriar</u> chamber
   (b) <u>antirier</u> or posterior   (d) the <u>anterier</u> section

7. (a) <u>antysocial</u> actions   (c) <u>antisotial</u> nature
   (b) <u>antysotial</u> behavior   (d) <u>antisocial</u> personality

8. (a) <u>milligram</u> of gold   (c) <u>milligrame</u> of medicine
   (b) <u>miligramm</u> of powder   (d) <u>miligram</u> of metal

9. (a) his <u>aggresive</u> disposition   (c) <u>agressive</u> language
   (b) her <u>aggressive</u> behavior   (d) those <u>agresive</u> gestures

10. (a) eight-room <u>duplecks</u>   (c) furnished <u>duplexe</u>
    (b) inexpensive <u>doplex</u>   (d) the empty <u>duplex</u> apartment

11. (a) <u>agravate</u> his ulcer   (c) <u>aggravvate</u> babies' skin
    (b) to <u>aggravate</u> my rash   (d) <u>aggrivate</u> and disrupt

12. (a) his famous <u>monologue</u>   (c) her boring <u>monalogue</u>
    (b) her entertaining <u>monnolog</u>   (d) your humorous <u>monalog</u>

13. (a) a wedding <u>proccession</u>   (c) the graduation <u>proccesion</u>
    (b) the honorary <u>procesion</u>   (d) a funeral <u>procession</u>

Name _____

Read each set of phrases. Fill in the circle next to the phrase with an underlined word that is spelled correctly.

14. (a) the delicate epidermis   (c) a sensitive epidermise
    (b) the thick eppidermis   (d) a snake's scaly epadermis

15. (a) the student's benefactar   (c) the elderly benafactor
    (b) the generous benefactor   (d) the unknown benefacter

16. (a) crime and diception   (c) diceiption and lies
    (b) your evil deceiption   (d) greed and deception

17. (a) miriad of talents   (c) myriad of excuses
    (b) miryad of cultures   (d) miried of performers

18. (a) the colision damage   (c) his colission report
    (b) an unavoidable collission   (d) the collision site

19. (a) the proud desendant   (c) an English decendent
    (b) an unknown descendent   (d) a proven descendant

20. (a) contredict the report   (c) contradict her testimony
    (b) contradick the statement   (d) contridick her findings

21. (a) antecedent behavior   (c) the antecedant event
    (b) anticident conditions   (d) antacedent factors

22. (a) contrarey to the truth   (c) contrary to rumors
    (b) contrery to popular belief   (d) his contrerry nature

23. (a) the mallevolent dictator   (c) the maleviolent character
    (b) the malevolent kidnapper   (d) his malevolant captor

24. (a) her cruel prejudiss   (c) his unfair prejudice
    (b) predjudice and greed   (d) their unwarranted predjudiss

25. (a) her professional coleague   (c) an active collegue
    (b) an affable colegue   (d) their mutual colleague

Name _____

Read each sentence and set of words. Fill in the circle next to the word that is spelled correctly to complete the sentence.

1. Dishonesty and _____ are abhorrent characteristics.
   - ⓐ desrespect
   - ⓑ disrispect
   - ⓒ disrespect
   - ⓓ desrispect

2. The executive jogs daily as a way to reduce _____ .
   - ⓐ anxiety
   - ⓑ anksiety
   - ⓒ angziety
   - ⓓ anxiaty

3. Censorship is a _____ issue that is often debated.
   - ⓐ contravercial
   - ⓑ controvercial
   - ⓒ contraversial
   - ⓓ controversial

4. Before making that _____ , the President consulted his advisors.
   - ⓐ decision
   - ⓑ dicision
   - ⓒ desicion
   - ⓓ disicion

5. The bride and groom prepared for _____ .
   - ⓐ matrimoney
   - ⓑ matramony
   - ⓒ matramoney
   - ⓓ matrimony

6. The physician wanted to _____ the accident victim.
   - ⓐ hospitalize
   - ⓑ hospitelise
   - ⓒ hospatalize
   - ⓓ hospatalise

7. While in _____ , that poet wrote his most poignant ballads.
   - ⓐ siclusion
   - ⓑ seclusion
   - ⓒ seclussion
   - ⓓ siclussion

8. The fraternal twins were _____ in appearance.
   - ⓐ disimilar
   - ⓑ dissimilar
   - ⓒ disimillar
   - ⓓ dissimiler

9. A defensive player intercepted the quarterback's _____ pass.
   - ⓐ lateral
   - ⓑ laterel
   - ⓒ latarel
   - ⓓ lataral

10. Our _____ payment is due soon.
   - ⓐ morgage
   - ⓑ morgaje
   - ⓒ moregage
   - ⓓ mortgage

Name _____

Read each sentence and set of words. Fill in the circle next to the word that is spelled correctly to complete the sentence.

11. Professionals were hired to _____ the termites.
   ⓐ extermanate   ⓒ exturminate
   ⓑ eksterminate   ⓓ exterminate

12. The governor assessed the cyclone's _____.
   ⓐ distrucsion   ⓒ destruction
   ⓑ destrucsion   ⓓ distruction

13. Registration for first-aid _____ will take place on Tuesday.
   ⓐ instrucsion   ⓒ enstrucsion
   ⓑ instruction   ⓓ enstruction

14. A throat culture will _____ whether harmful bacteria is present.
   ⓐ dettermine   ⓒ dittermine
   ⓑ ditermine   ⓓ determine

15. The ambitious student researched the topic _____.
   ⓐ independently   ⓒ independantly
   ⓑ indipendently   ⓓ indipendantly

16. Each design consists of seven _____ circles.
   ⓐ concentric   ⓒ consenteric
   ⓑ concenteric   ⓓ consentric

17. Please do not _____ me.
   ⓐ interupt   ⓒ interrup
   ⓑ interrupt   ⓓ inturupt

18. Your answers were too _____.
   ⓐ vague   ⓒ vage
   ⓑ vaeg   ⓓ vagau

19. The circus was quite a _____.
   ⓐ spectacel   ⓒ spektakle
   ⓑ specktacle   ⓓ spectacle

20. He did _____ well on the test.
   ⓐ expecially   ⓒ especially
   ⓑ especialy   ⓓ especailly

Name _____

Review Test (Side A)

Read each set of words. Fill in the circle next to the word that is spelled correctly.

1. ⓐ imobilize   © immobilize
   ⓑ imobelize   ⓓ immobilise

2. ⓐ moleculer   © moleccular
   ⓑ mollecular   ⓓ molecular

3. ⓐ coherrent   © cohirent
   ⓑ cohirrent   ⓓ coherent

4. ⓐ parralel   © parallel
   ⓑ parlel   ⓓ paralelle

5. ⓐ economicle   © economical
   ⓑ economicall   ⓓ economecal

6. ⓐ oppulent   © opullent
   ⓑ opulent   ⓓ opulant

7. ⓐ democracy   © demmocracy
   ⓑ dimocracy   ⓓ democcracy

8. ⓐ symmetry   © symetry
   ⓑ simtry   ⓓ simmetry

9. ⓐ anestesia   © annesthesia
   ⓑ anisthisia   ⓓ anesthesia

10. ⓐ metropolous © metropollis
    ⓑ mettropolis ⓓ metropolis

11. ⓐ aeranautics © aeronautics
    ⓑ aironautics ⓓ aerenautics

12. ⓐ inaccurate   © inacurrate
    ⓑ innacurate   ⓓ innacurat

13. ⓐ coincide   © coinside
    ⓑ coneside   ⓓ coincid

Review Test (Side B)

Read each set of words. Fill in the circle next to the word that is spelled correctly.

14. ⓐ symbolise   ⓒ symbulise
    ⓑ simbolise   ⓓ symbolize

15. ⓐ thermastat   ⓒ thermstat
    ⓑ thermustat   ⓓ thermostat

16. ⓐ criticize   ⓒ critisize
    ⓑ critecize   ⓓ critticise

17. ⓐ negligient   ⓒ negligent
    ⓑ neglegent   ⓓ negeligent

18. ⓐ enthuisiasm   ⓒ enthusasm
    ⓑ enthusiasm   ⓓ inthusiasm

19. ⓐ coordinate   ⓒ coordnate
    ⓑ cordinate   ⓓ coordinat

20. ⓐ exhilerated   ⓒ exhilarated
    ⓑ exhilareted   ⓓ exilarated

21. ⓐ documentary   ⓒ documentery
    ⓑ documentarry   ⓓ documentry

22. ⓐ nonexistent   ⓒ nonexistant
    ⓑ nonexistint   ⓓ nonnexistant

23. ⓐ dielog   ⓒ dialoge
    ⓑ dialogue   ⓓ diulogue

24. ⓐ exorbitent   ⓒ exorbetant
    ⓑ exxorbitant   ⓓ exorbitant

25. ⓐ parrable   ⓒ parble
    ⓑ parable   ⓓ parabble

Name _____

Review Test (Side A)

Read each set of phrases. Fill in the circle next to the phrase with an underlined word that is spelled correctly.

1. ⓐ the gymnast's flexibility   ⓒ extreme flexability
   ⓑ increased flexibillity   ⓓ scheduling flexxibility

2. ⓐ a satisfactery job   ⓒ satasfactory food
   ⓑ the satisfactery apartment   ⓓ their satisfactory performance

3. ⓐ a jubilent winner   ⓒ the jubilant recipient
   ⓑ jubelant cheers   ⓓ those jubilante fans

4. ⓐ a dexterous surgean   ⓒ an expensive surgan
   ⓑ the charitable surgeon   ⓓ the heart sergeon

5. ⓐ opague windows   ⓒ the opake paint
   ⓑ an opaque material   ⓓ his opaqe sunglasses

6. ⓐ to coordinate schedules   ⓒ different scedules
   ⓑ their busy skedules   ⓓ crazy scheduls

7. ⓐ complementary food   ⓒ her complementery mug
   ⓑ this complimentarry shirt   ⓓ some complimentary tickets

8. ⓐ the complicated accesory   ⓒ an attractive accessory
   ⓑ the useless accessery   ⓓ a ridiculous acessory

9. ⓐ unmistakable simmilarity   ⓒ note the similarity
   ⓑ uncanny similarrity   ⓓ very little simillarity

10. ⓐ a dependant pet   ⓒ the dependent gosling
    ⓑ deependant kittens   ⓓ their deppendent children

11. ⓐ a disasterous accident   ⓒ disastrus test results
    ⓑ the dizastrous trip   ⓓ with disastrous effects

12. ⓐ the competant scientists   ⓒ a compitant employee
    ⓑ a competent professor   ⓓ with compettent skill

13. ⓐ an extrordinary writer   ⓒ her extraordnary art
    ⓑ the extrordenary museum   ⓓ with extraordinary talent

Name _____

Read each set of phrases. Fill in the circle next to the phrase with an underlined word that is spelled correctly.

14. ⓐ an observant scientist ⓒ observent birdwatchers
    ⓑ the observint sleuth ⓓ remaining obzervant

15. ⓐ one's own individuality ⓒ her own indaviduality
    ⓑ having individuelity ⓓ without any indeviduality

16. ⓐ playing crocquet ⓒ a croqet ball
    ⓑ his croquet mallet ⓓ a crocquette lawn

17. ⓐ her porcelan vase ⓒ a porcelain doll
    ⓑ porselain tiles ⓓ smooth as porcelin

18. ⓐ with legandary stories ⓒ a legendery king
    ⓑ his leggendary adventures ⓓ a legendary athlete

19. ⓐ an old infirmery ⓒ visited the infermary
    ⓑ outside the infirmerry ⓓ the college infirmary

20. ⓐ the benefactor's generosity ⓒ his kind generousity
    ⓑ appreciated the gennerosity ⓓ generrosity of others

21. ⓐ a scarcity of food ⓒ scarsity of supplies
    ⓑ the unfortunate scarecity ⓓ an unavoidable scaresity

22. ⓐ econamize their time ⓒ greatly ecanomise
    ⓑ if we economise ⓓ need to economize

23. ⓐ the boss's aveilability ⓒ availabylity of resources
    ⓑ its apparent avalability ⓓ lack of availability

24. ⓐ courses in ettiquete ⓒ proper etiquette
    ⓑ having good etiquete ⓓ to teach ettiquet

25. ⓐ those tranquill mountains ⓒ the tranquel colors
    ⓑ a tranquil setting ⓓ trenquil resorts

Name _____

Read each sentence and set of words. Fill in the circle next to the word that is spelled correctly to complete the sentence.

1. The _____ of the shop is a kind old man.
   - ⓐ proprieter
   - ⓒ propriotor
   - ⓑ proprietor
   - ⓓ proprioter

2. What is an _____ sentence?
   - ⓐ interrogative
   - ⓒ interogative
   - ⓑ interoggative
   - ⓓ interogativ

3. The famous museum hosts a special _____ .
   - ⓐ exibit
   - ⓒ exhibbit
   - ⓑ exhibit
   - ⓓ exibitt

4. Many authors write under a _____ .
   - ⓐ psuedonym
   - ⓒ sudonym
   - ⓑ psudonym
   - ⓓ pseudonym

5. Serena completed the _____ of four years of college.
   - ⓐ equivalant
   - ⓒ equivelant
   - ⓑ equivelent
   - ⓓ equivalent

6. I must take my sick dog to the _____ .
   - ⓐ veteranarian
   - ⓒ vetterinarian
   - ⓑ veterinarian
   - ⓓ vetrinarian

7. *Sputnik* was an early Russian _____ .
   - ⓐ satelite
   - ⓒ sattelite
   - ⓑ satellite
   - ⓓ sattleite

8. His long-winded _____ made us all very tired.
   - ⓐ narrative
   - ⓒ narative
   - ⓑ nartive
   - ⓓ narrativ

9. This invisible _____ lives in the water.
   - ⓐ microorganism
   - ⓒ microrganism
   - ⓑ microorgnism
   - ⓓ microorgansm

10. The famous _____ was in a popular movie.
    - ⓐ comedien
    - ⓒ comedianne
    - ⓑ commedian
    - ⓓ comedian

Name _____

Read each sentence and set of words. Fill in the circle next to the word that is spelled correctly to complete the sentence.

11. Where is that _____ odor coming from?
    ⓐ peculier   ⓒ peculiar
    ⓑ peculierre   ⓓ peculiarre

12. A _____ doesn't have an electrical charge.
    ⓐ nuetron   ⓒ neutron
    ⓑ newtron   ⓓ nutron

13. A rhyming _____ is commonly used in poetry.
    ⓐ cuplet   ⓒ couplet
    ⓑ couplette   ⓓ cuplette

14. I'm afraid I don't have a _____ to your problem.
    ⓐ solution   ⓒ sollution
    ⓑ solushun   ⓓ sulution

15. My dental _____ says I should brush my teeth more often.
    ⓐ hygenist   ⓒ higenist
    ⓑ hygieneist   ⓓ hygienist

16. Look up the _____ in a dictionary.
    ⓐ definition   ⓒ defenition
    ⓑ defnition   ⓓ definnition

17. This organization is known by an _____ .
    ⓐ acranym   ⓒ acronym
    ⓑ accronym   ⓓ acronim

18. His sore _____ was a result of his loud shouting.
    ⓐ larnyx   ⓒ larnx
    ⓑ lerynx   ⓓ larynx

19. It is necessary to learn _____ when learning a foreign language.
    ⓐ grammer   ⓒ gramer
    ⓑ grammar   ⓓ gramar

20. A fable is a kind of _____ .
    ⓐ allegory   ⓒ allegorey
    ⓑ alegory   ⓓ aleggory

Review Test
Answer Key

Lesson 6

1. b	11. b	21. d
2. d	12. d	22. c
3. d	13. a	23. a
4. a	14. b	24. a
5. d	15. a	25. c
6. d	16. a	
7. c	17. d	
8. a	18. b	
9. b	19. a	
10. c	20. d	

Lesson 12

1. a	11. b	21. a
2. b	12. a	22. c
3. c	13. d	23. b
4. c	14. a	24. c
5. d	15. b	25. d
6. a	16. d	
7. d	17. c	
8. a	18. d	
9. b	19. d	
10. d	20. c	

Lesson 18

1. c	11. d
2. a	12. c
3. d	13. b
4. a	14. d
5. d	15. a
6. a	16. a
7. b	17. b
8. b	18. a
9. a	19. d
10. d	20. c

Lesson 24

1. c	11. c	21. a
2. d	12. a	22. a
3. d	13. a	23. b
4. c	14. d	24. d
5. c	15. d	25. b
6. b	16. a	
7. a	17. c	
8. a	18. b	
9. d	19. a	
10. d	20. c	

Lesson 30

1. a	11. d	21. a
2. d	12. b	22. d
3. c	13. d	23. d
4. b	14. a	24. c
5. b	15. a	25. b
6. a	16. b	
7. d	17. c	
8. c	18. d	
9. c	19. d	
10. c	20. a	

Lesson 36

1. b	11. c
2. a	12. c
3. b	13. c
4. d	14. a
5. d	15. d
6. b	16. a
7. b	17. c
8. a	18. d
9. a	19. b
10. d	20. a

List Words

Word	Lesson	Word	Lesson	Word	Lesson	Word	Lesson
abandon	1	applicable	14	competent	25	detour	11
abhor	9	aquamarine	13	complex	14	device	35
abolish	9	aquarium	13	complication	14	diagnose	31
abrupt	14	aquatic	13	complimentary	27	dialogue	23
absolve	9	arbitrator	32	compromise	25	dilapidated	29
abstain	9	archaic	22	compulsory	27	dilemma	35
abstract	9	architect	22	concentric	15	diminish	17
absurd	9	archive	22	conferred	5	disadvantage	11
academy	22	aristocrat	23	conjunction	34	disastrous	29
acceptance	3	artificial	2	conqueror	4	dismal	2
accessory	29	ascertain	1	consolidate	1	dispute	11
accidental	2	assistance	3	conspiracy	16	disrespect	16
acquitted	5	attendant	29	contemporary	27	disrupt	14
acronym	34	auditor	21	contraband	10	dissatisfaction	11
administrator	32	availability	26	contradict	10	dissimilar	13
admitting	5	bankrupt	14	contrary	10	dissolve	11
advisory	27	barbecue	1	contrast	10	distort	11
advocate	15	barometer	23	controller	5	documentary	21
aeronautics	22	benefactor	10	controversial	17	dominate	1
affable	9	benefit	10	cooperative	19	dominion	21
affidavit	1	benign	10	coordinate	19	drizzle	3
affiliate	9	bibliography	33	copilot	19	duet	7
affirmative	9	biography	23	cordially	3	duplex	7
affluent	9	biological	23	corrupt	3	duplicate	14
aggravate	9	bouillon	28	corsage	28	eccentric	15
aggressive	9	boycott	3	cosmopolitan	22	eclipse	22
allegory	33	bureaucracy	22	cosmos	22	economical	22
allergy	31	cancellation	3	couplet	33	economize	25
alligator	4	capability	26	courtesy	17	elastic	22
alliteration	33	capitalization	34	criminal	2	electrician	32
allotted	29	caricature	33	crisis	22	eligibility	26
anagram	22	carpenter	32	criticize	22	eloquent	17
analogy	33	centigrade	7	croquet	28	eminent	17
analysis	22	centimeter	7	cruel	17	emphatically	29
analyst	32	centralize	15	curiosity	1	endive	28
anarchy	20	cerebral	2	customary	17	enterprise	25
ancestors	4	chemist	32	customer	17	enthusiasm	23
anchor	4	chronic	23	decade	7	entirely	17
anemia	20	clockwise	25	decanter	11	epidermis	8
anesthesia	20	coauthor	19	deceased	11	epilogue	8
angular	4	coexist	19	deception	11	episode	8
annex	9	coherent	19	deciliter	7	epistle	8
annihilate	9	coincide	19	decimal	7	epitaph	8
annotate	9	collaborate	10	decimeter	7	equally	17
announcement	9	collateral	19	decision	17	equivalent	35
announcer	32	colleague	10	decline	11	especially	17
annul	9	collection	10	decompose	11	etiquette	28
anonymous	20	collision	10	defenseless	17	eulogy	10
antecedent	8	colossal	2	deferred	5	euphoria	10
anterior	8	comedian	32	definition	34	eventuality	26
anteroom	8	commemorate	1	democracy	22	excess	17
antibiotic	9	commencement	10	dependent	25	excitable	17
antihistamine	9	comment	10	deplete	11	exclamation	34
antisocial	9	commerce	10	depression	3	exclude	16
anxiety	17	commitment	10	descendant	11	exclusive	16
apologize	25	commodity	10	destruction	14	exhibit	35
apostrophe	34	communal	10	determine	15	exhilarated	21
appetite	1	commute	10	deterring	5	exorbitant	21

106

List Words

Word	Lesson
expectation	16
expelled	5
expenses	17
experimental	2
expire	16
exposition	33
exposure	1
exterminate	15
extraordinary	27
fallacy	17
fascinate	29
fiancée	28
fiction	33
finesse	28
fiscal	2
flexibility	26
forbidden	5
formality	26
fragment	34
franchise	25
friction	31
fulfilled	29
fungus	31
generosity	26
geographical	23
geological	23
gerund	34
glacier	4
gladiator	4
glossary	34
grammar	34
gratitude	1
guardian	1
handicapped	5
harmonize	25
homonym	34
hospice	13
hospitality	26
hospitalize	13
hostage	13
hostel	13
hostile	13
hydrant	23
hygienist	32
hysterical	2
idiom	33
immaculate	20
immense	3
immigration	3
immobilize	20
impatiently	20
impending	14
impersonate	20
implicate	14
imposter	4
impromptu	20
imprudent	20
inaccurate	20

Word	Lesson
inactive	20
including	16
incognito	20
incubator	4
incurred	5
indecisive	20
independently	14
indigestion	31
individuality	26
inexplicable	14
inferiority	26
infinitive	34
infirmary	27
insecticide	21
inspection	16
inspiration	16
installation	1
instruction	14
integral	2
interrogative	34
interrupt	14
introductory	27
invalid	20
investor	4
iodine	31
itemize	25
jeopardy	29
jubilant	25
junior	4
juvenile	21
kiloliter	7
kilowatt	7
laboratory	35
larynx	31
lateral	13
legality	26
legendary	27
lengthwise	25
liability	26
liberal	13
liberate	13
librarian	32
linear	4
literal	2
literature	33
logical	2
magnetic	22
maladjusted	11
malevolent	11
malfunction	11
malice	11
mandatory	27
manicurist	32
marionette	28
marriage	35
maternal	16
maternity	16
matrimony	16

Word	Lesson
matron	16
maximum	21
menu	28
metabolism	11
metamorphosis	11
metaphor	11
metropolis	22
metropolitan	35
microorganism	31
milligram	7
milliliter	7
miniature	35
mobility	26
moderator	4
modifying	34
molecular	21
monarch	7
monetary	27
monolith	7
monologue	7
monopoly	7
monotone	7
mortal	13
mortgage	13
mortician	13
mortuary	13
murmur	4
myriad	7
narrative	33
necessary	27
necessity	3
negative	20
neglect	20
negligent	20
neon	23
neutron	31
nonchalant	20
nonexistent	20
notarize	29
observant	25
observatory	27
obstacle	35
occasionally	5
occurring	5
octagon	23
omitted	5
opaque	28
opportunities	35
oppose	35
oppress	3
optician	21
optimistic	35
option	21
opulent	21
ordinance	21
ornament	1
overlapping	5
parable	23

Word	Lesson
parallel	23
paralysis	23
paramedic	32
paraphrase	34
parasite	23
parenthesis	34
parody	33
participle	34
particular	4
patrolled	5
peculiar	35
pendant	14
pendulum	14
perennial	31
permanent	25
permitted	5
perpendicular	4
perpetual	2
perplexing	14
personality	26
personification	33
perspective	16
pharmacist	32
pharmacy	23
physics	31
pleasant	25
poetic	33
politics	22
pollen	3
porcelain	28
possession	3
practicality	26
preamble	8
precinct	29
preclude	16
predicate	34
preferred	5
prejudice	8
preliminary	27
prelude	8
premature	8
premier	8
premonition	8
preposition	34
presuppose	8
prevalent	25
primary	27
primitive	35
procedure	35
procession	8
professor	4
propeller	5
prophet	8
proposal	8
proprietor	32
prose	33
protégé	28
protocol	8

List Words

Word	Lesson	Word	Lesson	Word	Lesson	Word	Lesson
protrude	8	schedules	29	survival	2	turbine	31
proverb	33	scheme	35	suspended	14	tweezers	4
provoke	15	seclusion	16	suspense	14	tyranny	29
prudent	25	semiannual	7	syllable	19	umbrella	29
pseudonym	33	semiprecious	7	syllabus	19	undoubtedly	1
psychology	31	sensational	2	symbolize	19	unforgettable	5
publicity	21	several	35	symmetry	19	unilateral	13
punctuality	26	significant	25	symphonic	19	upheaval	2
quadrilateral	13	similarity	26	symposium	19	vaccinate	31
quarantine	21	simile	33	symptom	19	vagabond	15
racquet	28	simulate	13	synagogue	19	vagrant	15
rationalize	25	simultaneous	13	synchronize	19	vague	15
recital	2	situation	35	syncopate	19	variation	15
reflector	4	solution	35	syntax	19	variety	15
regime	21	sonnet	33	synthesis	19	various	15
relevant	25	sophomore	17	technicality	26	vendor	32
representative	32	soufflé	28	technician	32	verdict	21
Republican	21	source	17	televise	23	vermin	21
researcher	32	souvenir	28	tendency	1	veterinarian	32
respiration	31	specifications	1	terminal	15	vinegar	4
résumé	28	spectacle	16	terrace	15	visibility	26
resurrect	1	speculate	16	terrain	15	vocabulary	27
revival	2	spiritual	16	territory	15	vocalize	15
revoke	15	stanza	33	theology	22	vocation	15
revolutionary	27	structural	14	therapist	32	voltage	31
sanctuary	27	subsidiary	27	thermos	23	voluntary	1
satellite	31	suburban	21	thermostat	23	vulnerable	29
satisfactory	27	successive	3	tranquil	29	wharf	29
saturate	1	succulent	3	transfusion	31	wholly	3
sauté	28	summon	3	transitive	34	withholding	3
savory	27	superiority	26	transmitter	31	yeast	29
scallop	28	supplemental	2	transmitting	5	zinc	35
scarcity	29	suppress	3	transpired	16	zinnia	29
scavenger	28	surgeon	28	tropical	2	zoology	31

Bonus Words

Word	Lesson	Word	Lesson	Word	Lesson	Word	Lesson
abacus	26	arcade	11	canopy	14	colonnade	11
a cappella	10	arduous	20	cartel	31	colony	1
addiction	32	arthritis	32	celestial	33	combustion	35
adjective	5	articulate	20	censorship	17	commentaries	17
ad-libbed	13	atoll	21	centrifugal force	33	commissioner	3
adverb	5	attorney general	3	chandelier	14	commonwealth	1
affiliation	31	audition	13	Chile	16	commune	1
alluvial	21	automobile	2	chiropractor	8	conduit	35
altruistic	20	auxiliary verb	5	cholesterol	32	confederation	31
ambassador	3	avalanche	21	cinema	19	confrontation	15
amethyst	28	bivouac	15	classical	10	conglomerate	25
amphibious	2	boisterous	20	clause	5	conservatory	10
amphitheater	19	borough	1	cliché	9	convalescent	22
amplification	29	broadcasting	13	clique	31	Corinthian	11
amplifier	13	buttress	11	closed circuit	13	coroner	3
anachronism	23	cadence	10	coliseum	19	corporation	25
analytical	26	calculus	26	colloquial	9	correlation	26

Bonus Words

Word	Lesson
courier	15
crescendo	10
crevasse	21
critique	19
crystallize	28
dauntless	15
davenport	14
decrescendo	10
dental hygienist	8
depressant	32
desperation	15
diamond	28
dietitian	8
dispensary	22
dispersion	28
distribution	17
diversify	25
Doric	11
draperies	14
dynamic	20
editorial	17
electromagnetic	35
El Salvador	16
embryo	7
encapsulate	33
enunciate	29
enzyme	32
epigram	23
epithet	23
erosion	21
escapade	15
euphemism	23
fabricate	35
façade	11
facets	28
facility	34
faction	31
fertilization	7
fetus	7
finite	26
franc	27
fraternal	7
fraternity	31
frequencies	13
frieze	11
gargoyle	11
gasoline	2
genetics	7
geodesic	11
geometric	26
geyser	21
Guatemala	16
guild	31
guilder	27
gurney	22
harrowing	15
heredity	7
horticulturist	8

Word	Lesson
hydraulic	35
hydroplane	2
hypertension	32
identical	7
igneous	21
implement	35
impurity	28
inaudible	29
incinerator	35
indictment	4
Indonesia	16
inertia	33
inflation	25
interjection	5
interrogative	5
interscholastic	34
intonation	29
intramural	34
intravenous	22
intrepid	15
investigative	17
Ionic	11
jargon	9
journalism	17
judgment	4
judicial	4
lacrosse	34
lathe	35
laudable	20
libelous	17
liquidate	25
lira	27
lithography	17
logarithm	26
luminosity	33
magistrate	3
mahogany	14
mandate	4
mark	27
mathematician	8
mechanical	35
melodrama	19
memoir	23
mercantile	25
mesa	21
metallurgist	8
meteorologist	8
mimicry	23
misdemeanor	4
module	33
momentum	33
Morocco	16
muckrake	17
municipality	1
musician	8
nebula	33
negotiation	25
nicotine	32

Word	Lesson
nominative	5
numerical	26
obituary	17
objective	5
obsidian	28
obsolete	9
ottoman	14
pageant	19
Pakistan	16
paradox	23
parquet	14
participation	34
pedestal	14
pediatrics	22
peso	27
petition	4
philharmonic	10
physical therapist	8
planetarium	33
plaque	32
Portugal	16
possessive	5
pound	27
pregnancy	7
production	13
prologue	19
property	4
proprietary	25
propulsion	2
province	1
proxy	25
psychiatrist	8
racquetball	34
radiology	22
redundant	9
refraction	28
rehabilitate	22
relativity	33
reproduction	7
residential	1
reticent	29
reverberate	29
rhetoric	23
ruble	27
rugby	34
rupee	27
rural	1
sapphire	28
sarcasm	23
scenario	19
schooner	2
secretary	3
securities	25
sedimentary	21
shekel	27
Sierra Leone	16
singular	5
skiing	34

Word	Lesson
slang	9
sojourn	15
soliloquy	19
soloist	10
sorority	31
stagecoach	2
statistical	26
staunch	20
stimulant	32
strident	29
subpoena	4
suburb	1
superfluous	9
superintendent	3
supervisor	3
surgery	22
syndicate	31
synonymous	23
syringe	22
taciturn	29
technological	13
telecast	13
therapeutic	22
timbre	29
tolerance	32
topography	21
tournament	34
transcontinental	2
treacherous	15
treasurer	3
trespass	4
tributary	2
trigonometry	26
trite	9
troupe	31
turquoise	28
umbilical cord	7
unscathed	20
upholstery	14
urban	1
vaudeville	19
veneer	14
ventilator	35
verbose	9
vernacular	9
vessel	2
vibrato	10
vice-president	3
videotape	13
vindictive	20
virtuoso	10
vociferous	29
volleyball	34
warrant	4
winsome	20
yen	27
Yugoslavia	16
Zimbabwe	16

Spelling Enrichment

Group Practice

Crossword Relay First, draw a large grid on the board. Then, divide the class into several teams. Teams compete against each other to form separate crossword puzzles on the board. Individuals on each team take turns racing against members of the other teams to join list words until all possibilities have been exhausted. A list word may appear on each crossword puzzle only once. The winning team is the team whose crossword puzzle contains the greatest number of correctly spelled list words or the team who finishes first.

Proofreading Relay Write two columns of misspelled list words on the board. Although the errors can differ, be sure that each list has the same number of errors. Divide the class into two teams and assign each team to a different column. Teams then compete against each other to correct their assigned lists by team members taking turns erasing and replacing an appropriate letter. Each member may correct only one letter per turn. The team that is first to correct its entire word list wins.

Detective Call on a student to be a detective. The detective must choose a spelling word from the list and think of a structural clue, definition, or synonym that will help classmates identify it. The detective then states the clue using the format, "I spy a word that. . . ." Students are called on to guess and spell the mystery word. Whoever answers correctly gets to take a turn being the detective.

Spelling Tic-Tac-Toe Draw a tic-tac-toe square on the board. Divide the class into X and O teams. Take turns dictating spelling words to members of each team. If the word is spelled correctly, allow the team member to place an X or O on the square. The first team to place three X's or O's in a row wins.

Words of Fortune Have students put their heads down while you write a spelling word on the board in large letters. Then, cover each letter with a sheet of sturdy paper. The paper can be fastened to the board with a magnet. Call on a student to guess any letter of the alphabet they think may be hidden. If that particular letter is hidden, then reveal the letter in every place where it appears in the word by removing the paper.

The student continues to guess letters until an incorrect guess is made or the word is revealed. In the event that an incorrect guess is made, a different student continues the game. Continue the game until every list word has been hidden and then revealed.

Applied Spelling

Journal Allow time each day for students to write in a journal. A spiral bound notebook can be used for this purpose. Encourage students to express their feelings about events that are happening in their lives at home or at school. Alternatively, they could write about what their plans are for the day. To get them started, you may have to provide starter phrases.

You may wish to collect the journals periodically to write comments that echo what the student has written. For example, a student's entry might read, "My brother is suceptible to infecshuns. He will probable need to see the doctor again today." The teacher's response could be, "People who are susceptible to infections will probably need to visit their doctors regularly to stay well." This method allows students to learn correct spelling and sentence structure without emphasizing their errors in a negative way.

Letter to the Teacher On a regular basis, have students each write a note to the teacher. At first the teacher might suggest topics or provide a starter sentence, including words from the spelling list. The teacher should write a response at the bottom of each letter that provides the student with a model of any spelling or sentence structure that evidences need of improvement.

Daily Edit Each day provide a brief writing sample on the board that contains errors in spelling, capitalization, or punctuation. Have students rewrite the sample correctly. Provide time later in the day to have the class correct the errors on the board while students self-correct their work.

Spelling Notebook Have students use the Spelling Notebook in the student book, a stenographer's notebook or pages of the reproducible Spelling Notebook stapled together (see page 111 in the *Teacher's Edition*) to keep record of words they encounter difficulty spelling. Tabs could be added to some pages to separate a large notebook into sections for each letter of the alphabet. Use students to use a dictionary or ask the teacher to help them spell words with which they are having trouble. Periodically, allow students to work in pairs to test each other on a set of words taken from their personal word

Acrostic Poems Have students write a word from the spelling list vertically. Then, instruct them to join a word horizontally to each letter of the list word. The horizontal words must begin with the letters in the list word. They could be words that are synonyms or that describe or relate feelings about the list word. Encourage students to refer to a dictionary for help in finding appropriate word. Here is a sample acrostic poem:

Evade
Lose
U-turn
Dodge
Escape

Poem Exchange Provide students with copies of a familiar poem. Discuss how some of the words can be exchanged for other words that have similar meanings. the students to rewrite the poem exchanging some of the words for other words.

Spelling Notebook

Name

			Pretest	Final Test	Bonus Test
Lesson 1	Syllabication				
Lesson 2	Words Ending with the Sound of əl				
Lesson 3	Double Consonants				
Lesson 4	Words with the Sound of ər				
Lesson 5	Doubling Final Consonants				
Lesson 6	Lessons 1–5 • Review		■		
Lesson 7	Prefixes for Numbers				
Lesson 8	Prefixes **ante, epi, pre, pro**				
Lesson 9	Prefixes **ab, af, ag, an, anti**				
Lesson 10	Prefixes **bene, beni, coll, com, contra, eu**				
Lesson 11	Prefixes **mal, meta, de, dis**				
Lesson 12	Lessons 7–11 • Review		■		■
Lesson 13	Latin Roots				
Lesson 14	Latin Roots				
Lesson 15	Latin Roots				
Lesson 16	Latin Roots				
Lesson 17	Challenging Words				
Lesson 18	Lessons 13–17 • Review		■		
Lesson 19	Prefixes Meaning "Together"				
Lesson 20	Prefixes Meaning "Not"				
Lesson 21	Words of Latin Origin				
Lesson 22	Words of Greek Origin				
Lesson 23	Words of Greek Origin				
Lesson 24	Lessons 19–23 • Review		■		
Lesson 25	Words Ending in **ize, ise, ent, ant**				
Lesson 26	Noun-Forming Suffix **ity**				
Lesson 27	Words Ending in **ary, ory**				
Lesson 28	Words of French Origin				
Lesson 29	Challenging Words				
Lesson 30	Lessons 25–29 • Review		■		
Lesson 31	Words from Science				
Lesson 32	Words from Occupations				
Lesson 33	Words from Literature				
Lesson 34	Words from Language Arts				
Lesson 35	Challenging Words				
Lesson 36	Lessons 31–35 • Review		■		■

Lesson	6	12	18	24	30	36
Standardized Review Test						